To my daughter
Sarah
and all the children of the world
So that the world may be a better place to fall in love

In memory of
William Masters, M.D.
An accomplished pilot, a state champion boxer, and a true gentleman
He was the greatest contributor to the science of sexuality

Barbara McDowell
My dear friend and secretary who called me George

Resurrecting
SEX

Also by David Schnarch

Constructing the Sexual Crucible: An Integration of Sexual and Marital Therapy

Passionate Marriage: Keeping Love and Intimacy Alive in
Emotionally Committed Relationships

Resolving Sexual Problems and Rejuvenating Your Relationship

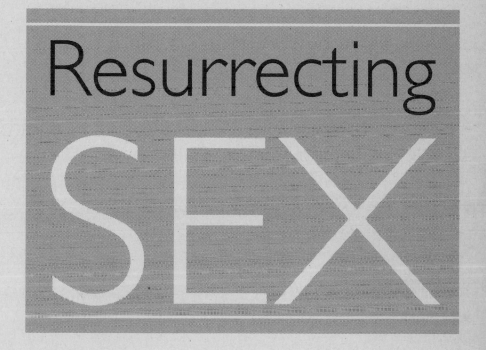

Resurrecting SEX

DAVID SCHNARCH, PH.D.

Scribe Publications
Melbourne

Passionate Marriage, Passionate Couples, Sexual Crucible, Crucible, Sexual Crucible Approach, Crucible Approach, Resurrecting Sex, and Intimate Proposals are trademarks owned and pending by David Schnarch, Ph.D. Programs, trainings, services, and materials using these trademarks can be provided only by the Marriage and Family Health Center of Evergreen, Colorado, and its authorized designates. Web site: www.passionatemarriage.com

Scribe Publications Pty Ltd
PO Box 523
Carlton North, Victoria Australia 3054
Email: scribe@bigpond.net.au

First published in Australia and New Zealand by Scribe Publications 2002
Published by arrangement with HarperCollins Publishers, New York

Copyright © David Schnarch 2002

Designed by Jessica Shatan

Printed and bound in Australia by Griffin Press

National Library of Australia
Cataloguing-in-Publication data

Schnarch, David Morris, 1946- .
Resurrecting sex : resolving sexual problems & rejuvenating your relationship.

Includes index.
ISBN 0 908011 73 3.

1. Sex instruction. 2. Sex in marriage. I. Title.

306.7

www.scribepub.com.au

Contents

Part III: Medical Options

Part IV: Couples in Search of Solutions

Appendixes

Acknowledgments

Writing about a living process has been a process in itself. Like watching my adolescent daughter, Sarah, rapidly become a woman, I have seen this book change its shape and tone more times than I could have imagined. I worry about what I see happening to many couples today. This book is my attempt to make things better for my daughter.

I also worry about what will become of the two sciences I love most, sex therapy and couples therapy. With the death of Dr. William Masters and the retirement of founding members of both disciplines, these two fields now flounder in midadolescence, struggling to develop second-generation approaches. This book attempts to resurrect sex and marriage in contemporary society by changing how we think about them. It also tries to set a direction for tomorrow's therapists, who are the future of my beloved sciences.

I want to thank my good friend and colleague Dr. James Maddock for his participation in the early planning stages of this book. We collaborate in developing workshops for therapists and counselors, and it is a treat to teach with Jim from twin podiums. He is one of the real thinkers in psychotherapy today, and a good man to boot. I have been enriched by his wisdom, his counsel, and his friendship.

The process of actually developing and writing this book has been a solitary one. I withdrew into myself for many months, trying to distill what to say and how to say it. I emerged with four goals: I wanted to write something that really helps you resolve sexual problems. I wanted to show you how to do this in a way that could broadly improve your life. I wanted to get closer to you, the reader, than I had in my previous books. And I wanted this to be kinder and more compassionate than anything I'd done before. In the end, I decided to share with you my understanding of how sex, intimacy, partnership, and spirituality all come together.

No one else, not even my wife, Ruth Morehouse, saw this manuscript until it was completed. In the last months, Ruth has been trying to sneak peaks and teasing me: "What if it isn't any good?" I'm respectful that I've had the opportunity to carry this baby. Now it's time to send it off into the world. One hundred thousand sheets of paper later, and here you have this book.

I want to thank Josh and Peggy Golden for their review of the manuscript. Their friendship and kindness has warmed me so often that I automatically relax in their presence. Josh's comments on medically related matters were especially helpful.

This book also benefited from the wonderful editorial guidance of Gail Winston, executive editor at HarperCollins. My literary agent, Owen Laster of William Morris Agency, handled contract negotiations and sales. My appreciation goes out to these two consummate professionals.

There are not enough ways to thank my wife Ruth. I am indebted to her in the way a long-term partner's debts are never paid: She has weathered my (limited) growth from impatience to gratitude. The more I grow up, the more I appreciate Ruth as my taste of the feminine Divine. I get great pleasure in respecting her as a partner, a therapist, and a copresenter. I am grateful for Ruth's comments on the manuscript. The more I feel the same about her comments about me, I am the better for it.

The longer I live and the more clients I see, the more I am thankful for my parents, Stan and Rose Schnarch. Of all their many wonderful traits, their basic decency, integrity, and goodness are beyond compare. Being parents I can respect and honor has been the greatest of their many gifts to me. If you need the image of parents wishing you well as you read this book, borrow mine.

I also want to acknowledge my brother, Steve Schnarch, for helping me maintain my perspective and direction while writing this book. Steve is my "quality of life" adviser and the most good-hearted and right-minded guy I know. If he were not my brother, I would be honored to have him as my friend. Having him as my brother has been a blessing.

The other blessing in my life is my daughter, Sarah. Sarah is the kind of child parents are fortunate to have. She sings happily to herself as she goes through the day, and she lights up our house. Her current life goals include going to college, mastering one-handed cartwheels, and exploring the strange world of boys.

When this book was almost finished, I asked Sarah who she thought it should be dedicated to. *Constructing the Sexual Crucible* was primarily dedicated to my parents, and *Passionate Marriage* was dedicated to my wife, Ruth. Sarah thought for a moment, and then she smiled and said, "Dedicate it to your brother, Steve!" When I refer later to operating from the best in you, this is what I mean.

Sarah has been frustrated at times by having parents with unusual jobs. Ruth and I figure she'll get over it, since she assured her teacher that we'd see her and her husband in therapy if they ever needed help. To see Sarah proud of our work, and proud of herself, is a joy any parent can appreciate.

Given all this, it won't be too strange for Sarah to learn that this book is dedicated to her. She already told me, when I asked, that she doesn't plan to read this for several years. That's fine with me. This is for Sarah, when she gets older. If you read this book now, and she reads it later, I will have accomplished what I wish for her. This book is my attempt to make the common experience of love and intimacy much happier, kinder, and more rewarding. My hope is that Sarah may grow up in a world that is a good place to fall in love.

David Schnarch
Evergreen, Colorado

Resurrecting
SEX

Introduction

Once upon a time two frogs fell into a large pail of buttermilk. Frantically the frogs climbed on each other, splashed furiously, and did whatever they could to stay afloat. As they grew weary and ever more fearful of drowning, they thrashed about more desperately. Finally approaching exhaustion, the frogs ceased struggling and prepared for the worst. Only then did they realize what their terrified minds never saw: All their seemingly futile and frustrating struggles had started turning the buttermilk into butter. Their random efforts were creating a platform on which they could float.

The frogs saw new purpose to their struggles and renewed their efforts with determination and collaboration. They kicked with less angst and paddled with greater ease. Eventually their efforts allowed them to rise above the milk. What once threatened their very existence became a resource for survival.

When you finish this book, you'll understand why we are all frogs in the buttermilk. You will have an entirely new understanding of sexual problems and how to deal with them.

What Is This Book About?

Resurrecting Sex deals with sexual problems that plague couples around the world. Every couple has sexual problems at some point. You could be a woman who never feels highly aroused or has difficulty lubricating. Maybe you have pain during sex or difficulty with orgasms. Or you could be a man who has problems getting or maintaining erections. Maybe you find it hard to have orgasms, or maybe you have them too quickly. Sexual desire is a common problem for women and men alike. Perhaps you don't want sex as often as your partner does, or vice versa. Or maybe you don't want to do it the same way or at the same time of day. Maybe you don't want to do it at all.

You could be celebrating your fiftieth wedding anniversary, or living together, or single and dating. You might be middle-aged and raising a family, or young and starting your first serious relationship. Maybe you're an empty-nest couple, struggling now that your kids have gone. Or perhaps you're approaching retirement and thrilled to finally have the house to yourself. Maybe you are newly single after your divorce or you're just starting to have sex. *Resurrecting Sex* covers sexual problems that surface in all stages of relationships.

Sexual problems are normal and so are their impacts: Once your sexual problem exists for a while, you're dealing with more than a penis or a clitoris that won't obey its owner. The matter involves two people with very complex feelings about themselves and each other. Because genitals are connected to people, it can be hard to turn sexual problems around.

Sexual problems happen to real people—people with real anxieties, insecurities, disappointments, resentments, autonomy struggles, and dependency needs. Very often, real people with sexual problems become real stubborn and set in their ways. You and your partner may feel inadequate, or fight with each other, and then wonder what's wrong with your relationship.

Many couples find it hard to talk about a sexual problem—or even admit they have one. Even if you're willing to talk about it, it's hard to know what to say or do. It is common to feel like you're flailing around to no avail, drowning in your problems. On top of that, you're struggling with the very person you want to feel and make love with.

Sexual problems happen in relationships, and context is everything. Your sexual problem shapes your relationship, and your relationship shapes your sexual problem. Resurrecting your sexual relationship often involves more than getting your body to do what you want. You have to get your relationship to a state that supports good sexual functioning.

Often sexual problems can signal the death knell of a relationship.

Far too frequently such problems turn into divorce, separation, or long-term emotional alienation. There are, however, far more pleasant deaths: the death of the relationship as you've known it, and the birth of one far better. Resolving sexual problems can change you, your relationship, and your life.

What Does This Book Offer?

Resurrecting Sex offers straight talk about sex, intimacy, and relationships. You'll find the latest facts on medical difficulties and cures, as well as thorough coverage of relationship problems and ways to change them. Count on realistic solutions and case examples of couples putting them into action. You'll also find a whole lot more.

Resurrecting Sex offers hope. It contains a revolutionary understanding of common experiences in emotionally committed relationships. What you'll learn can help you hang on through tough times and use them to advantage. It can turn commitment into an adventure, rather than servitude to past promises.

Resurrecting Sex builds partnership. Sometimes partnership requires discussing and doing things together. Other times partnership requires functioning independently when your partner is not at his or her best. It frequently involves compassion for your partner in the midst of difficult times. You won't find trite sermons about love and compassion in this book. You'll find effective ways to create hope and put it into action.

Resurrecting Sex is a book within a book. We'll talk about sexual difficulties and how to solve them, but we'll also reflect on life, relationships, and anxiety and how they all fit together. It's easier to go through bad times when you recognize them as part of the power and elegance of intimate relationships.

How Is This Book Unique?

Lots of self-help books offer tips, tricks, secrets, exercises, homework assignments, and sure-fire sex techniques. But books with easy-as-pie attitudes can backfire, leaving you feeling more inadequate when their simple solutions fail to bring expected results. Maybe you've been liberated and rejuvenated. Maybe you've raised your consciousness and become more politically correct. Even exploding your myths, exposing your hang-ups, and exorcizing your inhibitions may not solve your problem. What do you do then?

Resolving sexual problems often requires more than new sexual positions or techniques like "sensate-focus" exercises or going out on dates. Books on how to be your own sex therapist presume you and your partner are cooperative patients. Many couples don't want more techniques or find improved sexual function doesn't help their relationship (or doesn't last). You or your partner may not be motivated to do things to improve your situation, whether or not you'd succeed.

Resurrecting Sex offers you new and different solutions. These are the product of my twenty years' experience as a certified sex therapist and a marriage and family therapist. What you'll read here is widely considered the cutting edge in these professions. In 1997 the American Association of Sex Educators, Counselors, and Therapists honored me with its first Professional Standards of Excellence Award, in part for the kinds of innovations this book contains. *Resurrecting Sex* is based on the first comprehensive second-generation approach to sex and marital therapy. (The work of Masters and Johnson defined the first generation in the 1960s.)

What you'll find here (and what you probably need) is a holistic, realistic, refreshingly straightforward approach. Couples do better with a holistic approach that doesn't reduce sexual problems to generalities like "power struggles," "communication difficulties," "deprived childhood," or "sexual abuse." In *Resurrecting Sex* you'll find a holistic approach that looks at the purposeful ways intimate relationships operate.

Holistic strategies work on several aspects of your problem simultaneously. You'll probably find treating sex, love, and intimacy as integrated processes more appealing than approaching sex as something that just happens between your legs. But you also don't want what's (not) happening between your legs to get lost in lectures about sex being primarily between your ears. *Resurrecting Sex* addresses emotions, thought, feelings as well as the physical dimensions of sexual problems.

Sexual problems have histories that shape how things look to you. After a while your problem takes on a life of its own. You (and your partner) begin to adjust to your problem both in and out of bed. This makes things somewhat more tolerable, but the adjustment process kills intimacy and passion. It's not just couples who can't adjust who have sexual problems. As you will see with couples you meet in these pages, decades of adapting to problems with orgasms, erections, or low sexual desire have an impact!

Resurrecting Sex gives you a sophisticated picture of relationships and shows you how to apply this to your specific situation. By the time you're done, you'll have new respect for things you probably think are "defective" in your relationship. Equally importantly, you'll learn things you can apply elsewhere in your life.

Resurrecting Sex is the next logical step after my last book, *Passionate Marriage: Keeping Love and Intimacy Alive in Emotionally Committed Relationships* (Owl, 1998). *Resurrecting Sex* applies the same core Passionate Marriage® Approach, this time to common sexual problems and how to solve them. Readers unfamiliar with my work will find *Resurrecting Sex* comprehensive in itself. Readers of *Passionate Marriage* will find previously unpublished material, together with familiar ideas applied in new ways. Although there's plenty about sex in *Passionate Marriage, Resurrecting Sex* is for the millions of couples and singles who need specific information about sexual dysfunctions and dead or dying sexual relationships.

In brief, *Resurrecting Sex* covers

- How your genitals work

- How sexual relationships operate

- How marvels of sexual medicine, like Viagra, weave their magic

- What to do about your sexual problem, how to do it, and how to motivate yourself to do it

This Will Be Personal

I plan to keep this personal. As we consider the stresses and challenges of intimate relationships, I'll focus on what it feels like to go through them. I'll also help you consider the specifics and history of your own unique relationship.

This book is also personal for me. I know what it's like to scour books for solutions to personal sexual problems and come away feeling inadequate, defective, and diseased. The medical model of sex reinforces your worst fears. ("It works if it's OK, and if it doesn't, then something's wrong.") Researching your problem in textbooks will convince you that you're as screwed up as you feared. You're someone with "unconscious hostility" toward your spouse (or parents)—or worse. If you want to preserve some sense of health—or if you want warm and tender sex—you're out of luck.

I know this because I've been there. There was a time when I was the patient rather than the doctor. In the course of my life I've had almost every sexual dysfunction a man can have. As a young adult I had premature orgasms. At different times I've had difficulty getting and maintaining erections. Sometimes I couldn't have an orgasm if my life depended on it. I know about embarrassment, self-rejection, blaming myself or my partner, and withdrawing when I "failed."

Having looked for information and felt patronized, dehumanized, and pathologized, I've made sure this book offers you a different experience. This book is what I wished someone would have given me. It's the book I want my daughter to turn to when she and her partner have sexual problems. I will share with you things I want her to know someday, including a healthy, hopeful, and humane perspective.

First and foremost, your sexual problems won't be treated like diseases. Your problems won't be treated as if they stem from sexual ignorance, hang-ups, or flaws in your relationship. There will be no talk of "psychopathology." This is a nonpathological approach.

In *Resurrecting Sex* you'll learn that sexual problems are normal, but not simply because they happen to just about everyone. Sexual problems are normal because of basic ways that healthy relationships evolve. This culture-transcending view of relationships, I believe, is the basis of the international interest in *Passionate Marriage* (which has been translated into Italian, Japanese, and Polish). I've felt honor-bound to make *Resurrecting Sex* easy to read so that this vital information will be accessible to a wide audience.

I Will Be Realistic and Optimistic

As a married man in a fifteen-year relationship, I know personally what it's like to have sexual problems. I also know how lots of other people feel about it too. My work as a therapist provides unique opportunities to look deeply into how sexual relationships and sexual problems operate. Twenty years' experience has allowed me to see beyond couples' immediate problems and understand *normal* patterns of intimate relationships. Sharing people's lives as they go through predictable sexual dilemmas has become my life's work. It's happy and exciting work, even though couples look like gloom and doom when they first enter my office.

I'm optimistic about what you can get from this book because I've seen how much my clients have accomplished. I've watched them do remarkable things, achieving far more than they (and, at first, I) ever imagined. Many couples resolve long-standing sexual and marital problems. Relationships on the brink of divorce have turned around. Have hope.

You might think the best part of my work is listening to sexy details of clients' doings. For me, it involves watching the best in people stand up. Any spirituality I have comes in large part from observing countless acts of heroism in my office. I watch people refuse to give up on themselves in the face of their sexual problems. I see people confront their fears, shortcomings, and limitations—all legitimate and understandable—when things boil down to maintaining personal integrity and self-respect. Witnessing this time and again increases my awe for the miracle of self-transformation and the power of intimate relationships.

I also know that what my clients accomplish takes hard work. Many feel resolving their sexual problem is one of the best things they've ever done, because it brings incredibly rewarding experiences and new growth. Some also feel it's the hardest thing they've ever done. If you want similar results, start by accepting three simple truths about sexual problems.

- There are often no simple answers or solutions.

- You don't need easy or simple solutions—you just need solutions that really work.

- A solution that's an emotional stretch for you and your partner is often the best solution to your problem.

As long as I'm telling the truth, I must disqualify myself as an expert on female sexuality. I've talked with hundreds of women about the intimate details of their lives. I have learned enough to know I am—and always will be—an outsider. I will never know basic things women take for granted, whether it concerns their bodies, having sex, or being female in contemporary society. Despite my limitations, I've tried to be a good student. Later on I'll talk about similarities in men's and women's sexuality. I'm open to ways they are different.

You Can Be Realistic Too

You can be realistic about yourself too. You don't have to pretend you're dying to change things. This book is written for someone whose motivations for change are counterbalanced by motivations to keep things the same. You probably have hesitancies and ambivalences about changing your relationship. Maybe you're still deciding which way you want to go. Couples don't live long with the problems we'll discuss without hurt feelings, resentments, and defensiveness.

You don't have to be "comfortable dealing with feelings." Some of my clients fear disturbing the powder keg of pent-up problems in their marriage. Others want to avoid their emotional life altogether. If you're like this, you may not have to dwell on your feelings or your past to improve sex. There are lots of things you can (and need to) do in the present to turn things around. This book's third section deals at length with medical and bionic solutions. If you worry about lifting the lid on your situation, *Resurrecting Sex* will give you a peak at what might await you. If you decide to improve your relationship, this book will show you how to do it.

You don't have to pretend changes will be easily made (or eagerly sought). I also won't make idealistic assumptions about where things stand between you and your partner. I don't presume your partner is eager to collaborate in your sexual restoration project. That's why I'll show you things you can apply by yourself, whether your partner participates or not. (If you and your partner are completely emotionally gridlocked, you may also want to read *Passionate Marriage,* which addresses this at greater length.)

I understand sex probably isn't the only issue in your relationship. You don't need a perfect relationship to apply what you read here. The solutions I offer are for real couples with real problems. These solutions are elegant because they simultaneously

- Resolve the complex causes of sexual problems

- Repair the negative impact sexual problems create

- Make you able to have a better relationship than you had before

How to Use *Resurrecting Sex*

I suggest you start at the beginning and read through to the end. Figure your first reading will give you an overview of your problem and what you can do about it. Don't worry if you read more than you can digest on one pass. You'll get a deeper understanding of how everything fits into the big picture on your second reading. By then you'll have the overall framework in mind, making it easier to add new details to your mental map. And new things will jump out at you on your second time through.

Read couples' stories even when their problems or personalities appear different from your own. This book is not a collection of chapters on different topics. *Resurrecting Sex* lays out a complete system by developing ideas early on in the book that you'll need in order to fully understand later chapters. If you are serious about changing your situation, take the time to learn about yourself and your relationship. If you want to pursue particular topics on second reading (or jump around on your first), consult the index in the back.

If Your Situation Is Bleak

Forget about reading from start to finish if your problem feels overwhelming, or if you're upset, or if your relationship is in crisis. Read Part 2 first. It will help you settle down so you can read the book in a quieter frame of mind. From the outset, you'll find new ways to understand your sexual problem and your sexual relationship. By midbook you'll be into powerful and creative solutions. Reading further, you'll realize you've stumbled onto a whole lot more. We're going to take buttermilk and turn it into butter. The more you are drowning in sexual problems, the more you should stop thrashing about and read on.

Read from the Best in You

One final suggestion: I want to talk to the best in you. This is the part of you that can do something about your situation. If you've got an easy time ahead of you, your strengths will get you through in the shortest time possible. If things are going to be tough, you want the best in you leading the way.

Here's how you can tell if you're reading from your best. If you have a running commentary in the back of your mind, is it your best or your worst self talking? Are you looking for holes in what I say or confronting yourself with the parts that fit your situation? The best in you can take what I say to heart, even if my shortcomings are obvious. The best in you can even do the same with your partner.

So stop trying to "do better" sexually so that you can finally feel "good enough." Stop trying to be a "better person." Just let the best in you stand up. It often happens, much to people's amazement, when they don't think they're measuring up at all.

As we begin, I want to be talking with the best in you. If you are like my clients, you're in for a very interesting time!

PART I

A Crash Course in Sex

I

A Second Chance at Sex

*In its essence, the delight of sexual love, the genetic spasm, is a
sensation of resurrection, of renewing our life in another, for only
in others can we renew our life and so perpetuate ourselves.*

—Miguel de Unamuno, *The Tragic Sense of Life* (1913)

What is it you seek? Are you looking for happiness? Peace? Passion? Solid connection with your partner? Sexy sex?

What do you currently have? Loneliness? Frustration? Failure? Boring, sad, empty sex? Painful sex?

We tend to believe couples don't typically have significant sexual problems. When we are unhappy, we think it's because of how we're uniquely screwed up. It is hard to believe unsatisfying and disappointing sex is normal. We try to live up to our distortions by hiding our own difficulties. Until recently, the full extent of common sexual unhappiness remained hidden from view.

Public discussions of sex have become more common over the last four decades (perhaps even too much so). The constant barrage of sexual information, advertising, and sex-laced entertainment in mass media makes it feel somehow inappropriate to have sexual problems in our liberated times. In spite (or because) of this, there exists a vast underground of couples with sexual problems who have gone unrecognized and unserved.

As a sex therapist, I've long known that sexual unhappiness is widespread. Sexual dysfunctions and dissatisfactions are rampant among normal healthy couples. My view of marriage differed so much from prevailing stereotypes that at times I felt alienated from society.[1] That is, until two technological marvels, Viagra and the Internet, showed up.

Incredible initial sales of Viagra, the first readily accessible and easily administered erection medication, made everyone wonder where these pills were going. Journalists did the math and started tracking prescription patterns. Feature articles in *Time, Newsweek, USA Today,* and every small-town newspaper helped spread public awareness. Gradually, John and Jane Doe began to realize what was (and wasn't) going on in many couples' beds.

The Internet, for all its wonders, became a new sewer for the sexual unhappiness and dissatisfactions in bedrooms around the world. Up sprang porn Web sites offering clip art, still photos, Java script images, and steaming streaming video. Sexually oriented chat rooms—meaning just about any chat room given half a chance—surfaced on major Web portals. Therapists started hearing complaints from clients that spouses (or they themselves) preferred masturbating online to having partnered sex. As complaints grew, the scope of unhappy marriages and sexually barren relationships became more apparent.[2]

The problem is not Internet technology per se. The Net benefits desperate people looking for factual sex information and support. Unfortunately, the modem connection that carries a support group for adolescent burn victims also delivers clandestine e-mail from "Internet affairs." The unhappiness in people's bedrooms that propelled initial Viagra sales now also drives the Internet.

How Common Are Sexual Difficulties?

Although sexual problems have plagued men and women throughout history, scientific incidence data is sparse. Studies vary in their estimates due to differences in assessment methods and the people studied. Overall, however, results suggest that anywhere from 10 percent to 52 percent of all men and 25 percent to 63 percent of all women have sexual problems. An estimated 15 million men in the United States have significant erection problems and another 10 million have partial difficulty. One man in three has some difficulty with erections by age 60. These staggering figures explain why more prescriptions were written for Viagra when it was initially released than for any other new drug.

The 1999 mail survey of 1,384 adults (ages 45 and older) conducted by the Association for the Advancement of Retired Persons (AARP) and *Modern Maturity Magazine* provides a similar view: The majority of men and women sampled said a satisfying sexual relationship was important to their quality of life. One in four men surveyed (26 percent) reported complete or moderate difficulty with erections, but less than half these men ever sought treatment. Overall, the AARP study noted that only a small minority of people who have sexual problems ever seek treatment. Only 10 percent of men and 7 percent of women in this study had taken medication, hormones, or other treatment to enhance their sexual performance. (A majority of those who did reported increased sexual satisfaction and improved relationships.)

Inside Your Neighbor's Bedroom
You can see widespread sexual problems in the results of the 1992 National Health and Social Life Survey (NHSLS) epidemiological study of 1,749 women and 1,410 men ages 18 to 59. The demographics of the people studied match the general public at large, meaning that the results probably represent an accurate picture of what's happening across the United States: 43 percent of women and 31 percent of men reported having a sexual problem *in the prior year.* Given people's tendency to under-report such problems, the study's findings probably are on the low side.

Stop for a moment and consider what this really means. When you realize that a third of all men and almost half of all women have had a sexual problem recently, that's a whole lot of couples struggling with a sexual problem in one partner or the other. You can visualize what's going on in bedrooms everywhere when you consider the actual sexual problems reported in the NHSLS study.

One out of five women doesn't enjoy sex. Fully 19 percent of women report difficulty lubricating and 15 percent report pain during sex. This means that lots of women aren't having a particularly good time in bed, and it's doubtful that their partners are either. Regardless of whether their partners reach orgasm or not, there isn't going to be a lot of inti-

macy, passion, tenderness, or affection for anyone involved. Look
behind the numbers and think of the disappointment, frustration, and
tears they represent.[3]

Next, consider the implications of other findings that a quarter of all
women report having difficulty reaching orgasm. Aside from the impact
this has on women's self-esteem and enjoyment of lovemaking, think of
what this means in bedrooms across the country tonight. One out of
four women may be lying there, lost in her own private mental world,
wondering if she'll reach orgasm and worrying about how her partner
will respond if she doesn't. Lots of people will be working in bed when
they could be relaxing. Many of them will feel miles apart during what
is supposedly the most intimate thing two people can do. Some will give
up on themselves or their partner, disappointments will be common, and
many will become discouraged and turn away from each other.

Thus, it's not surprising that the NHSLS study found a third of all
women weren't interested in sex. Only 16 percent of men reported low
sexual desire—but that is still a large number of guys. My clinical experience suggests more men struggle with low sexual desire than the study
found. I'd guess sexual disinterest occurs equally frequently among men
and women.

According to the study's actual findings, half of all people have difficulty with sexual desire. In practical terms, this means lots of households in which one partner goes to sleep later to avoid sex, lots of "Not
tonight, dear," and lots of arguments about who's frigid and who's
obsessed with sex. When you put the whole picture together, it isn't surprising that half of all men report extramarital affairs and women are
rapidly achieving parity.

For another vantage point, consider the NHSLS findings about male
sexual difficulties. Twenty-five percent of men struggle with rapid
orgasm. Once again, visualize what this means in real time: One out of
four men gets into bed anxious and ready to fail, trying to keep from
getting "too aroused" by the very person he's trying to make love with.
Whether distracted by his fears of failure or his own attempts to delay
orgasm, every fourth guy having sex tonight is out of contact with his
partner. Next, imagine their partners trying to figure out whether to
shut up, speak up, or soothe their man's disappointments. Not a very
romantic picture, is it?

Also, 17 percent of men and 11 percent of women report being anxious about their sexual performance. That adds up to lots of nervous people trying to do what's supposed to be easy and carefree. My clinical experience suggests these figures are an underestimate. I've encountered lots of men who are so frightened during sex, they can't allow themselves to realize how nervous they are. Moreover, people who have no overt sexual dysfunctions often have insecurities about being good in bed. This makes for lots of sweaty sex, caused more by fear than by sexual athletics. When people fear being found inadequate, they usually are not eager for intimacy (that is, being known) during sex.

Unfortunately, all this and more is happening tonight in many homes in your community. Since you are reading this, something similar probably happens in your home, too.

It's Normal to Have Sexual Problems

Realizing the misery, disappointment, and heartbreak behind the results of the NHSLS study may make you more charitable toward yourself and your partner. We'll talk about compassion for you and your mate later in this chapter (and throughout this book). But know from the outset that this compassion comes from a realistic assessment of the scope of the problem, rather than bleeding-heart liberalism or "wounded-child" self-indulgence. Sexual problems are common among healthy couples who are normal in every other way—so common, in fact, that they are arguably a sign of normality.

You don't have to be defective to have sexual difficulties. Believing you are defective is normal too. Moreover, ferreting out your defects won't necessarily resolve your sexual problems. It probably won't make you interested in sex or good in bed, either.

Who Wants a Second Chance at Sex?

Between how little we've known about human sexuality and intimate relationships, and how many people suffer between the sheets, lots of couples and singles are looking for a second chance at sex. You (and most people you know) are probably one of them.

Resurrecting your sexual relationship can offer you more than better or more frequent sex. It is a chance to stop the disappointments, dashed hopes, and heartbreaking squabbles that usually come with repeated sexual problems. The key to success involves believing in yourself and going forward from what is good and solid in you. Resolving your sexual problems creates opportunities for peace.

Viagra sales indicate lots of guys want a second chance at sex. And if you add up the figures from the NHSLS study, you'll see that lots of women do, too. Women have more sexual problems than do men. Actually, we know the least about those who need sexual health care the most. Recently, needed research about women's sexuality is emerging because of economic incentives to sell them Viagra and other drugs. Armed with knowledge gained about men's erections, pharmaceutical companies are eagerly developing more elaborate applications for women. They know they have a ready market of eager buyers.

Many couples want a second chance at sex because the secondary impacts of sexual problems reverberate in ways that destroy intimacy, fun, and joy. Nights that otherwise could hold soft embraces or passionate athletics are filled with awkwardness and emotional estrangement. Too many partners turn away from each other in large and small ways. Too often we turn to others outside our home for what we thought our relationship would bring in the first place.

Many older couples want a second chance at sex. Realizing you won't be here forever makes intimacy more intense and the need for it more pressing. Mortality makes you want to figure out the dear stranger lying beside you, before one of you has to bury the other. Likewise, current social attitudes offer the gray contingent more freedom to explore sex than when they were younger. If you think time is slipping away and Eros has already passed by, you're among the horde of people who want a second chance at sex.

You are also never too young for a second chance at sex. Young people often delay seeking treatment because they feel they shouldn't have difficulties until they get old. Some have sexual problems from their first sexual experience and throughout their lives. The NHSLS study found adults of all ages experience sexual problems, and some (rapid orgasm for men and lack of orgasm for women) are particularly common among young people.

Who Are "Couples with Sexual Problems"?
All couples have difficulties with sex and intimacy at some point in their relationship. When I speak of "couples who have sexual problems" I'm not pointing to a group of couples who differ from those who don't. I

simply mean "when couples are at that point in their relationship," rather than distinguishing a "kind" of relationship (that has sexual problems) from a different kind (that doesn't).

Let me tell you about some couples who want a second chance at sex.

- **Betty and Harry** are a young couple struggling through serious medical problems. At first this severely curtailed their sexual relationship. Ultimately they stopped having sex altogether. Now they'd like to pick up their sex life where they left off, and maybe take it further. Betty still has difficulty getting aroused.

- **Alexia and Martin** spent years locked in a war of independence, destroying what was once a fairly satisfying sexual relationship. Now older, more mature, and surer of herself, Alexia wants to make up for lost time. Martin, however, is still gun-shy around her and doesn't really feel interested in sex. He has difficulty with erections and thinks Alexia should be more understanding. They fear the process of trying to improve their sexual relationship could ignite World War III.

- **Peter and Judy** never had much of a sexual relationship to begin with. Sex was dismal from the start and got worse. To the rest of the world, Peter and Judy are the perfect couple because they always get along. This part of their lives is their dirty little secret. They cringe every time friends complain about missing the early passion they once had in their own marriages. Having nothing to "go back to," Peter and Judy despair of ever getting things going. Judy has difficulty with arousal and orgasms but doesn't want to experiment.

- **Cindy and Boyd** both come from troubled households. Cindy was sexually abused as a child and now has disturbing orgasm trigger fantasies. She has difficulty having orgasms with Boyd but no difficulty by herself. Boyd recently discovered Cindy was having clandestine Internet affairs. Both are itching for some adventurous sex, although they haven't shown this "hidden" side of themselves to each other.

- **Byron and Vern** got together later in life. Vern lost her husband to illness, and Byron was divorced. Byron has difficulty with erections, and Vern doesn't want to marry him if it continues. Vern's husband never had difficulty with erections, and Byron had this problem in his marriage. Neither one knows quite what to do or what to make of it.

- **Jack and Vicky** have struggled with Jack's premature orgasms for over forty years. Neither one anticipates success at this point. Vicky still smolders over the years Jack refused to get treatment and ignored their problem. Jack is so sensitive about his problem he doesn't deal with it at all.

Throughout *Resurrecting Sex* you'll meet lots of other couples. Some who sound similar to you may have different kinds of problems. Likewise, some who have similar difficulties may seem very different from you. Seeing parts of yourself in different examples can expose your assumptions about people and sex that may be getting in your way.

Shed Your Stereotypes but Not Your Dreams
Reading this book will probably shatter some of your fondest dreams and illusions about relationships. However, your dreams about what marriage can be won't be shattered. This book is a manual for how you can begin to live these dreams. Clinically, I've observed that long-term emotionally committed relationships are where people often have the most intense sex of their lives.

When I talk about a second chance at the relationship you've dreamed of, I'm not referring to naive fantasies. Further on you'll encounter a starkly realistic view of marriage, but it isn't a pessimistic one. I encourage you (and will help you) to pursue everything good you thought your relationship could be.

So now that you have been encouraged to keep your dreams for your relationship alive, what illusion is most likely to bite the dust? It's how you think this incredible relationship is supposed to happen. This will be the focus of the second part of this book.

Resurrecting Sex: New Solutions and New Hope

Resurrecting Sex reflects my two decades of experience helping couples with sexual problems. This is my life's work. Clients are surprised that I can often describe the full measure of their dilemma better than they can. This gives my optimism about their situation some credibility and confuses them at the same time. How can I understand the complexities of their situation better than they can and still be optimistic? Clients say this makes them feel like I know something they want to learn.

You probably want your problem to be gone long ago. While I can't immediately end your discomfort, I can offer you ways to give it purpose. (In Chapter 6 I refer to this as "self-soothing," the all-important process of comforting yourself.) First I'll show you how the causes and results of sexual problems all fit together in an intricate process. Then I'll help you use this process to bring alive the best in you and your partner. This will help you better tolerate your situation and use it to good advantage.

Resurrecting Sex contains methods I've developed for resolving sexual problems. People who use these methods report rapid improvement in sexual functioning and increased satisfaction with themselves, their partner, and their relationship. This is the same approach used in Passionate Marriage® Couples Enrichment Weekends and nine-day Couples Retreats, and the Marriage and Family Health Center intensive therapy program. Clients' satisfactions go beyond the fact that they no longer feel defective. They are grateful for many other benefits they gain along the way.

This book contains a complete system that can help you resolve sexual problems and a lot more. You'll find

- An unflinching look at what really goes on when couples have sexual problems

- An unwavering conviction that you can accomplish tremendous things while you're in the (sexual) pits

- Ways to use your sexual problems (actually, your sexuality per se) to grow in ways that bring sexual happiness, deep intimacy, and joy

If this appeals to you, read on.

A Second-Generation Approach
In subsequent chapters you'll encounter a revolutionary approach to sex and intimacy. It differs from the rightfully well known works of Drs.

William Masters, Virginia Johnson, and Helen Singer-Kaplan. It probably differs from what you have learned or believe. Lots of people say it fundamentally disagrees with everything they've been taught about sex, love, and relationships and makes more sense than anything else they've encountered.

During the last half century, modern sex therapy evolved technology that jump-starts your body while interfering with intimacy at the same time. This realization comes as a shock to many people (including some therapists). Suggesting that conventional sex therapy unwittingly undermines intimacy at least *sounds* different from what has come before. But given the avalanche of books claiming to be new, revolutionary, and groundbreaking, how new and different can this be?

How Different Is "Different"?

Consider *the* most common sex therapy intervention: sensate-focus exercises developed by Masters and Johnson. In this activity, you and your partner take turns focusing on your own physical sensations while being touched. You are supposed to lie back, relax, not focus on your partner, and tune into your body. For most people, this is antithetical to intimacy.[4]

Moreover, troubled couples often find sensate-focus exercises uncomfortably similar to the "cadaver sex" they're already having. In many bedrooms, one partner tunes out his or her mate and focuses on physical sensations, leaving the other partner feeling ignored and used. When the first partner "gives feedback" about the kind of touch he or she wants, it doesn't always receive a rosy reception. You need something different (like what you'll learn here) if your relationship has been troubled for some time.

Another common approach encourages you to fantasize about sex with someone other than your partner. This is to "bypass" negative feelings you harbor toward your mate and get your motor going.[5] Unfortunately this destroys intimacy with your partner, whether you do this on your own or your therapist prescribes it. When you think your partner is fantasizing about other people during sex with you, does that make you feel more intimate, passionate, compassionate, or loving?

Finally, consider the most common methods of treating premature orgasm, the "squeeze" and "start-stop" techniques.[6] Whether or not these stop ejaculation, both approaches kill intimacy. Imagine having sex with someone who stops in the midst of sex to give his organ a mighty squeeze! He stopped focusing on you long before that, awaiting the proper moment to administer the sexual "Heimlich maneuver." The stop-start approach isn't much better, unless you like sex with someone who freezes in place, like a deer in the headlights, just when you're really getting started.

Common preoccupation with genital performance keeps us from realizing sexual "cures" often haven't been much better or much different than the problems themselves. However, the approach you'll learn here doesn't interfere with intimacy to begin with, and offers powerful ways to increase it.

This intimacy-based approach is a 180-degree shift from traditional methods. For instance, most therapies suggest emotional estrangement comes from "lack of connection" with your partner. In Chapters 6 and 7 you'll learn it's caused by emotion "fusion" with your partner (connection without separateness). I realize this may not make immediate sense, but that's part of finding something different that can help you. These two chapters will help you accomplish this complete reversal in perspective. *Resurrecting Sex* will show you how to:

- Develop an effective mind-set that facilitates intimacy and profound sexual union

- Resolve sexual dysfunctions and desire problems

- Explore your sexual potential and maximize your physical and emotional pleasure

In subsequent chapters I'll walk you through the process of how relationships really change, and help you motivate yourself to make that happen. We'll accomplish all this by shifting your attention from fixing "defects" to developing your capacity for intimacy, eroticism, passion, and love.

One common outcome of this is increased peace when you are with your partner—not just some kind of temporary truce, but a profoundly solid and deeply meaningful ease, so tangible you can relax into it. Peace that surfaces outside the bedroom in a casual touch, a warm smile, and enough sureness of intent that it's safe to kid around. (When was the last time you or your partner laughed during sex and no one felt defensive?)

What's in Store

Resurrecting Sex is organized into four parts. Materials in each part are arranged in a logical sequence of topics, each building on prior sections. Each of the four parts I'm about to describe takes the mystery out of sexual problems and helps you explore the mysteries of intimacy and love.

Part 1: Human Sexual Response and Sexual Problems

It's hard to help yourself if you don't understand what causes your sexual problem. Sex remains a mystery for many of us, even after the magic of sex has long passed. The first thing we'll explore is what makes your genitals "work," so you'll know what to do when sexual dysfunctions occur.

Think of Part 1 as a crash course in sex. There you will learn a simple new model of human sexuality. Once you learn it, you'll never forget it. This will help make sense of your current and past sexual experiences and give you ideas about what to do in the future.

This book will show you how everything in sexual relationships fits together like a system. Sex, intimacy, love, passion, partnership and compassion all work together in harmony, even when it doesn't look like it. Part 1 starts this process with a holistic picture of human sexuality that reveals how different sexual dysfunctions are basically pretty similar. In contrast to hoopla about men and women being from different "planets," you'll see that men's and women's sexualities are more similar than not. By the end of Part 1, you'll have the holistic solution strategy for resolving sexual problems that we'll use throughout *Resurrecting Sex*.

Part 2: Intimate Relationships

Now let's say you've taken the first step: You know what to do to get your body to function. How do you get this to happen when you are with your partner?

Changing your relationship can be a daunting task. Couples struggle with sex for years because they don't know how, or aren't able, to change their relationship. It's hard to change any relationship when strong feelings are involved. Given the emotionally charged aspects of your sex life, sexual relationships are often particularly hard to change.

Part 2 teaches you about how intimate relationships work. You'll learn things about changing your relationship (and yourself) that, by themselves, make this book worth reading.

Part 2 considers your sexual relationship in two different ways: First we'll explore the process of changing any sexual relationship. Then we'll consider what happens when there's a sexual problem involved. By the time we're through, you'll understand why your relationship operates the way it does and what's likely involved in changing it. When you finish Part 2, you'll appreciate moment-to-moment interactions between you and your partner as never before. You'll also learn things you can immediately apply to every relationship in your life.

Part 3: Medical Options
Before rearranging your sex life, you should consider all your options. In Part 3, we'll review medical solutions like surgery, medications, and over-the-counter sexual aids. There's a whole chapter on Viagra and other oral medications. You'll learn how these options work as well as their benefits and limitations. Equally important, you'll know how best to use them and how they can impact your relationship.

Part 4: Resolving Specific Sexual Problems
Part 4 integrates material from the preceding sections and offers solutions for the major sexual problems that plague men and women. You'll find holistic solutions that can resolve easy and difficult sexual problems alike. You'll read detailed examples of couples changing their sexual relationships, and changing their lives along the way. Here's where your questions about the "working-through process" will be answered.

Part 4 addresses what to do and how to do it. Men's and women's arousal problems are covered in Chapter 11. Chapters 12 and 13 detail solutions for orgasm problems. Chapter 14 takes a final look at what's involved in changing your particular relationship.

Dealing with Your Partner While You Are Reading This Book

In Part 2, I'll offer you lots of ideas about how to conduct yourself as you change your sexual relationship. You can also probably use some suggestions from the outset. Here are some things to keep in mind for now.

Don't Worry If One of You Isn't Eager to Change

Nobody really likes to change, especially when we're talking about changes that are transformative. Mind you, most of us wouldn't mind being transformed—if we could snap our fingers and be done with it. Unfortunately, becoming an adult isn't simply fun and games.

It's understandable that you and your partner aren't dying to change your sexual relationship. Chapters 6 and 7 address this very topic, so from the outset, don't pressure your partner for a "commitment" to change. Here are three important reasons: (1) This will make your partner more resistant to change. (2) If your partner is going to change, what's important is what he or she does, not what he or she says. (3) Making your own efforts contingent on your partner's efforts keeps you stuck.

Be Prepared to Read on Your Own

Many couples who read *Passionate Marriage* to each other have said this was a wonderful shared experience. You might consider doing this with *Resurrecting Sex*. However, don't make this a prerequisite for you reading this book. If your partner isn't interested, but you'd like him or her to read this, be smart about how to handle yourself. Don't try to make your partner read this book. A mention that you are reading it is cordial. Recommending it once to your mate is what friends do with something good. Give him or her a copy if you think it's prudent. (In some relationships, this is "pushing.") Beyond that you've made your point, so leave it alone. Focus on your own efforts. Resist the temptation to ask your partner for a reading progress report.

The Person Who Wants to Change Always Has the Most Control

I'm not saying you shouldn't try to influence your partner, only that there are often smarter (and less belligerent) ways to do it. Changing yourself always pressures your partner to change, because that's how intimate relationships work. But here's the really important thing that may help you stop pushing your partner to change: *The partner who wants to change things always has the most control.* That's because you can change your relationship unilaterally by simply changing yourself. The status quo only exists as long as you and your partner agree it does.

Three powerful changes occur when you understand this point: (1) You don't have to struggle with your partner if he or she doesn't want to change. (2) You are more likely to treat your partner kindly rather than being insulting or demeaning. (3) You will approach your decisions and actions thoughtfully (rather than frantically) because you don't feel helpless or controlled.

Don't Give Ultimatums

Ultimatums are binding only on the person who issues them. People who constantly issue ultimatums are usually bullies and cowards who lack personal integrity. There is no point in threatening your partner. If you are determined to change things, you don't give ultimatums or warnings. Confronting yourself and soothing yourself—whether your partner does likewise or not—tells your partner loud and clear that he or she better pay attention. Your shouts and threats say it's safe to ignore you.

Remember, You're Dealing with Another Human Being

When you've struggled with sexual problems for some time without success, it's easy to forget your partner is another human being. By this I mean being mindful that your partner is someone separate from yourself, another member of the human race. As a fellow married person, I understand how hard this can be. It's hard when your partner is indifferent to your discomforts and dissatisfactions or goes out of his or her way to hurt you. We all want to be happy and avoid pain and suffering. Often we interpret the fallout of our partner's (ineffective) attempts at self-protection as a response meant to hurt us. Of course it's natural to see things this way (Part 2 will explain why), but it doesn't help. Your partner is often just trying to avoid discomfort as best he or she can at the moment.

Compassion for Your Partner Is Kindness to Yourself

Likewise, don't be naïve. Later on we'll discuss normal marital sadism. I don't advocate "turning the other cheek" or endless apologies or patience. You don't have to always put your partner's feelings and needs first. Understanding your partner's situation and feelings doesn't involve giving up your own. Being considerate of your partner doesn't include perpetually backing away from an issue he or she wants to avoid. Considerateness has to do with how you treat him or her when you are speaking up.

Offering your partner kindness, generosity, and friendship doesn't mean you have to be a saint. Simple self-interest is all you need. The Dalai Lama says compassion for your partner is really compassion for yourself.[7] Righteous indignation still involves personal suffering.

Be kind to your partner while you're reading *Resurrecting Sex*. This will shape the meaning of the changes you make. You're likely to find your partner more responsive (or at least pleasantly confused).

Give Yourself Time

Compassion for yourself involves appropriate expectations. Give yourself time to grasp the whole picture this book presents. Allow yourself to reflect on what you've read. Let it sink in before taking a stand. If the best in you is reading this, you won't use this time to avoid facing what you don't want to face.

Conclusion

Sexual relationships are journeys that traverse landmark issues and conflicts. Knowing you've reached a marker or milepost is helpful, particularly when you can't stand where you are. It's one thing to tough it out when you're in a rough spot. It's entirely more upsetting and anxiety-provoking if you think you're off the path. Most couples don't figure they'll end up bedeviled by sexual disappointments. Since you're reading this, you're probably at a place you didn't think was on your itinerary.

There's an old saying: It's the journey, not the destination, that's important. Easily said when you feel like you are on solid ground. It's a different story when sex seems like a struggle, a chore, an embarrassment, or a total disaster. Most of us don't like going forward when our relationship is troubled, the path is rocky, and the emotional weather is inclement. We want stability, familiar emotional terrain on which to rest before we move on. Unfortunately, you never have this option, because that's not the way life works.

You can't keep your relationship stationary, even if you feel stuck. So *Resurrecting Sex* offers you another alternative: You can study the terrain ahead so you can deal with it in the best way possible. Think of *Resurrecting Sex* as your guidebook. What you'll find here, essentially, is a map. Many people find this map helpful when they feel like a stranger in a strange land.

You are about to embark on the sexual road less traveled. It is the path hidden within every sexual relationship, within every couple's sexual problem. Prepare to abandon familiar ways of understanding what's happening.

The process of changing yourself and your sexual relationship has begun!

2

How Sex Works

Sex, a great and mysterious motive force in human life, has indisputably been a subject of absorbing interest to mankind through the ages.

—U.S. Supreme Court Justice William J. Brennan, in his dissenting opinion on the 1957 5–4 ruling establishing a new legal standard defining obscenity

Amanda was starting to worry. She was only 55 years old, and this seemed too young for sex to disappear. She hadn't said anything to her husband, Cole, but she suspected he'd already noticed the change in her. Amanda used to like sex and it usually didn't take much to get her started.

Amanda just wasn't interested in sex any more, and she had increasing difficulty having orgasms. She and Cole squabbled like couples do, but that didn't seem serious enough to cause this. She still cared deeply about Cole, which is why she tried to hide her lack of desire. What caused her problem? What was her solution?

Lloyd wanted to know why lately he had increasing difficulty keeping his erection. It was becoming tough to get one to begin with, and his premature orgasms were happening more frequently. He and his wife, Peggy, hadn't said anything about it, but it was starting to distract and worry him. Was this the beginning of the end?

Every day people from every walk of life confront such questions. One by one they realize they know far less about human sexuality than they thought they did. Certainly, less than they need to know to solve their problem. So let me ask you:

What if, like Amanda, you realize you have no sexual desire? What causes something like that and what can you do about it?

What if you've never had an orgasm but you're dying for your first? Or you've had orgasms, but they are few and far between? How come trying harder and longer often doesn't work?

And what if, like Lloyd, you can't maintain an erection (or you have difficulty getting lubricated)? How can that happen when you're really feeling aroused? What do you do if you're not feeling aroused at all? And what if you reach orgasm so readily that the party's over as soon as you get started?

Conventional answers to these questions would make this book impossibly huge. Typically, lack of arousal, loss of erection, premature orgasm, and difficulty reaching orgasm are thought of as different "diseases" with different causes. Each disease would have its own chapter—much like medical problems such as asthma, diabetes, and high blood pressure. Instead, we are going to approach sexual problems holistically, using a framework I developed that ties them all together. This holistic framework is called the Quantum Model.

The Quantum Model[1]

The Quantum Model explains how complex aspects of human sexuality—like your health, physical stimulation, and subtleties like intimacy, desire, eroticism, passion, and love—fit together. It helps you understand and harness your uniquely human capacities (your sexual potential), and enhance your sexual pleasure and satisfaction. The Quantum Model helps you answer the question, What does it take for my body to respond the way I expect?

Answering this question is no small undertaking. For more than twenty centuries experts of the day have offered (dubious) explanations about what causes sexual *dys*functions. Most people know precious little about what causes sexual *function*. But understanding what you're trying to do when resurrecting your sexual relationship is essential.

No one event or factor usually determines how things turn out, whether we're considering erection or lubrication or a sexual relationship reaching "critical mass" and fundamentally changing (Chapter 7). When accumulated events or factors reach a particular level, however, new things start to happen (or stop). The Quantum Model is similar to quantum theory in modern physics, explaining how a system abruptly changes because of an accumulation of events that, by themselves, don't have sufficient impact.

Sufficient Stimulation

At its most basic, the Quantum Model is simply this: an explanation of how you function sexually—what's required to make your genitals "work" and reach orgasm. The basics are easy to learn and apply. Here is a way to picture the process. Getting your body to function is like pulling yourself (your arousal) up and over a high horizontal bar. That's easy enough to picture—and sometimes very hard to do.

Your body detects stimuli conducted through your nerves, muscles, spinal cord, and brain. Your body responds when it recognizes it is being sexually stimulated. When you are sufficiently sexually aroused for all the intricate processes in your body to take place, your genitals respond.

Genital response and orgasm are actually reflexes, acting much like any other reflex, such as your leg kicking out when your knee is tapped at just the right spot to trigger the patellar reflex. Lubrication or erection and orgasm generally feel better than a knee-jerk reflex (and are more likely to drive you nuts).

The key idea is that you have to be sufficiently sexually stimulated for your body to respond. This isn't as simple or obvious as it might seem at first. "Sufficient stimulation" for human beings involves a lot more than sensory input with a little mental fantasy thrown in.

Reaching Your Response Threshold

Now let's add another piece to the picture. Your body has two sexual trigger points, called "response thresholds." You have one response threshold for initial sexual arousal (genital response) and another for orgasm. These response thresholds are the imaginary horizontal high bar I had you envision earlier. Your response thresholds are the heights of arousal you have to reach in order for your body to function sexually.

When your total sexual excitement exceeds your arousal threshold, your body does what you expect. Your vagina lubricates if you're female, and your penis becomes erect if you're male. If and when your level of arousal exceeds your orgasm threshold, you experience the most pleasurable reflex in your body. Reaching your thresholds for genital response and orgasm creates what you probably consider "normal" sexual functioning. Difficulty reaching your response thresholds creates sexual dysfunction.

One implication of the Quantum Model is that sexual dysfunctions and desire problems are part of normal sexual functioning. This is more than reassurance that occasional sexual difficulties are perfectly normal and nothing to worry about. I'm saying that when your body doesn't "work right," it happens because you are *normal*, not abnormal. In two decades of clinical practice I've never seen a single instance where sexual difficulties didn't follow the rules.

Many of my clients are relieved to know this because it gives logic and reason to their sexual problems. It gives them hope and makes them feel less defective. Once you understand why things happen, you are more likely to relax and take effective steps to change them to your liking.

Sexual Stimulation

Now we'll add another layer to our picture. Let's examine what I mean by sexual stimulation. About half a million years ago, a new part of the human brain evolved: the neocortex. With this development came unique abilities . . . and problems. Our ancestors started talking and looking *into* each other during face-to-face sex. Sexual desire began to involve desire for a specific partner rather than just an urge to reduce sexual tensions. Human sexuality shifted from being primarily a reproductive function to a vehicle for intimacy and love.

Unfortunately, as our sex shifted from hormonally programmed reproduction to the ability to bring meaning to sex, humans became more susceptible to sexual dysfunctions and desire problems than any other animal on Earth. The same capacity that makes self-awareness and intimacy possible also lets you drive yourself crazy monitoring your sexual performance ("spectatoring"). Likewise, sex that lacks meaningful emotional connection can limit your satisfaction because of your biological capacity for intimacy.

The ability to bring meaning to sex makes our sexuality quintessentially human. We are meaning-making animals. That's why meanings present and absent during sex strongly determine how our bodies function and how satisfying this is. The same abilities that make you capable of spiritual and loving sexual union also make you vulnerable to every negative thought and feeling you bring to bed.

When people think of sexual stimulation they usually focus on touch and, to a lesser degree, on sight, taste, smell, and sound. But how you feel about your sensations, and the meanings they carry, can have greater impact on your overall arousal level than sensory stimulation itself. That's why touching your partner perfectly is often less important than showing your partner that you are really involved. Your current and past relationships and your relationship with yourself greatly shape the meanings and emotional contexts of your sexual experiences.

Human sexuality is so subtle that your partner's feelings can affect your sexual function and satisfaction. For example, when Mariel became aware (or imagined) that her partner, Nicholas, was bored or uncomfortable, she couldn't get enough physical stimulation to trigger her orgasm regardless of how long they kept at it. Sometimes Mariel had intermittent pain during intercourse because she had difficulty staying aroused. Mariel was perfectly normal. Her vagina did not stay lubricated ("wet") when she wasn't sufficiently aroused. But Mariel couldn't get aroused or reach orgasm when she sensed that Nicholas needed her turned on to prove his competency and her love for him. Try as she might to give Nicholas what he wanted, Mariel couldn't get aroused enough to do it.

Total Level of Stimulation

Sexual response requires sufficient stimulation to reach your arousal and orgasmic thresholds. Here, "sufficient stimulation" refers to total level of stimulation, which is determined by the interaction of three things:

- The sensory stimulation you receive

- Your body's ability to transmit and respond to this stimulation

- Your subjective emotional processes (how you feel about what you're feeling)

By considering these three factors, you can decipher sexual difficulties and develop an effective treatment strategy of your own. We'll revisit these three components of total stimulation later in this chapter (and throughout this book) to organize a general strategy for dealing with your sexual problems.

Sexual Dysfunctions

Now we can explain how sexual dysfunctions happen. When your combined physical sensations, feelings, and thoughts (i.e., your total level of stimulation) reaches your threshold for arousal or orgasm, the physical response you expect takes place. But if your total stimulation never reaches (or drops below) your arousal or orgasm threshold, the sexual response you are expecting never occurs (or stops or decreases). This is how sexual dysfunctions occur.

Some women have never had an orgasm because they've never been sexually aroused enough to reach their orgasm threshold. Some reach their orgasm threshold occasionally; these are the times they have a climax. When men's total stimulation isn't sufficient to reach their arousal thresholds, they don't get an erection. When their total arousal level drops below their arousal threshold (after they get an erection), their erections subside.

Some men and women have difficulties reaching their arousal thresholds all the time. If you're a woman, this means you never become highly sexually excited and your vagina doesn't spontaneously lubricate. If you're a man, this means you never get an erection.

On the other hand, you might have difficulty reaching your arousal threshold only with a particular partner, or in certain settings, or during the early (or later) parts of a sexual encounter. If you're a woman, you might be wet when you start having intercourse but you become dry later on. If you're a man, you might get an erection initially but lose it at some point—like when you insert your penis for intercourse. (You might think a man gets more aroused at that particular moment, but when you learn how anxiety affects total level of stimulation you'll understand why that's sometimes not the case.)

Some people have orgasms during masturbation but have never had one with a partner. Lots of women have difficulty reaching orgasm through intercourse. Some men have never reached orgasm in their partner's vagina or mouth. In each instance the person's total stimulation lagged below his or her threshold for orgasm.

Knowing about response thresholds and total level of stimulation helps you understand how some dysfunctions last a lifetime and others come and go. Mariel stopped feeling defective when she finally understood this. It helped her make sense of the way she felt and the way her body functioned. As she put it, at least she knew she was functioning "wrong" for the "right" reason.

Basic information makes a big difference. Nicholas turned out to have intermittent difficulty with erections. He was so sensitive about this, neither he nor Mariel mentioned it when they sought treatment for her arousal problems. Nicholas was greatly relieved to learn that losing his erection was no different than Mariel becoming dry midway through intercourse. Instead of feeling diminished, Nicholas felt more on an equal footing with Mariel. Nicholas and Mariel were able to make progress with both their problems when Nicholas didn't feel he was losing face in front of his wife.

Most sexual problems have counterpart male and female versions. Sexual problems highlight how remarkably similar men and women are. Erection problems are no different than female arousal and lubrication problems. And men and women have difficulty reaching orgasm for any number of similar reasons. Male and female sexual functions and dysfunctions are not only equivalent; they involve similar physiological processes and corresponding anatomical parts.

Components of Your Total Stimulation

Now that we've explained how sexual function and dysfunction occur, let's explore what you can do to solve sexual dysfunctions. Your solution involves modifying the three components of your total stimulation: body responsiveness, physical stimulation, and emotions, thoughts, and feelings.

Body Responsiveness

The first major component of your total stimulation involves your body's ability to respond. For you to have "normal" sexual function, your body must transmit your sensations from remote parts of your body to your spine and brain and then back to your genitals. Your genitals have a complex biochemistry all their own that must be intact. Anything along the way that interferes with this whole process can reduce your total stimulation, your sexual responsiveness, and your sexual function and satisfaction.

Response Thresholds Differ

People differ greatly in how much total stimulation it takes to make their bodies respond. For example, Joyce was blessed with a very *low* threshold for orgasm. She could have what are known as "mental orgasms." When she focused her thoughts and feelings (including very vivid fantasies), she needed very little physical stimulation to reach her threshold. Tensing her thighs together was enough to do it. (Research indicates these kinds of orgasms are physiologically undistinguishable from masturbatory orgasms induced through manual stimulation.[2]) At the other end of the continuum, only a third of all women are able to achieve orgasm during intercourse. That's because intercourse is less effective than direct clitoral stimulation in helping women reach their orgasm threshold.

Response Thresholds Change

Not only do people differ in their threshold for genital response and orgasm. Aging, medical problems and treatments, medications, and recreational drugs can all raise response thresholds, and when this occurs you are more likely to have sexual problems. We'll discuss the affects of aging here and consider medical factors in Chapter 3.

Aging slows your body's responsiveness, because your response thresholds rise. As women age, they need more stimulation to reach their arousal thresholds and the speed of their physical responsiveness slows. Some women also require more stimulation to reach orgasm as they get older. This pattern can be accentuated by menopause or hysterectomy.

The same is true for men with regard to the speed and firmness of their erections. Furthermore, it happens earlier than is commonly thought. Although lots of men continue sexual activity, including intercourse, until well into their seventies, many notice changes in erections and orgasms by age 50. As men get older, they may not get full erections until shortly before orgasm. Although their erections may be firm enough for intercourse, they may feel "less sensitive" because of decreased rigidity and upsetting emotions.

Aging itself never destroys your capacity for sex. Nor are arousal problems an inevitable consequence of aging. In fact, the increased emotional maturity and capacity for intimacy that can come with age can make for some of the best sex of your life. Men often let themselves relax and be held in bed for the first time in their lives, and many older women become aroused and reach orgasm more readily because they are more comfortable with their eroticism. That's a good thing, because women and men who are more sexually active (either by themselves or with a partner) have less genital atrophy than those who aren't.

Take Gordon, for example. Although age-related shifts in functioning are perfectly normal, his erections became less reliable and he became increasingly distracted, embarrassed, and anxious. At first the changes were so subtle that Clare was unaware this was happening. Gordon said nothing and went about "doing his duty" during sex. Intimacy faded and Gordon's sense of isolation increased, creating further negative impacts. All of this diminished his total level of stimulation, and whenever it dipped below (or never reached) his arousal threshold, Gordon lost (or never got) an erection.

Eventually, Gordon had to aim and support his penis when attempting intercourse. This had a huge impact on him because he lived by the motto, Don't start what you can't finish. His increasing avoidance of sex further diminished his self-respect. Gordon's ensuing fears about "the beginning of the end" were creating a self-fulfilling prophecy.

Like many men and women, Gordon was not really aware of what was happening to him during sex. He used sex to escape from reality. For years he got into bed, tuned Clare out, and focused on the sensation in his loins. As long as he could get an erection on his own, she was willing to accommodate him with intercourse. However, now, when he couldn't "get it up" just by lying naked next to his wife, Gordon's strategy for sex closed in on him. He felt like his whole life was falling apart.

Clare and Gordon were not what you'd call intimate friends. Clare had settled for what little intimacy Gordon could handle and she made the best of it. Clare always hoped there would be more between them, and she realized that in an odd way Gordon's sexual problem was an opportunity for this to happen. Clare thought about Gordon, sex, and their marriage for months. Finally, she took matters into her own hands. She became more aggressive in stimulating Gordon's penis when they had sex. She stopped counting on him getting a spontaneous full erection or maintaining it throughout their encounter.

Gordon's first reaction was to become threatened and upset. He never needed "help" before, and it embarrassed him to need it now. But Clare persevered. Gordon finally let her help him insert his penis when they began intercourse. In short order, he had no difficulty with erections. The increased ease and decreased anxiety of intercourse, together with their markedly improved emotional connection, boosted Gordon's total level of stimulation well above his arousal threshold. Going through this was a big event in Gordon's life, and a turning point in their relationship.

Adapting to normal aging-related increases in response thresholds requires changing your sexual behavior. This creates tensions if you're in a sexual relationship that is (typically) limited and inflexible. It can lead either to celibacy or to more intimate sex, depending on how you handle it.

Physical Stimulation

The second major component of your total stimulation involves the amount and quality of sensory input you receive during sex. You can receive more than one type of stimulation at a time. Generally speaking, the more types of stimulation you receive, and the better each one is, the greater your total stimulation.

However, it's not as simple as how many places you're touched, or how fast or how long or how hard. A setting that is comfortable, pleasant smelling, and a joy to the eye works better than rumpled bedsheets and smelly socks, even if you are a fantastic lover. And different sensory inputs have to blend harmoniously in your mind if they're going to actually help. So, while one partner may get off having sex with the stereo blaring, this sensory input may overload or distract the other.

Most people figure out where to rub, more or less. Typical styles of touch range between "fairy tickles" and dermabrasion, unless someone's getting ticklish or chaffed. In therapy I've had to tell couples,

"Slow down!" more often than I've said, "Rub there!" I also have to talk with folks about looking where they are touching. If you hate touching your partner's (or your own) genitals, you're not going to touch him or her (or yourself) like you've discovered something you treasure!

Throughout this book we'll discuss different aspects of increasing the quality and quantity of physical stimulation you receive. However, we won't be focusing on erogenous zones or sexual positions. You can read about these elsewhere, and I've found these instructions generally don't help. Instead we'll focus on more important and rarely covered aspects of physical simulation, like subtle but profound nuances of connection with your partner.

Sharon and Reggie are a perfect example of what I mean and illustrate why I don't use exercises and techniques. Sensate-focus exercises don't work for everyone. Sharon and Reggie were an African American couple who sought treatment with me. It turned out Sharon felt she was *supposed* to lubricate when Reggie deliberately touched her and told her to "focus on her sensations."

For years Sharon avoided saying anything about this or about feeling rushed into intercourse. She didn't want to hurt Reggie's feelings. She knew his sexual competency hinged on knowing how to please a woman. Reggie got angry or depressed if she expressed displeasure with how he touched her.

Like many people, Reggie was attempting (without realizing it) to capitalize on the fact that physical sensations *and* emotions determine total level of stimulation. When he sensed things weren't going well sexually, he tried to compensate by rubbing or humping harder.

Although Sharon became progressively less aroused during sex as their relationship evolved, she had sex anyway to keep Reggie emotionally propped up. Eventually, Sharon couldn't do it anymore. Their sex was becoming increasingly uncomfortable and her patience was wearing out. More important, she loved Reggie and she wasn't willing to have her relationship with him fall apart.

Sharon told Reggie that the way they had sex just wasn't working. She reassured him that she loved him and found him attractive, but they needed to have sex differently. The next several weeks were tough while Reggie faced up to what he already knew: Sharon was going through the motions to please him. He could either accept Sharon's invitation to work on things together, or they might divorce and his son would grow up without a father in the house, just like he had.

Reggie wasn't a slob or an insensitive guy. He rushed Sharon into intercourse because he was afraid of losing his erections. And it wasn't that he didn't listen to Sharon's instructions about how she liked to be touched. He just got so nervous that he couldn't pay attention to what he was doing.

Reggie rose to the occasion and things turned around. He stopped trying to make Sharon have orgasms and stopped rushing her into intercourse. Sharon was touched by Reggie's efforts to keep his insecurities under control, and she liked when he touched her slower and longer. Sharon started getting more aroused and had no difficulty staying lubricated during intercourse. Moreover, her total arousal level was often high enough that her orgasms became more frequent. Reggie became less defensive and their relationship blossomed. They worked much better together when Sharon stopped trying to push out an orgasm and let herself be with the man she loved.

Emotions, Thoughts, and Feelings

The third component of your total stimulation involves your emotions, feelings, and thoughts. Your mind plays a critical role in your ability to recognize your sensations. "Receiving" sexual stimulation is a very active process. Physical sensations have to be organized into a pleasurable experience. If you are upset or distracted, for example, sexual stimulation may not feel good to you at all. At such times sexual behaviors that usually work no longer do. It's not as simple as some kinds of touch being better than others. If your partner starts to touch you in situations you deem inappropriate, for example, your physical sensations become less arousing and less likely to produce genital response and orgasm. (However, if you're turned on by the idea of "breaking the rules," this can be highly arousing.)

Feelings, emotions, and thoughts can so profoundly impact your sexual function that you'd swear you have a serious physical problem when none exists. Some people have come to see me, mistakenly reporting they feel "absolutely nothing" or have "absolutely no response" during sex.

Amy frequently had difficulty reaching orgasm with a partner. She'd had this problem with other men too, but it was much less a problem with Fred—at least at first. Why did this problem always come up, and why was it surfacing *now*? Amy wasn't sure what she was more scared of—never finding answers or what those answers might be. Could her pattern mean she had an emotional problem with men?

Amy's intermittent problem reaching orgasm wasn't happening because of some mysterious unconscious process or emotional problems. When Amy finally relaxed and let Fred take care of her while he gave her oral sex, she had no difficulty reaching orgasm. Fred didn't have to change how he pleasured her. Amy knew Fred was great at oral sex. That, in fact, made it harder for her to accept it. It was *so* good she felt inadequate receiving it. In retrospect, Amy realized how difficult it was for her to let Fred love her. She learned that receiving can be a gift we give others and ourselves.

So why did Amy have this problem less with Fred than with her prior partners, and why was this coming up now? Before Fred, Amy tended to pick guys with whom she never felt secure. She was usually a bundle of nerves in bed, trying to prove herself through sex and make her partners want her. Fred, however, was a very different choice for Amy. He loved her and he was the most stable guy of the lot. That's why at first sex with Fred was like magic. Amy had no trouble having orgasms with a man for the first time in her life. However, as their relationship continued and Fred became increasingly important to her, Amy's insecurities were triggered.

This relates to Amy's situation and her total level of stimulation: Amy had an inkling she needed to get more aroused—she just wasn't sure how she could do it. Repeatedly having sex until one of them (usually Amy) was sore proved that harder, longer, and faster stimulation wasn't going to help. It wasn't until Amy realized how isolated she felt from Fred during sex, and how frightened and demoralized she was, that things started to turn around.

Amy realized she wasn't dealing with the problem she thought she was. In the past, Amy thought her problem stemmed from her fears of rejection. But this time she faced a new problem. She finally had found someone who loved her and she couldn't accept it. The real question wasn't whether Fred would reject her, but rather, would she let him love her and would she love him back? Amy settled down and realized this question involved more than sex.

All her life Amy was afraid to consider whether or not she was really capable of loving someone *deeply*. It was easier to hide behind her fear that someone would not love her. I helped Amy see how her unconfronted fears of being too shallow, selfish, and immature to really love anyone made her doubt another's love for her. Were it not for her determination to preserve the best relationship of her life, Amy might have continued running away from herself, all the while insisting that Fred wasn't doing enough to make her feel "secure."

As Amy confronted these issues her arousal during sex improved. Reaching her sexual response thresholds became easier and happened more frequently. Fred enjoyed how Amy seemed more involved and present when they made love. Their sex blossomed, as did many other aspects of their relationship. Amy not only liked sex a whole lot more, she also had more respect for herself.

Maximize Your Total Stimulation

So now you know about your two sexual response thresholds—genital response and orgasm—and your total level of stimulation. You know that your total level of stimulation is composed of three parts: your body's ability to respond, the physical stimulation you receive, and your emotions, thoughts, and feelings during sex.

It will take many pages to flesh out this simple framework. In the next two chapters, we will discuss sex and sexual problems in greater detail. For example, what exactly is an orgasm? What actually causes vaginal lubrication and erections? What kinds of medications often interfere with sexual function? What are common problems with emotions, thoughts, and feelings? What actually causes premature orgasms in men?

But what we've already laid out has lots of relevance for understanding "sexual normality." Here's another piece. Many people develop a sexual style that generates just enough total stimulation to barely reach their threshold. They get aroused and reach orgasm—and as far as they are concerned they're "normal" because their genitals function as expected. They certainly are normal because this is what most people do. However, "good-enough sex" creates a precarious situation. All you need is a minor change in touch, situation, or meaning to reduce your total stimulation below your threshold. Suddenly, you have a sexual dysfunction. Unfortunately, most of us are sexual accidents looking for a place to happen.

Conversely, pursuing your sexual potential and developing a robust sexual relationship makes your sexual functioning more resilient. If you develop a sexual relationship that generally gets your total stimulation *way* above your response thresholds, then occasional distractions, arguments, or fatigue will be less likely to cause sexual problems.

In other words, whether you've had a sexual problem for some time or you want to avoid developing one, your strategy will be the same. The best way to avoid sexual problems is also the best way to solve them once they occur. You want to send your total level of stimulation through the roof. The solution involves having the best sex of your life!

What Is Happening When You Can't Get Aroused?

Before marriage, a man will lay awake all night thinking about something you said; after marriage, he'll fall asleep before you finish saying it.

—Helen Rowland

Wendy was starting to wonder if sexual dysfunctions were contagious. She and Jonah had been together for ten years, and it seemed like she was catching his problem. Jonah had difficulty with erections throughout the course of their marriage. Increasingly, Wendy had difficulty getting aroused when they had sex. She never knew what was going to happen when she and Jonah got into bed. Often she didn't feel very into it, and she had a hard time getting turned on.

Wendy's mind often wandered during sex, although she tried to not let Jonah know it—he was having enough sexual difficulties of his own, and she didn't want to burden him further. Besides, Jonah was already jealous and worried Wendy might find other men attractive. They didn't need more problems just now.

Jonah joked that his penis had a mind of its own, but he really didn't think it was funny. In most of their sexual encounters Jonah lost his erection during intercourse. Although Wendy was reasonable and understanding about this, sometimes Jonah avoided sex because he felt so inadequate. Occasionally Jonah had no difficulty with erections from start to finish, but frequently he went soft just as Wendy was getting into it. Why did this keep happening?

Do You Pole-vault into Bed or Get Wet Like Morning Dew?

Let's start at the beginning. What is sexual arousal? How can you tell when you're getting aroused? Is there a difference between physical arousal and subjective arousal? Where does sexual desire fit in? The first part of this chapter will answer these basic questions. In the second section you'll find an overview of different kinds of sexual arousal problems. We'll conclude by looking at causes of arousal problems through the framework we developed last chapter.

Typical Signs of Sexual Arousal

In the 1960s and 1970s, Drs. Masters and Johnson first documented the changes that occur in people's genitals as they become aroused.[1] When your total level of stimulation exceeds your arousal threshold, your genitals go through a cascade of dramatic and subtle physical changes.

For instance, when Wendy got aroused she had all the normal physical reactions: The increased blood flow to her genitals created a "sweating" response in her vagina that released natural lubricant. Spontaneous vaginal lubrication in women occurs the same way men get an erection from blood rushing to their penis. Wendy experienced this as "getting wet."

Moreover, Wendy's body went through numerous other changes that often escaped attention: her vagina enlarged and increased in muscle tone, her labia enlarged and turned darker in color, and her uterus elevated. As she became more highly aroused her clitoris retracted into the skin around it. Her vagina "deflated" in later stages of arousal and contracted during orgasm.

Wendy's clitoris, like Jonah's penis, was endowed with a rich supply of nerves and had the ability to swell (become erect). When stimulated and engorged with blood, Wendy's clitoris became more sensitive. The clitoris, labia, and entrance to the vagina are the most sensitive parts of a woman's genitals. The walls of the vagina are less sensitive to touch, but deep pressure often yields pleasant sensations.

Jonah's penis went through similar changes that were no less wondrous. When his total level of stimulation exceeded his arousal threshold, two spongelike tubular spaces within the shaft of his penis engorged with blood, which caused his penis to become erect. This was the equivalent of Wendy's lubrication response. In some ways, erection may seem like a simple hydraulic process compared to all the changes that occur as a woman becomes aroused. However, erections are equally incredible (and, to most of us, equally mysterious). The difference, perhaps, is that major changes are far more obvious.

Arousal Problems

Almost all men and women have arousal problems at one time or another. Arousal problems can involve absence of physical or subjective arousal and excitement. Arousal problems for women include partial or total lack of physical response, surfacing as lack of vaginal lubrication (wetness) or genital swelling, and discomfort or pain during sex. It can also involve persistent lack of subjective sexual excitement and pleasure during sex. Both men and women can have physical arousal without subjective arousal, and vice versa.

Men's sexual arousal problems include difficulty getting and maintaining an erection sufficient for completion of sexual activity and lack of subjective arousal. This can involve many different patterns. Some men never get a full erection. Others get a good one at first but lose it at some point before they reach orgasm. Onset of intercourse is the most common time for erection problems. This is due to the distracting mechanics of intercourse, particularly inserting the penis. Men often feel a dramatic increase in anxiety caused by pressure to perform.

Here's how our discussion from Chapter 2 applies: If you have an arousal problem in a given sexual encounter, your total level of stimulation never reaches your arousal threshold and the genital response you expect doesn't occur. Or, it reaches and then drops below your arousal threshold, at which point your initial genital response stops.

Arousal problems usually happen early in sexual encounters, in the initial stages of shifting from everyday reality to a mind-set conducive to sex. Jonah and Wendy referred to this as difficulty getting turned on.

However, arousal problems can happen at *any* point in a given sexual encounter.

You could get adequately aroused at the outset, but your total level of stimulation could drop below your arousal threshold later on. For example, you could become bored during sex if you don't like the way your partner touches you. If you think arousal problems occur only at the outset of sex, you can feel "messed up" (i.e., defective or pathological) when they show up later in the midst of things. By knowing arousal problems occur whenever your total level of stimulation drops below (or never reaches) your arousal threshold, you're more likely to handle it better.

Physical Arousal vs. Subjective Arousal

Many people complain of a lack of subjective arousal. Although you might expect subjective arousal to happen automatically when your genitals respond, this doesn't always occur. Limited subjective arousal and enjoyment usually accompanies lack of physical response, but you can have one problem and not the other. In fact, the whole relationship between physical and subjective arousal is not as clear as you might presume. Research indicates people's subjective experience and what their bodies are doing (e.g., heart rate, vaginal engorgement, pelvic contractions) often don't match.[2] A large part of our discussions will involve getting your mind and body in synchrony.

There is a complex link between physical and subjective arousal, particularly among women. Some women are poor judges of how physically aroused they become, according to laboratory measures of their genital response. Other women track their level of arousal quite well but find it takes longer to get emotionally involved than it does to get physically aroused. In fact both women and men who have no difficulty getting their bodies to respond physically may feel no subjective (emotional) arousal. They have no overt sexual dysfunction, but their own lack of passion, desire, and eroticism is bothersome. Their resulting low sexual desire can, in turn, further reduce their physical and subjective arousal.

Wendy had no difficulty becoming physically aroused during the early years of her marriage. It always seemed easy for her to get wet. In fact, sometimes this became a source of pressure for Jonah, because he thought this meant she was highly aroused and ready for action. However, Wendy's physical response often outstripped her subjective arousal, occurring long before she was ready for intercourse. Although they never discussed this, this was the complete opposite of how Jonah saw things.

Jonah was intimidated because Wendy always seemed to be ready to go. He was always trying to catch up to Wendy's arousal, and felt one-down because of it. (Many women have exactly the same experience as Jonah, with partners who readily become erect.) It made Jonah feel pressured to get an erection so they could have intercourse, which made his problem worse.

The difference between subjective and physical arousal regularly surfaced in Jonah's arousal problem. Although his total arousal level often declined below his arousal threshold during intercourse, Jonah felt a subjective sense of arousal just the same. The disparity between his subjective arousal and his diminishing genital response made Jonah really wonder what was wrong with him.

Some men and women who have difficulty with their genital response feel turned off. Others, like Jonah, feel subjectively aroused even when their genitals don't respond as expected. Other peripheral signs of physical arousal include increased heart rate, breathing rate, and pupil dilation. Recognizing these signs of physical arousal helps some people relax because the problem seems more limited. However, they made Jonah feel crazier. "If I wasn't responding at all, this would make more sense," he told me. "When I feel like my motor's running but my penis stops working, I feel like something inside me is broken!"

Sexual Desire

At the point they came to see me, Wendy was having increasing difficulty getting aroused and her desire for sex was diminishing. Subjective arousal and sexual desire are often closely related, so we ought to stop for a moment and clarify these terms. *Subjective arousal* has to do with what you're feeling (or not) about what your body's doing. *Sexual desire* has more to do with your interest in engaging in sexual behavior. "Low desire" is always relative to other factors, like your age, sex, health, and life context (which also affect your sexual functioning). However, low sexual desire generally shows up as persistent lack of sexual fantasies and disinterest in sexual activity.

Sixteen percent of the men in the NHSLS study reported having low sexual desire in the prior year. So did a third of the women. From my experience, this represents gross underreporting of the problem among men (thus illustrating the problem itself). Men are more loath to report sexual desire problems than women, although they are equally likely to experience them. Other research suggests that the incidence of low sexual desire among women is closer to 50 percent. Sexual desire problems are one of couples' most frequent sexual complaints.

Another kind of sexual desire problem is far less common but no less important. *Sexual aversion* involves extreme reactions to and avoidance of sexual contact. True sexual aversion—like getting violently anxious to the point you throw up—is exceedingly rare. Aversion also shows up in repeated hysterical sobbing and full-blown panic attacks when sex is imminent. Wendy went through periods where she didn't want Jonah to touch her, but this pales in comparison to real sexual aversion.[3]

How Common Are Sexual Arousal Problems?

Men's Arousal Problems
A 1994 study called the Massachusetts Male Aging Study (MMAS) sheds some light on men's arousal problems. Fifty-two percent of male subjects ages 40 to 70 reported difficulties with erections. Mild erection problems were equally common among older and younger men alike (17 percent). More severe problems were two to three times more common among older men (15 to 34 percent) compared to younger men (5 to 17 percent). Overall, 35 percent of all subjects had moderate to severe erection problems. Major factors were diabetes, heart disease, hypertension, and medications used to treat these diseases. Prostate cancer treatment (radiation, surgery) and spinal cord injury were among the many other causes. Extrapolating from this study's findings, 20 to 30 million men in the United States have erection problems. At least 20 percent of men over age 50 have this difficulty.

Women's Arousal Problems
Sexually active women of all ages report arousal difficulties. In the 1994 NHSLS nationwide study, 19 percent of women between ages 18 and 59 reported lubrication difficulties. The rate of lubrication problems among postmenopausal women goes up to 45 percent. A 1978 *New England Journal of Medicine* study of 100 "normal" couples reported

that 48 percent of women had difficulty getting excited and 33 percent had difficulty staying excited. While these results are striking, also consider this: 86 percent of these women said their sexual relationship was satisfying, and only 15 percent of their husbands knew their wives had these problems!

In the past women's subjective arousal difficulties were not considered problems in themselves. Women's arousal problems usually surfaced as low sexual desire, pain during intercourse, and vaginismus. However, women no longer have to tolerate being told to "have a drink and relax" in order to get through sex. In countries where women enjoy some measure of equality, women's subjective sexual arousal and satisfaction increasingly shape their sexual relationships. And with the advent of Viagra and the discovery of the biochemistry of sexual response, women's arousal problems are now receiving more attention.

Stereotypes that women are slower or more difficult to arouse than men turn out to be untrue. Many couples find these roles reversed. Differences in arousal speed show up between lesbian and gay partners too. Masters and Johnson demonstrated that women become aroused just as quickly as men do if they are "effectively involved."

Patterns of Arousal Problems
Arousal problems can be lifelong or start later in life. Most sexual problems are intermittent or situational, but some are pervasive (meaning they happen every time you have sex). A woman with a pervasive, lifelong problem, for example, would be someone who never became sexually aroused and lubricated at *any* point under *any* circumstances in her life (including masturbation). For a man, this would mean he never became aroused or had an erection under any circumstance (including morning erections). These kinds of sexual difficulties are rare (especially in men) and often involve underlying medical problems.

Other arousal problems continue without letup once they start. They can be constant in all sexual experiences, regardless of circumstance or situation. They can result from such medical problems as neurological damage from alcoholism, adolescent-onset diabetes, or hysterectomy. Hormonal difficulties also tend to be persistent once they start. Long-standing sexual or interpersonal concerns can also create seemingly invariant arousal problems.

Most arousal difficulties are intermittent. Any number of things can periodically interfere with your total stimulation reaching your arousal threshold. These can be episodic arguments about gridlocked issues in your relationship (Part 2) or undisclosed relationship conflicts. Maybe you're ruminating about something unsettling at work, or the phone rings in the middle of sex. It doesn't have to be the same cause each time. Situational problems usually involve things that compete for your attention and keep you tense, such as the baby crying in the next room, your parents sleeping at your house during a visit, or running out of birth control pills.

Sexual Pain Disorders

Occasional arousal problems are common and nothing to worry about when infrequent. However, when the severity and frequency increase, it's time to act. Painful sex (dyspareunia) is not something you should ignore or tolerate.

Think of arousal difficulties and pain disorders as two separate but typically related problems. Arousal problems can cause painful sex, and pain of any kind can cause difficulty with physical and subjective arousal. Though pain usually kills arousal, many women carry on. Painful sex shows up in these women as difficulty having orgasms.

Women's sexual pain consists of surface pain at the entrance to the vagina or pain deeper within. Arousal problems frequently show up as friction pain (being rubbed dry) at a woman's clitoris and labia. Pain deeper in the vagina can be caused by insufficient arousal, positional pain (e.g., a thrusting penis hitting the woman's cervix), and other physical causes such as endometriosis, prolapsed uterus, vaginal scarring, and unusual skin sensitivity.

Sexual pain is far less common among men. Only 3 percent of men in the NHSLS study reported sexual pain in the last year, compared to over 14 percent of women. Male sexual pain arises from medical problems like infection, inflammation, priapism (prolonged erection), or Peyronies disease (bends in the penis).

Both men and women can develop hypersensitivity to even slight discomfort from repeated painful sexual experiences. A degree of friction some couples experience as pleasant "tightness" might feel intolerable to people with a history of painful sex. Pain sensitivity is as important in the experience of pain as the physical stimulus itself.

Some men experience penile discomfort as a result of extreme interpersonal anxiety or sexual aversion. For instance, Chen reported pain during intercourse and had difficulty reaching orgasm inside Li's vagina. He preferred to stroke his own penis when they had sex because Li "didn't do it right." Li was at a loss because no matter how she touched Chen's penis, he said it hurt. He was often "twitchy" when Li touched him anywhere on his body, and he found hugging unpleasant. Chen focused on what Li was doing wrong and attacked her adequacy, but he lacked the slightest awareness of how highly anxious and overreactive he was. He often felt cornered and saw no room to acknowledge his contribution to their difficulties.

Women can develop hypersensitivity to pain too. Eleanor created a self-induced pain syndrome after several months of painful sex brought on by a vaginal infection. For the next several years Eleanor douched daily. This upset the natural environment in her vagina, causing further discomfort during intercourse. Eleanor's "solution" was to use lots of extra lubricant during sex, which led to more douching. Sexual anxieties and discomfort with her own body contributed to Eleanor's problem, as did the subsequent negative impact on her relationship.

Repeated painful sexual experiences can create another physical problem, which becomes its own pain-producing mechanism: vaginismus. This is a recurrent involuntary spastic contraction of the muscles surrounding the outer third of a woman's vagina, which makes insertion painful and interferes with or prevents intercourse. Vaginismus develops from recurrent sexual pain, sexual trauma, rape, incest, strong sexual inhibitions, panic about intercourse, and phobias about sex. Although vaginismus occurs less commonly than dyspareunia, it still happens to 10 to 15 percent of women.

Cases of vaginismus vary widely. Some preclude any kind of vaginal entry (e.g., speculum insertion, Pap smear, or tampons), whereas others are situation-specific (e.g., intercourse). Some women with vaginismus avoid dating or sexual relationships for decades. Some are married and have sex without intercourse, while others are celibate. Some reach orgasm with oral sex. A number only come for treatment because they want a baby or their marriage is falling apart. Some do not have intercourse with their partners even when their vaginismus is resolved.

The therapeutic view of vaginismus has changed markedly in the last fifty years. It was initially considered a severe personality disorder and thirty years ago it was (naively) thought to be an easily reversible, purely physiological problem. However, vaginismus produces a pain-tension-pain cycle that can be hard to break. Women who have severe phobic reactions in addition to vaginismus may need medication or systematic desensitization.[4] Long-term interpersonal impacts of vaginismus can be hard to repair. Tension in the relationship, embarrassment, disappointment, low desire, arguments about sex, and conflicts outside the bedroom are common.

Causes of Arousal Problems

Using the framework developed in the last chapter, we can organize the many causes of arousal problems into three categories:

1. Medical and physical difficulties that interfere with sexual response

2. Insufficient physical stimulation

3. Emotions, feelings, and thoughts that diminish arousal and enjoyment

Arousal problems can result from any one of these three categories or some combination thereof. For example, difficulties with erection and lubrication can result from physiological causes (vascular, neurological, hormonal), your thoughts and feelings during sex, insufficient physical stimulation or any combination of these. Although some arousal difficulties originate from drug side effects, they can develop an additional psychological basis due to your emotional reactions and remain after a problematic medication is discontinued. Keep in mind that things that cause arousal problems can also cause problems with orgasm and desire.

Physical Problems Limiting Your Response to Sexual Stimuli

Aging and medical problems are two major factors that can affect your responsiveness. In Chapter 2 we discussed how aging raises your response threshold and predisposes you to arousal problems. I won't repeat this here except to note that how you adapt to aging largely determines the impact it has on you.

Medical illnesses and treatments, medication side effects, and hor-

monal changes can also limit your total level of stimulation and ability
to respond to it. They can raise your threshold or make it difficult for
your body to transmit stimulation. It gets harder for you to trigger the
complex cascade of chemical, vascular, and neurological changes that
creates sexual function.

Many things can impair your body's ability to receive and process
sexual stimulation: neurological disorders, vascular problems, heart disease, hormonal imbalances, surgery, congenital abnormalities, injuries,
pelvic vascular insufficiency, prescription medications, recreational
drugs, fatigue, stress, and lots more. Some medical conditions have pervasive effects, while others cause intermittent problems. The partners of
people with these disorders can also develop arousal problems from the
secondary impact of their mate's sexual problems and the demands of
their medical conditions.

Menopause and Hormones

Hormonal factors are particularly important for women, especially during and after menopause. Estrogen depletion reduces vaginal lubrication
and increases vaginal irritation (atrophic vaginitis) in 10 percent of
postmenopausal women. This in turn can cause pain during intercourse
and decreased desire. Estrogen replacement can improve women's vaginal lubrication and reduce atrophy, but this doesn't necessarily increase
desire or sexual activity.

Testosterone also gradually tapers as women go through menopause.
(It drops precipitously with hysterectomies that include removal of the
ovaries and with some chemotherapies.) Testosterone deficiency can
reduce a woman's sexual desire and fantasies; decrease the sensitivity of
her clitoris, vagina, and nipples; and make it harder for her to become
highly aroused or reach orgasm. If testosterone-deprived women reach
orgasm at all, their orgasms are shorter, weaker, less "global," and less
pleasurable.

Hysterectomy

A small percentage of women who have hysterectomies experience subsequent differences in sexual response. Because of scar tissue their
vaginas may not "balloon" as fully; they may also experience reduced
sensation and pain. Without a uterus, congestion of blood in their pelvis
is reduced, and uterine contractions during orgasm are absent. The rea-

son for their hysterectomies can also affect their sexual adjustment. Hysterectomies for benign disorders (the major reason for hysterectomy) usually have less impact than those conducted for cancer. Older women often adjust better than younger women, who lose the opportunity to give birth. If hysterectomy cures distressing symptoms, such as chronic pain, endometriosis, or uterine bleeding, or if it reduces cancer risk, it can markedly improve a woman's sexual function and interest.

Medication Side Effects

You'd be amazed how many popular medications negatively impact sexual function and desire—so much so that the major categories of medications have evolved second-generation versions that have significantly fewer sexual side effects. The most popular drugs on the market can really screw up your sexual response. Most drugs for hypertension, depression, and anxiety can interfere with arousal, orgasm, and desire.

This turned out to be Connie's problem. Connie thought her reduced desire and arousal was related to menopause. However, she had started taking Prozac because she had been worrying about financial problems and her mother's declining health. While the drug helped her overall mood, it also increased her thresholds for arousal and orgasm and diminished her subjective desire. When she didn't feel herself getting physically aroused and lubricated like she used to, this further increased her anxiety, reduced her desire, and killed any chance of orgasms.

Once I suggested this possibility to Connie, she talked with her physician. They decided to try another medication with fewer sexual side effects. Pretty soon Henry was teasing her that she was back to her "old raunchy self."

Recreational and Over-the-Counter Drugs

If you have difficulty getting aroused or reaching orgasm, consider the impact of nonprescription medications, recreational drugs, and alcohol. For example, some men find they can't reach orgasm when taking particular over-the-counter cold remedies. Excessive alcohol consumption can suppress your arousal for an evening. Chronic alcohol abuse can create nerve damage that impairs your genital response for the rest of your life.

The nicotine in tobacco is a vasoconstrictor, which is why tobacco smoke causes heart and lung disease. But nicotine also reduces blood flow to a man's brain and genitals and increases outflow from his penis. Women experience similar impacts, as well as fertility problems. None of these encourage robust blood flow to your pelvis (which is what you want if you want to get physically aroused). Kissing increases your total level of stimulation, and smoking discourages kissing. All things considered, smoking is a lousy aphrodisiac.

Quality and Quantity of Physical Stimulation

The second major source of arousal problems involves insufficient physical stimulation. In the language of today's computer world, problems with physical stimulation involve "operator errors." For instance, arousal problems sometimes result from repeatedly being rushed into sex by your partner.

Stereotypically, men rush women into intercourse, but some men develop difficulty with erections because they feel obligated to start intercourse when they think their partner is ready. Women can feel rushed if they're with a partner who rapidly reaches orgasm. Men who have premature orgasms often *do* rush themselves and their partner into intercourse. Many women and men who have difficulty getting aroused rush themselves during masturbation too. That's why couples often need to slow things down rather than finding new "magic" erogenous zones.

Sufficient physical stimulation is not simply a matter of duration. The quality of stimulation is critical. This involves more than being touched in the right spots with techniques you like. It involves the degree of positive emotional connection between you and your partner and your willingness to give and receive pleasure.

There are good answers to age-old questions like, "Why must I keep telling you what I want?" "Why do you keep changing what you're doing?" "Why do you keep doing it too hard (or too soft) even when I show you?" The answer isn't necessarily that your partner is brain-dead, deaf, or passive-aggressive. (We'll consider these possibilities later.) More often it's that he or she can't feel you. There's no positive visceral connection between the two of you, so she or he has no internal sense to go by.

For example, if your partner touches you but doesn't *feel* you, sometimes no amount of touch gives you threshold levels of arousal. Touching without feeling is fairly common. It shows up as touch that feels mechanical, wooden, or dead. It often involves the same spot being rubbed over and over again and feels irritating both physically and emotionally. Repetitive motion results from boredom (or anxiety) in the toucher, and induces mind wandering and frustration in the touchee. This is not the kind of stimulation you want to pay attention to.

Many therapists address this as a "communication problem," encouraging you to tell your partner what you want. This often fails because it focuses on talking and listening. The real issues have to do with limited positive emotional contact and the absence of a collaborative alliance. Often partners are well aware of each other's feelings and thoughts about what's going on—and it isn't very positive.

If you and your partner are emotionally "fused" (Part 2), you probably spend lots of time buffering the emotional impacts you have on each other and little time reveling in the pleasure of each other's touch. If you or your partner anticipate more criticism or an argument, telling your partner what you want often doesn't bring results you like.

Insufficient high-quality stimulation can often be resolved if couples discuss this openly without dodging or overreacting. This is a big *if*. What might seem on the surface like a necessary straightforward conversation between adults is difficult for many couples. My clients often find that this conversation is a turning point in their relationship and personal developments. That is why I don't presume you and your partner will have this conversation if I simply say you should do it. It involves more than giving your partner the technical specifications on the kinds of touch you want.

Speaking up is itself an act that changes sexual relationships. That's why it is difficult to do. Later on I'll explain why it's so important that you do it, without expecting your partner to accept what you say or applaud you for saying it. This has more to do with holding on to yourself better around your partner than it does with "better communication." The fact that you're learning to validate and soothe yourself is the message.

Psychological Factors

Arousal disorders can be caused by acute or chronic stress and undetected or untreated depression. Marital discord, money problems, health crises, and work troubles are common causes of arousal problems. Positive and negative aspects of your current relationship have a big impact on your emotions, feelings, and thoughts during sex. Struggling with your partner over commitment issues, for example, doesn't generally help sexual arousal. Neither do the common and necessary struggles over sexual preferences.

Unresolved emotional struggles about sexual orientation, gender identity, and social roles can also surface as distractions during sex. Child or adult sexual abuse can also be a factor. Negative body image is a serious problem for many women, and aging, illness, surgery, and obesity reinforce this. Limited sexual knowledge and unrealistic expectations can also have an impact.

Although most of what I just described are present-time issues, childhood sexual abuse may stand out for you because it involves the past. As you'll learn in Part 2, your past does *not* create all the dynamics in your relationship. Everything is not a replay of your childhood or an expression of your unconscious fears or wishes. Your past colors the meaning you give to natural and predictable relationship processes as they play out. This is not the same as saying your past "causes" the things that happen in your marriage. It does shape how you interpret inevitable developments in every relationship and ways you become emotionally blind or hypervigilant.

When you can't get aroused after an argument with your partner, it's easy to see what's causing it. But sometimes situational and intermittent problems can be hard to figure out. Many couples have no idea what is causing their arousal problems (although these invariably seem obvious in retrospect). Even simple notions like "strict religious upbringing" fall apart when you try using it to explain why problems happen intermittently.

Phil and Mary's pattern was invisible to them because the emotional interaction between them was the key. Phil almost always had difficulty maintaining an erection during intercourse. Typically, he would withdraw, feeling inadequate, frustrated, and guilty because he couldn't stay erect. If they tried again later and Mary consoled him for half an hour, Phil would reliably get and maintain an erection without difficulty.

Although they repeated this pattern about forty times a year for over twenty years, neither Phil nor Mary realized how his sexual functioning hinged on receiving consolation and validation from Mary. Yes, they recognized that the second try always seemed to work. However, they never looked into what was really going on between them.

Phil was anxious and insecure about letting Mary get emotionally close to him. His anxiety made it hard for him to keep his total stimulation above his arousal threshold. When Mary didn't react angrily and helped him calm down, a little oral sex and a few words of endearment produced a reliable erection. Phil thought of this simply as getting from Mary the "support" he needed. Phil willingly acknowledged his insecurities, but there was more going on.

In every sexual encounter, Mary had to put her feelings aside and dote on Phil. Phil presented her with the choice between putting herself second or going without sex. This was the indirect result of Phil's inability to deal with his own fears of being controlled by Mary. When she let herself get swept up in the power of her own sexuality, Phil felt intimidated. As long as Mary deferred to him sexually, he could relax and *feel* her on the second try at intercourse. However, Mary was inadvertently being conditioned to never relax or get too aroused, and it eventually took its toll.

Mary and Phil didn't understand what was happening, but it still had an impact on her. Mary had no difficulty lubricating when Phil touched her, but their interactions reduced her subjective arousal, her desire for sex, and her desire for Phil. Basically, Mary felt Phil was terribly self-centered and inconsiderate. In turn, Mary didn't want Phil to really connect with her during sex because she didn't want him to know what she was feeling.

Phil and Mary demonstrate why seemingly commonsense solutions often don't work. Although Mary's support and consolation helped Phil keep his arousal level up on the second pass, it was also the reason their problem continued for over twenty years. The more Phil demanded "support" from Mary, and the more she gave it, the more he feared losing her and being controlled by her. When Mary deferred her own wishes and consoled and supported Phil, it briefly eased his fear of being dominated by her—and made him more insecure and dependent on her the next time.[5]

How did Phil and Mary turn things around? Eventually their situation "ripened" to the point that they could no longer keep their old patterns going. Mary's lack of desire became so obvious that she told Phil the truth. This kicked off predictable processes in their sexual relationship.

With some help from me, Phil and Mary were able to recognize their pattern and break it. Phil acknowledged their sexual interactions reflected much of the dynamics in their whole relationship. Phil figured he was in for a "raft of grief" from Mary, now that the truth was out. However, instead of blasting Phil, Mary started asking herself why she'd been willing to go through this for so long. Mary didn't like the answer, but it wasn't hard for her to figure out. She always put everyone's interests before her own. Instead of getting angry, Mary just got quiet and introspective.

Instead of ducking for emotional cover, Phil got clear about what was really important to him. He calmed himself down because the possibility of divorce was increasing. He had no room for blaming, denying, or taking out his frustrations and fears on Mary. His options boiled down to confronting himself or breaking up their marriage. Going to Mary for soothing only replicated the problem they played out in bed.

Phil decided that if he lost his erection again, he would continue pleasuring Mary one way or another. It became a point of personal integrity for him. He couldn't repeat his pattern of twenty years now knowing what he was doing.

When they had sex that night Phil and Mary settled down in bed, making and keeping a sense of emotional connection from the outset. Phil had no hint of difficulty on their first attempt at intercourse. Or their second. Or their third, the next morning.

For a while Phil's problem showed up intermittently. However, they had turned a corner. Phil and Mary understood how his erections, their emotional functioning, and their relationship all fit together, and not just as a theory. They watched how their sex worked in real time.

Phil had to get over feeling controlled by his caring for Mary. Mary had to stop deferring at every turn. These were scary self-confrontations for both of them, but ones that were also surprisingly helpful. Like many couples, Mary and Phil found the outcome far better then they ever expected. In Parts 2 and 4 I'll explain how and why this happens.

If you happen to have difficulties with orgasm or sexual desire, you don't have to feel left out. You can go through this same process too. Orgasm problems will be the next chapter's focus. The process Phil and Mary went through is actually the core of *Resurrecting Sex*.

4

Do You Have Difficulty with Orgasms?

The orgasm has replaced the Cross as the focus of longing and the image of fulfillment.

—Malcolm Muggeridge, *The Most of Malcolm Muggeridge* (1966)

Do the mountains tremble and the heavens shake when you have sex? If the earth doesn't move you have lots of company. Orgasms are a mystery to many people, even to those who have them. We can use what we've said thus far to reduce some of the mystery: Orgasm is "just" a matter of having your total stimulation exceed your orgasm threshold. However, the diverse ways people have difficulty sending their bodies and minds into spasm are incredible. So are the complex reactions people develop around what is basically a psychobiomechanical twitch. (Alfred Kinsey, the great sex researcher, compared orgasm to a sneeze.)

And problems with orgasm don't always involve not having one. Many men reach orgasm too quickly. Only men have this problem, and it is the most frequent sexual problem they have.[1]

There are three reasons why you need to appreciate the variety and subtly of orgasm problems: First, if you understand the pattern of your particular problem, you can tailor your efforts to change it. Second, understanding your pattern of orgasm difficulty will help you resolve the impact it's had on you. Third, your pattern of difficulty reaching orgasm is a window into who you are (as is true of *everyone's* sexuality), and you can learn a lot about yourself through it.

What Is an Orgasm?

An orgasm is a sequence of physiological changes in your genitals, your brain, and throughout your body. These changes are accompanied by subjective experiences that can vary between intense pleasure and deep meaning, and utilitarian tension release and minimal satisfaction. People describe feeling increased physical tension and high sexual arousal, which build to a peak. When this peak reaches their threshold for orgasm, they have a sensation of release and "letting go." This coincides with brief genital contractions, which are rapidly followed by a sense of relaxation.

If you are a woman, when you reach orgasm the muscles in your uterus, vagina, and rectum rhythmically contract every eight-tenths of a second. If you are a man, your penis, scrotum, and rectum do likewise. Typically your face grimaces, muscles all over your body tense, and your stomach and buttocks muscles tighten. Some people have intense contractions; others don't. Some women and men experience orgasm as an overwhelming positive global experience; other people's orgasms are more like a brief shudder. Most people's orgasms vary in intensity between these two extremes.[2]

Sometimes your arousal level may stay high enough for another orgasm cycle to occur. This is known as "multiple orgasms" and is common among a minority of women and a few men.[3] Most typically, your arousal gradually declines after orgasm (especially as you age).

There are many profound orgasm experiences that have little to do with the number of orgasms. "Time stoppage" is a good example of a subjective experience that can accompany orgasm. Time seems to stop and hold your partner and you together in a private moment, separate from the rest of the world, which is moving in real time. Some people like sex for these experiences and are unhappy when their orgasms don't produce them. When you are not willing to lose yourself in the moment, however, sex can seem to be over in a flash: One laboratory study found women underestimated the duration of their orgasms by as much as half.

Difficulty Reaching Orgasm

Although most men and women have occasional difficulty reaching orgasm, persistent delay or absence of orgasm is a significant problem for some. Women and men who have difficulty reaching orgasm often feel tremendous performance pressure. That's partly because "success" is so clear (and supposedly so magical). Some people feel their own and their partner's sexual adequacy hangs on whether they "pop their cork." (That's why people fake orgasms.)

Here is another area where men and women are more similar than we realize. Because a man's difficulty having orgasms is usually called delayed *ejaculation* rather than delayed *orgasm,* it is harder to see.[4] Political correctness forbids calling women "frigid," but this hasn't yet caught up with pejorative labels like "retarded ejaculation" and "ejaculatory incompetence" for men.

So don't think of a man's problem as difficulty ejaculating. Think of it just as you would for a woman, as difficulty reaching orgasm. Both genders can learn to broaden the ways and increase the ease with which they have orgasms.

Sexologist Havelock Ellis shocked the nineteenth-century world by suggesting women's sexual responsiveness far exceeds that of men. However, sixty years ago, Alfred Kinsey found that one out of ten women in his surveys had never had an orgasm. Delayed orgasm is less frequent among men than it is among women, but this doesn't make it any easier to bear. Some women who have difficulty having orgasms talk with other women to find advice and support. If you're a man with this problem, you probably have never spoken a word about this to anyone (perhaps including your partner).

Many women are unable to reach orgasm during intercourse. This is a normal variation of female sexual response, especially if you can have orgasms with your partner using noncoital methods. Your level of sexual experience has to be taken into account. Younger women are more likely to have difficulty reaching orgasm, period. As women become more sexually experienced, they often have orgasms with forms of stimulation (including intercourse) that didn't "work" when they were younger.

However, at least half of all women have intermittent problems having orgasms in some situations or to some forms of stimulation (for example, oral sex or intercourse). Fully 10 percent have never had an orgasm under any circumstances.

In the 1994 NHSLS study, orgasm problems were the second most common complaint from women of all ages. One out of four women had this problem in the prior year. Other studies estimate 10 to 15 percent of women never reach orgasm with a partner, and another 25 percent have intermittent difficulty reaching orgasm during partnered sex. One study of 329 women ages 18 to 73 at an outpatient gynecological clinic found 29 percent had orgasm problems, 11 percent had frequent pain during sex, and 40 percent felt anxious or inhibited.[5]

According to the NHSLS study, one man in a dozen has difficulty reaching orgasm. A small percentage (3 percent) report pain during sex, which can interfere with orgasm. Male problems with delayed orgasm typically involve not being able to reach a climax after trying for some time. However, some men find their orgasm and ejaculation are "out of sync." Orgasm and ejaculation involve two separate (but usually synchronized) processes. One can be impaired, while the other remains intact. In other words, occasionally a man might experience orgasm but have no ejaculation, or the other way around.[6]

Some men, like some women, don't acknowledge difficulties having orgasms, especially if their self-worth is on the line. Some men try to turn it into a virtue, acting like "I'm a real stud who can last a long time." However, their lack of passion, their anxiety about failing, and the fact that their partners generally want things over sooner gives them away.

On the other hand, orgasm dysfunctions are not a problem for some couples. It's not that they don't occur, it's that they aren't terribly upset by them. In Chapter 3 you learned of one research study in which 86 percent of women who had difficulty with arousal said their sexual relationship was "satisfying." Maybe you won't be surprised by another study of "happy marriages" in which 63 percent of women reported orgasm and arousal problems and 85 percent reported being satisfied with their sexual relationship.[7]

Not having an orgasm doesn't have to be a catastrophe, and getting upset about it won't help. However, you don't have to be complacent about your problem. If you want more satisfaction than many women and men seem to expect, what you read next can help you.

Never Had an Orgasm at All
Some people have never had an orgasm in their lives and are still trying to have their first one. If you've ever had an orgasm, whether by masturbating or while sleeping, or by any means whatsoever, you're not a member of this group. Lifelong total lack of orgasm frequently occurs among young and middle-aged women. Their likelihood of success is so great therapists refer to them as "pre-orgasmic," implying that they are at a normal midpoint in their sexual development.

Women in this category simply need encouragement, more (and better) stimulation, and some lubricant to reach their goal. Rarely does complete lack of orgasm in women have a medical basis. It is most easily and readily resolved through well-informed masturbation. Masturbation groups and books for women on masturbation and sexual self-care flourished in the 1960s. Although the groups vanished along with psychedelic T-shirts, masturbation has stood the test of time as a way to have your first orgasm.

On the other hand, not all cases of total lack of orgasm are easy to resolve. A man who has not had an orgasm (ejaculation) at some point is quite rare. Boys are frequently embarrassed by nocturnal emissions because they are almost automatic in adolescence. Complete lack of orgasm in men can be caused by severe hormonal, chromosomal, congenital, or interpersonal problems, which require specialized treatment by a competent team of experts.

Medical problems, conflicts about sex, and interpersonal difficulties sometimes interfere with women having their first orgasm. These kinds of things made it harder for Rhonda, for example, to turn things around. Rhonda was a college cheerleader who looked like a sex kitten but who had never had an orgasm. Three things kept her from her goal:

Ineffective stimulation. Rhonda typically "gave up" after stimulating herself for 10 minutes. She wasn't afraid to have an orgasm.

It was that she lost hope, her wrist got tired, and her clitoris became sore.

Emotions, feelings, and thoughts. While Rhonda masturbated, she pressured herself to have an orgasm and castigated herself for not "scoring a touchdown."

Physical responsiveness. Rhonda was taking antidepressant medication. Her boyfriend had recently ended their relationship. Rhonda believed this stemmed, in part, from her sexual difficulty. The load of appearing the ever-perky campus queen, while hiding her sexual "secret," was getting to her. Her medication (known to impair orgasm) probably masked any improvement Rhonda made with her physical stimulation and her thoughts and feelings during masturbation.

Rhonda turned things around by addressing each layer of her problem. First, she confronted herself about feeling like a fraud and her dependency on men's approval. Confronting her emotional weakness helped her see her own personal strengths. As she began to feel better about herself, she stopped taking medication. Moreover, Ronda became more observant of the *tone* of her masturbation. When she started pressuring herself to reach orgasm, she took a brief break rather than stopping altogether. She also bought herself some personal lubricant at her drugstore. All told, this allowed her to stimulate herself longer and better without rubbing her clitoris into oblivion. This multilayered solution helped Rhonda have orgasms and became a pathway to a new way of life.

Pervasive Orgasm Difficulties Starting Later in Life
What if you had your first orgasm, but somewhere down the line you run into difficulty having your next one? This is the most common orgasm problem, in part, because so many different things can cause it. These difficulties can be as simple to resolve as in Rhonda's case, but sometimes they are more complicated. That's because there is more involved than learning how to have an orgasm. Situations and relationship difficulties that can limit your total stimulation during sex can also be hard to change, as we'll discuss in Part 2.

Orgasm problems can be pervasive once they start (meaning you never have another orgasm again) or they can be intermittent. The causes of these problems can also be obvious or obscure. Pervasive and unrelenting orgasmic difficulties starting later in life frequently arise from medical problems. Injuries and medical treatments such as surgery and radiation treatments can create neurological (e.g., severed nerves) or vascular changes that also impair orgasms.

For example, having the saphenous vein in the upper thigh harvested for heart bypass surgery can decrease blood flow to the genitals.[8] The pudendal nerve and its pathways up the spine are also involved in having an orgasm. Lower back or pelvic injuries can damage these nerves, resulting in reduced genital sensations and the need for massive stimulation to reach orgasm (if even possible). Removal of a woman's cervix when hysterectomy is performed may also decrease her ability to orgasm.[9] All of the above can affect sexual function and desire through our thoughts and feelings too.

Medications

Many medications commonly prescribed for anxiety, depression, psychosis, and hypertension can directly and indirectly impair orgasm. An estimated 80 percent of people who take SSRI antidepressants experience delayed orgasm and reduced desire.[10] Unfortunately, these are more likely to be women. However, Conner, a 65-year-old man taking high blood pressure medication, found out medications can affect a man's functioning too.

Having taken his medication for years, it didn't register as the cause when Conner became unable to have orgasms. Even though his physician had recently increased the dosage, Conner just thought his whole body was wearing out, and he became distraught. Once Conner confided his sexual difficulty to his doctor, a minor adjustment brought his orgasms back to life. It was a good thing Conner didn't get too upset because this could have perpetuated his difficulty after his medication was no longer interfering.

Illness and Medical Procedures

Medical problems are more likely to cause pervasive sexual difficulties because their negative impacts tend to last for long periods with little variation. However, early stages of diseases like multiple sclerosis and diabetic neuropathy sometimes first surface as intermittent difficulty reaching orgasm. Diseases that come and go (e.g., myasthenia gravis, genital herpes, or depression) and episodic medical procedures (e.g., chemotherapy) may cause intermittent problems.

Menopause and Hormonal Problems

As women settle into menopause, reduced hormone levels create pervasive difficulties reaching orgasm for some. The secondary impacts of menopause cause intermittent orgasm problems for others. For example, Candice and Regina's relationship conflicts were growing over differences in their sexual desires. In addition to hot flashes, Candice's sexual desire and orgasms decreased markedly with menopause. Treating herself homeopathically had reduced her hot flashes, but her diminished responsiveness remained.

On top of this, Candice's labia and the entrance to her vagina often became irritated and raw when she had sex. She tried to deal with the ensuing skin irritation and discomfort by attempting to cut sex short. Repetitive pain also caused her to anticipate pain, heightened her anxiety, and diminished the intimacy she had with Regina during sex. All of this made it hard for Candice to get aroused enough to trigger her orgasm.

Regina was at her wit's end because she didn't want to go without sex forever. On the other hand, she didn't want to be a source of pain for Candice. Regina hated pushing Candice for sex and she didn't want to feel like a sexual "oppressor." Accepting sex from Candice felt like she was taking "pity handouts."

Candice wasn't happy about her own two-choice dilemmas.[11] On the one hand, she didn't want to switch to hormone replacement therapy because she didn't want to put drugs in her body. On the other hand, Candice saw homeopathy wasn't helping her sexual problems. Homeopathy and sex had become battlegrounds where she and Regina fought out who was going to control whom. She didn't want to give in to Regina, but she didn't want Regina to leave.

After three years of tears and arguments, Regina announced she was leaving and forced Candice's hand. Candice could no longer put off her decision. All things considered, she decided to rethink her stand on homeopathy. Hormone replacement therapy helped Candice reach orgasm, her vaginal irritations decreased, and her interest in sex returned. This, and dealing with their (self-) control struggles, led to a more satisfying relationship. Like many couples, Candice and Regina used the information you'll learn in Part 2 to turn a relationship on the brink of divorce into a robust and resilient one.

Occasional Difficulties Reaching Orgasm

Everyone has difficulty reaching orgasm sometimes. Intermittent difficulty can stem from medical problems (although this is more rarely the case). For example, women who have intermittent pain during sex (e.g., from endometriosis) frequently have difficulty reaching orgasm. In men, painful ejaculation (e.g., due to chronic prostatitis and urethritis) can cause similar orgasm problems.

Trans-urethral resection of the prostate (TURP), a common treatment for prostatitis, can indirectly cause orgasmic difficulties in some men.[12] Richard developed "retrograde ejaculation," a common secondary impact of TURP. When he had an orgasm, his ejaculate went backward into his bladder rather than out his penis. Richard was in his fifties and wasn't trying to have more kids, but he was a high-strung guy who reacted strongly to this change. The result was that he could not reach orgasm when he got upset about it during sex. Some men develop rapid orgasm or difficulty with erections, while others take the whole thing in stride. Learning this helped Richard realize his problem reaching orgasm stemmed from his emotional reaction to retrograde ejaculation, rather than damage to his ability to have orgasms, per se.

Situation-Specific Difficulties

For human beings orgasms are more than a biomechanical process. Orgasms are interpersonal events whether you are with a partner or masturbating. For women and men alike, your emotional frame of mind, your relationship, and your environment play big roles in your ability to climax.

For instance, if you are due at a gala dinner in an hour and your partner decides it's time for hanky-panky, you may not be able to have an orgasm while the countdown is running in your mind. And the first time you have sex after a serious argument may not be when you hit your heights. Hearing your baby cry or your mother-in-law cough in the next room may also kill things for that encounter.

Intermittent situational difficulties reaching orgasm are a universal experience. These invariably involve emotions, thoughts, and feelings that limit your total level of sexual arousal. How, when, and why you have this problem reflect who you are. What happens when you think you may not have an orgasm in a particular encounter? Some people get very upset about this, while others do not. Some aren't able to overcome this, while others go on to climax.

Difficulty with Specific Partners

Severe relationship problems can create orgasm difficulties that may last for years. Such problems usually have slower onset than those from medications, illnesses, and injuries, although there are exceptions. For example, Denise had stayed in her marriage for the benefit of her children. She withdrew completely from her husband upon the sudden death of their youngest daughter. Her interest in sex disappeared and her thoughts during sex were about her dead child. Denise's depression decreased her desire as well as her ease, enjoyment, and frequency of orgasms.

When couples don't repair relationship damage caused by "dealbreaking" developments (e.g., extramarital affairs or chronic drug abuse), residual thoughts and feelings can cancel out the arousal value of any physical stimulation they exchange during sex. People can become unable to reach orgasm with their partner although they can climax during masturbation.

Some people have never had an orgasm with a partner, period. For some it's the fact of another person being present. For others, it's about allowing (depending on) someone else to provide (control) the stimulation. Similarly, you can have more difficulty (or greater ease) reaching orgasm only with particular categories of people because of the meanings and roles involved. The problem surfaces (or disappears) with partners who fit a special stereotype. There are men like Steve, who could reach orgasm only with prostitutes, because he felt they were "trash." Paula had multiple orgasms when she was in an affair with a married man. She had difficulty having orgasms with her husband, unless she fantasized about her affairs. "Getting away with something" had turned her on since she was an adolescent.

However, orgasm difficulties can be limited to one specific partner. Maybe you don't like his or her sexual style and technique. Maybe you don't like or feel comfortable with him or her at all. Perhaps it's nothing about the person per se, but something in your relationship distracts you.

Jesse, for example, remarried late in life. Her first husband died after a long illness and her new husband was a very controlling man. He had definite ideas about what was all right to do sexually, and oral sex (which worked for Jesse) was not among them. He was defensive and closed to any suggestions from her. Jesse found she couldn't reach orgasm after they argued—which was typically when he wanted to have sex. Early in her second marriage, Jesse became unable to have orgasms with her husband.

As I said, the details of your problem, like intermittent difficulty reaching orgasm, reflect who you are. What's important is what's going on for you.

Stimulation-Specific Difficulties

Difficulties reaching orgasm with particular forms of stimulation are common, although people's patterns differ greatly. Stimulation that's not quite right usually comes to mind as an example of stimulation-specific problems. However, many orgasm problems are specific to particular sexual behaviors. Some women and men have lifelong difficulties reaching orgasm during intercourse, although they have no difficulty by any other means. For others it's exactly the other way around: They are able to reach orgasm *only* during intercourse.

The range of difficulties can be heartbreaking. Benson, for instance, never had a climax during oral sex, even though he regularly brought his wife, Betty, to orgasm that way. Betty was eager to return the favor, but Benson couldn't let himself be "taken." Another client, Sue, could reach orgasm only during intercourse because that way didn't trigger her discomfort with her own genitals. Then there was Bud, who had never been able to climax inside a woman's vagina. His wife spent years longing for Bud to release himself inside her. Another man, George, could reach orgasm only by dragging his penis along the sheet as he stood beside the bed. (He was living proof that your customary way of masturbating can condition your sexual response to patterns of stimulation you can't get with a partner.) In each case, people's difficulties occurred because some or many behaviors didn't provide enough total stimulation for them to reach their orgasm threshold.

When people have repeated difficulty having orgasms, there are often equally unhappy partners lying beside them. People like to use their partners' orgasms to bolster their own sense of sexual competence (Part 2). Men, as well as women, can feel pressure to reach orgasm. To some women, a man's ejaculation means completion and sexual communion. To others, ejaculation itself is no big thing, but repeated *absence* of ejaculation gets to them. Some men feel pressured to have an orgasm during intercourse because their partners want to get pregnant. Gay and lesbian couples go through similar games around orgasm.

Given the great weight attached to reaching orgasm with a partner, people who have no difficulty by themselves often feel defensive and inadequate. Early on I promised you a nonpathological approach, so let me share with you what I've learned since I stopped looking through the lens of pathology. Some men and women are simply better at having sex with themselves than with a partner. Sex with their partner may or may not be as good as other couples have. In some cases, it's better. It just doesn't provide the stimulation they need to reach their threshold for orgasm.

Four different things might give you better sexual function when you are on your own: First, you may be truly expert at stimulating yourself. Second, you may need incredible stimulation—you may have a high orgasm threshold and can reach orgasm only when you stimulate yourself. Third, you may have anxiety during sex with your partner, and sometimes you don't know it. It may always be present and you come to expect it without realizing it. Fourth, you may not be able to create the same highly erotic mind-set with a partner that you can when you're alone. Perhaps it's a way of touching yourself that you're embarrassed to reveal to your partner. Or it may be a fantasy world of taboo relationships and sexual behaviors that pales with your partner present.

As I said, some folks are incredibly good at masturbation. It's not necessarily a sign of narcissism or immaturity or difficulties in their relationship. It's a matter of good judgment. They are so good at masturbating that sex with other people isn't as "hot." If this is you, you know what you like and you don't have to apologize for it. Whether this represents a dysfunction or the side effect of a wonderful ability depends on how you feel about being able to have orgasms with a partner.

I've worked with clients who had great sex by themselves but who had difficulty reaching orgasm with their mate. This was a problem for them because they wanted to share this with their partners, and they felt limited because of this. If this is true for you, your task is to develop the same incredible sex with your partner that you have with yourself.

This process invariably involves personal growth on your part to make this possible. Turning the corner from feeling pathological to pursuing your sexual potential is always a pivotal step in personal development. Regardless of your pattern of orgasm difficulty, avoid assumptions and stereotypes about your problem. Pay attention to what you actually do and feel during sex. You need to know why your particular pattern of difficulty occurs as it does.

Premature Orgasm

Rapid orgasm (often called "rapid ejaculation") is the most common sexual dysfunction that men have. In Alfred Kinsey's 1950s surveys, 75 percent of the men reported reaching orgasm within 2 minutes. Other estimates suggest that 30 to 60 percent of men have premature orgasms. According to the NHSLS study, one in four men reached orgasm too quickly in the past year. Rapid orgasm is a normal pattern of male sexual function (although this doesn't make it enjoyable).

There is little gained debating how quick is too quick. Measuring it by minutes, thrusts, or the partner's satisfaction are useless common approaches. (In Part 2 I'll explain why measuring men's "successes" by their partners' sexual responses perpetuates sexual and relationship problems.) The "premature" in premature orgasm involves a climax with minimal stimulation that happens before a man and his partner want it. I suggest you approach premature orgasm as the absence of voluntary control of orgasm (within realistic expectations). Looking at this as the absence of voluntary control (1) underscores men's ability to develop voluntary control and (2) emphasizes what couples find most problematic.

A major aspect of premature (and delayed) orgasm is that you have no sense of control over what happens to you. This can play havoc with your sense of self-mastery, which is crucial to many people's self-worth. Like difficulty reaching orgasm, rapid orgasm can be pervasive or intermittent, and it can vary in severity. In severe cases, men ejaculate the moment (or shortly after) they start intercourse. As one man told me,

"When I repeatedly go to the penalty box the minute I start to play the game, after a while I don't feel like playing at all."

Not All Orgasms Are Fun

At first glance, premature orgasm may not seem to have a counterpart in women. Referring to it as rapid (or premature) *ejaculation* rather than *orgasm* blinds us to the similarities, because (most) women do not ejaculate. Men like Bill, who has rapid orgasms, are similar to women like Joan, who can reach orgasm after a minute or two of simulation. The difference is that Bill doesn't like his orgasm and Joan does. There are two reasons for this.

First, Bill has a "refractory period" after he orgasms (and Joan doesn't). Bill loses his erection and has to wait a while before his sense of arousal and erection can gear up again. As Bill has gotten older, his refractory period has increased from 15 minutes to several hours. After Bill has a climax his subjective arousal, excitement, and passion diminish. Even if he sticks around to help his partner have an orgasm, his energy declines. Bill and his partner can feel it and react defensively to it. Joan's partner, in contrast, is tickled when Joan has her orgasm. His pet nickname for Joan is "marathon woman."

Second, the components of Bill's total stimulation that drive him to orgasm are entirely different from what Joan has when she's "hitting her stride." Joan is relaxed and eagerly anticipating what (and who) is about to come. The stimulation that quickly drives her to orgasm is 100 percent pure carnal pleasure.

Bill, on the other hand, is anxious and tense. He's not looking forward to what he anticipates will happen next. His stomach churns, his hands and armpits are wet, his mouth is dry, and his heart is pounding. He is hyperalert and his adrenaline is pumping. He is already at a very high state of physical arousal. All he has to do is feel the warmth of his wife's vagina and he's a goner. Too much of the stimulation that brings Bill to orgasm is already present: It is *anxiety*. Cutting back on his pleasure doesn't make much difference because Bill's total stimulation is 98 percent anxiety and 2 percent pleasure. No wonder Joan is happy and Bill is crestfallen during their respective climaxes.

In some ways men with rapid orgasms are no different from women (and men) who have difficulty reaching orgasm. They all have difficulty letting themselves relax and be held or "taken in" during sex. It's hard to relax when you feel ashamed and humiliated, or frustrated and angry, regardless of your gender.

Stimulation-Specific Problems

Speed of reaching orgasm can vary with circumstance, partner, relationship, and time since your last sexual encounter. Some couples adopt the strategy of having sex twice in an encounter, figuring that the second time will take longer. However, some men *don't* have longer latency, because the same massive anxiety that quickly triggered their first orgasm is present the second time around. Some men struggle with rapid orgasms all their lives. Some find aging raises their orgasm thresholds and increases how long they can last.

Speed of orgasm varies greatly with the form of stimulation. Premature orgasms (like delayed orgasms) are often specific to intercourse. Men with premature orgasm (like men and women with delayed orgasm) often have better volitional control of their orgasms when receiving intense manual or oral stimulation. Moreover, they typically have much better control during masturbation. Many can last 10 minutes or more. However, some are done after a few seconds inside a vagina or just having their penis near one. Even if these men forgo all foreplay, it takes just brief intercourse to reach orgasm.

Anxiety, Sex, and Relationships

The major cause of premature and delayed orgasms is anxiety. Men with either problem have the most difficulty with intercourse, because it's "put up or shut up time" either way. There are an awful lot of anxious, awkward, uncomfortable guys in the bedrooms of America and throughout the world.

Consider the different ways anxiety impacts sexual function: On the one hand, anxiety generally reduces your total stimulation. Anxiety can interfere with reaching arousal and orgasm thresholds, creating erection (and lubrication) difficulties as well as delaying orgasm in some men (and women).

In premature orgasm, however, anxiety adds to, rather than reduces, men's total level of stimulation. Think of stimulation as physiological activation rather than something sexually arousing. Your body gets ticking when you're filled with either pleasure or dread.[13] Your orgasm won't be much fun because your arousal has more to do with anxiety than pleasure. The process can be hard to stop once it starts because your anxiety typically increases as you become more sexually aroused. (The same holds true, for instance, among women with delayed orgasm.)

If this sounds weird, realize that it's the *norm* that anxiety makes men reach orgasm quickly. Why men respond to anxiety one way or the other is not well understood. In fact, some men with severe anxiety may have more than one sexual dysfunction, and I've worked with some who have as many as three. At the outset of an encounter, for example, Kyle struggled with getting an erection. Once he started intercourse he became embroiled in trying not to reach orgasm quickly. If successful at lasting 5 minutes, he shifted to struggling to be able to have an orgasm. Needless to say, Kyle and his partner did not have fun in bed.

A Glimpse of What's Next

Men like Bill and Kyle often report having intercourse 10 to 30 minutes longer than their partners remember. However, the problem isn't simply that these men and their partners are in two separate realities. It's that they actually may not be separate enough.

Some guys are "emotionally fused" with a partner who has as much difficulty regulating her own anxiety as he does. When partners are emotionally fused, they infect each other with anxiety through their emotional connection. Some women pass their anxiety to their husbands, and both partners' anxiety keeps them from any awareness that this is happening.

For example, Esteban developed a sense of dread when he knew Carmela was interested in sex. Repeated experiences of premature orgasm and the emotional aftermath had left an impression. Carmela went into fits of anger and depression, questioning what was wrong with her—or Esteban. Was she bad in bed? Did Esteban want to get away from her as quickly as possible? Maybe Esteban didn't really care about her? Maybe he was just "using her for sex"?

Esteban was nervous to start with, and being in bed next to Carmela's anxiety was like getting a double dose. He wasn't about to ask her to relax, because this made her more nervous and defensive. Esteban's total stimulation quickly reached his orgasm threshold from all the anxiety they both felt, although Carmela saw it as Esteban's problem.

With this in mind, imagine what happens when men's and women's most common sexual problems (rapid orgasm and delayed orgasm) show up within a single couple. There's not much room for accommodation. A woman's first orgasm usually takes the longest, and men's first sexual encounters are usually their shortest. Many women know there's not much time to relax when you're trying to beat your husband's orgasm. In this contest between the tortoise and the hare, the hare "wins."

Then, think of a pair of single adults having sex for the first time. Imagine how much anxiety *both* partners carry. Women are often as nervous as the guys. Couples struggling with premature orgasm through fifty years of marriage face the same situation. There is more than enough anxiety and insecurity to go around.

The good news is that men can train themselves to delay orgasm in ways equivalent to how women (and men) learn to hasten theirs. Some men with premature orgasm probably have low orgasm thresholds, but most are average guys reaching orgasm too quickly because their anxiety spikes beyond their thresholds. If you have common sexual anxiety *and* a low orgasm threshold, you can spend your life struggling with rapid orgasms. You may think your problem is so severe as to make it unique, but your solution is the same: You need to learn how to better regulate your anxiety during sex.

5

Twenty-two Ways to Resurrect Sex

If venereal delight and the power of propagating the species were permitted only to the virtuous, it would make the world very good.

—James Boswell, *London Journal,* March 26, 1763

Welcome to graduation day of your crash course on sex! Let's review what we've learned. Basically, resolving sexual dysfunctions involves increasing your total level of stimulation, and doing what you can to ensure your body can respond to it. This increases the likelihood you'll reach your response thresholds and have the genital response or orgasm you want.

Sometimes you can accomplish your goal by improving only your physical stimulation. However, you are more likely to succeed, and more likely to enjoy doing it, if you have a better relationship with yourself and your partner. Likewise, improved physical stimulation and an improved relationship will have the biggest impact on your sexual function if your body is well prepared to respond. From this we evolved a basic three-part strategy for resolving sexual problems.

- Optimizing your body's ability to respond

- Optimizing the physical stimulation you receive

- Optimizing your feelings, emotions, and thoughts, including your relationship with your partner

Remaining sections of this book fill out this framework. Part 2 addresses how your sexual relationship operates. You'll learn why fairly predictable things happen between you and your partner regarding sex in particular and your relationship in general. And I'll show you how to implement necessary changes and transform your sexual relationship.

In Part 3, we'll explore medical marvels that might enhance your sexual response. We'll discuss surgical methods, oral medications like Viagra, and even Viagra usage by women. You will learn what bionic solutions can and cannot do and how best to use them.

Part 4 pulls the prior sections together. That's where you'll see the working-through process of putting these good ideas into action. You'll encounter many couples going through this process, just like you. We'll discuss how to deal with medical problems, ways to increase your physical stimulation, and how to get your relationship and yourself percolating. We'll also go deep inside the mental world of sex so you can further optimize your thoughts and feelings.

As we transition to Part 2, we'll use our three-part strategy in this chapter to organize some ideas for going forward. I'm going to give you twenty-two suggestions. Some are easier to implement and some are harder. Just like Nancy and Carl, a couple I'll tell you about, you can use these suggestions to keep your eye on your goal: resurrecting sex.

Optimize Your Body's Ability to Respond

Anything that interferes with your body transmitting or responding to stimulation can limit your sexual function. Here's how you can apply this idea to your situation.

Suggestion 1: Have a Complete Medical Evaluation
Do yourself a favor and have a thorough medical examination. Get one if you suspect or know you have medical difficulties, or if you just want peace of mind. Sexual dysfunctions and lack of desire can be early warn-

ings of brewing medical problems. For example, low sexual desire can be caused by low testosterone, which itself is sometimes secondary to a pituitary tumor. A clean bill of health clears the way to concentrate your efforts where they're likely to do the most good.

Consult your physician if you are taking medications. If this is the source of your difficulty, possibly your doctor can modify your dosage or shift you to other drugs. Be explicit and direct about your sexual symptoms. Don't wait for your doctor to ask, because she or he may be just as nervous as you about bringing up the topic. It's the doctor's responsibility to ask, but you lose out if he or she doesn't. (Lists of medical problems and medications frequently causing sexual difficulties appear in the appendixes.)

Suggestion 2: Don't Push for the Diagnosis You Prefer

A lot of maneuvering occurs around what diagnosis people want for their sexual problems. I've worked with many clients who sought purely physical explanations for their problems. Their goal wasn't to just find out if they had medical difficulties, they wanted to exclude the possibility of any emotional component whatsoever. Men in particular prefer to have physical problems, because they want to split mind and body in order to avoid any mental causes. In one couple, the husband wanted to avoid feeling inadequate. ("It's not my fault if it's medical.") In another case, the wife wanted a bullet-proof excuse to quit having sex. ("It's not my fault if it's medical.")

Give yourself a fair chance. Don't commit to one particular view of your problem prematurely. Don't assume a disease you have or a drug you take is the culprit in your case, just because it's known to cause sexual difficulties for other people. Don't assume that anything to do with thoughts and feelings automatically requires dredging up your past (read: childhood).

Suggestion 3: Remember Sexual Problems Always Involve Mind and Body

All sexual problems are physical problems because even emotion-based sexual problems have negative impacts through physical processes in your mind-body interaction. Similarly, *all* sexual problems have an emotional component—if not as a cause then certainly as a result. People invariably have emotional reactions to even purely medical problems.

There is much to be learned about the body's secrets, but a primarily physiological view of sex destroys the essence of human sexuality. Even if you have a medically based sexual problem, don't forget sex is a mind-body interaction.

- Resolving relationship and personal impacts of medical or drug-related sexual problems always involves using your brain and opening your heart.

- Your relationship situation and your emotional state tremendously impact how you and your mate deal with medical problems.

Suggestion 4: Do What You Can to Maximize Your Physical Health

If you have an illness or medical problem, do what you can to bring it under control. Take necessary medications in a timely fashion. Don't do things that exacerbate your condition. This sounds like common sense, but you might "compensate" yourself for your medical problems by indulging in ways that make your problems worse (e.g., not following dietary restrictions). Likewise, if you are at war with your body over your appearance, there's a tendency to abuse it or not keep it fit.

Suggestion 5: Pay Attention to Subtle Changes in Your Physical Response, but Don't Get Overly Preoccupied with Them

Some people experience subtle shifts in sexual sensations in the early stages of undiagnosed illnesses. A number of disorders frequently first manifest themselves sexually. If you notice changes in your sexual response or desire, don't ignore them.

On the other hand, don't let normal changes of aging command your attention. Your biological sex drive and the intensity of your sensations decrease as you get older. The process starts earlier and more subtly than many people realize. It is well under way for some folks by their thirties. The changes are often imperceptible at first. Eventually, these changes can distract you during sex and encourage you to withdraw from your partner and go into your inner world of fears. That, in turn, further decreases your total stimulation, and makes genital dysfunctions and diminished desire more likely.[1] When in doubt about whether your changes are normal or a sign of something more serious, get a medical exam.

Given that many of us no longer have bodies that defy the law of gravity and we're showing signs of wear-and-tear, how can I be encouraging you to have the best sex of your life? Aging itself doesn't destroy sex or diminish your capacity for (and interest in) intimacy, eroticism, and desire. In fact, these often grow as you get older. Your genitals reach peak responsiveness in adolescence, but it can take half a century to get your heart and judgment involved. Genital prime and sexual prime are entirely different, each occurring at opposite ends of your life span. People don't reach their sexual prime until their forties, fifties, or beyond. Cellulite and sexual potential are highly correlated!

If you want to be a sexy senior citizen, emotional maturity and connection with your partner must become driving forces of your sexuality. You'll inevitably discover sex diminishes as you age if you depend on horniness to carry you through half a century of marriage.

Suggestion 6: Expect to Change Your Sexual Style as You Get Older

If your sexual relationship stays the same, you are more likely to have sexual dysfunctions (and be bored to death). When your response thresholds exceed the total stimulation you get from "doing what you usually do," you'll start having sexual dysfunctions.

Likewise, think of medically related sexual problems as "problems given the way you usually have sex," as opposed to "intractable problems you'll have no matter what you do." In some cases medical problems can be compensated for by markedly increasing your total level of stimulation. Typically, this requires changing your sexual relationship and believing in yourself—and this means changing yourself in the process.[2]

Expect to have to shake up your sexual relationship every once in a while. I know that's exactly opposite what couples want to do. People usually like stability in their sexual relationships. Just incorporate episodic shake-ups into your notion of long-term stability.

The need for change and sexual growth is built into the way we humans evolve physically and emotionally throughout our lifetimes. You have dormant sexual potential that's ready and waiting to be developed. You can develop it through the personal growth called for in your relationship, made necessary by the way your body changes as you get older. This tendency for your physiology to call for growth and require changing your sexual behavior (relationship) is something you should note early on, because we'll return to this in later chapters of this book.

Optimize the Physical Stimulation You Receive

Optimizing your physical stimulation involves good will as well as good technique. Your partner's willingness to make you feel good is as important as your ability to relax and receive this. Relationship (re)building is often more crucial than tips on sexual positions or telling your partner what you want.

This was certainly the case for Nancy and Carl. They typically had sex two or three times a year, and nothing had happened in over ten months. Just getting things started was a major event. It wasn't as if Nancy or Carl didn't like sex. The sex they had was sort of okay—pretty awkward, actually. Not something either one wanted to do repeatedly. For the last two decades, Carl planted his garden instead, Nancy took their kids to the gym, and they let their opportunities drift away. Now Carl and Nancy sought treatment because they didn't want to continue this way for the rest of their lives.

Suggestion 7: Don't Assume You Connect Emotionally with Your Partner During Sex
When I listen to a couple's description of their sexual interactions, I figure out how much contact they really have with each other during sex. Use the following questions to make this assessment for yourself.

- Do you feel like you connect emotionally with your partner during sex?

- If so, how do you do that?

- What do you do when you lose contact with each other?

- Do you ever realize you've lost connection while it's happening?

- What do you do on those occasions?

- How have you been able to reestablish connection with your partner during the encounter?

- Do you cover over when you tune out, pretending you are really present? How (and how often) do you do it?

Think back to the last time you broke contact with your partner during sex. (For some of us, that's the last time we had sex.) Your answers will reveal who you are and what your relationship is like. Nancy and Carl were so struck by these questions they had sex to find out the answers. They walked into whole new dimensions of sex they never knew existed.

Nancy and Carl discovered they had much less actual contact during sex than they ever imagined. Nancy realized she had sex with Carl without the slightest sense of what he was thinking. She also realized the same was true in reverse. She often conducted mental dialogues with herself during sex. Carl went on as if Nancy was still with him, while she was mentally miles away. This revelation scared and electrified Nancy. This was a whole world she had never played with. It sounded sexy. It offered hope.

Suggestion 8: Increase the Quality and Quantity of Your Stimulation

By now this should seem obvious. However, if you've been celibate for any length of time, increasing the quality and quantity of your stimulation takes on a different meaning. Try reaching out to your partner one way or another. Your overture doesn't need to be blatantly sexual. What's important is that your reaching out be (1) clear and unambiguous and (2) heartfelt rather than obligatory.

Carl and Nancy might have had sex several times in prior months if they had responded quicker to each other's overtures. Neither wanted to reach out to the other if a warm response was not immediately forthcoming. Between tentative initiations and guarded responses, neither held themselves out long enough for the other to respond in time. However, this time Nancy reached out to Carl in such a guileless and open way, he almost grabbed her hand for fear of not responding quick enough and having everything fall apart. Nothing in their usual exchange said, "Yes, I'm nervous, too, but I love you and I'm trying." This time it was loud and clear. Carl reached out and kissed Nancy's hand and held it to his face. At that moment they were more together, and more aroused, than they had been in a long time.

Suggestion 9: Do Whatever Works

I suggest you not focus on intercourse to start with, because that's often the hardest way to establish emotional contact with your partner. Also, don't just focus on erogenous zones. Before you try holding each other's glands, try holding hands. If you and your partner are emotionally estranged, just reaching out and taking your partner's hand will bring your issues to the surface and give you practice making and maintaining contact. Soften your hand and let your body relax. Who is really holding whose hand?

Once Nancy and Carl passed the hurdle of getting started, they faced other problems. Their kisses and caresses were tentative and defensive, conveying their expectations that things were about to go downhill. Each was upset by the way the other acted. So Nancy and Carl moved forward by focusing on kissing. It was more like an evening of collaborative improvisation, rather than a refresher on technique. Nancy started kidding that they kissed like chickens. That led to playful demonstrations of a whole menagerie of kisses. Carl and Nancy spent an evening laughing and kissing, quite apart from their typical dismal sexual encounters.

Suggestion 10: Increase Contact with Your Partner During Sex: "Follow Your Connection"

Stop your mind wandering and increase your "in the moment" involvement during sex. Your involvement during sex can vary anywhere from "barely there" to "really there." You can be distracted with a sexual dysfunction, present enough to get aroused or reach orgasm, or so profoundly engaged with your partner and so deeply engrossed in the moment that sexual function isn't a question.

When your partner is touching you, focus your attention on the point of physical contact. As your partner's touch shifts, move your attention with it. Sometimes watching your partner touch you can help you stay focused. Don't just focus on the mechanics of his or her touch. Try to feel your partner's *intent*.

When you are touching your partner, focus your attention on the person inside your partner's body, rather than on the surface of his or her skin. Whether you and your partner just hold hands or touch everything you can reach, reach out to your partner in ways that convey you are trying to touch minds and hearts. Relax and let him or her *feel* you through your touch. Try to help your partner feel good, but don't presume you know what will do that.

In Carl and Nancy's case there was no presumption. They had no idea what the other really liked. But now they had a fledgling sense of connection in bed, and they didn't want to give it up. Nancy started looking at Carl while they had sex because she didn't know what else to do. Carl noticed this immediately and started paying attention too. Nancy said she just wanted to see him and reached out to touch Carl's cheek. There was no doubt in Nancy's or Carl's mind at that moment that they were very much together.

Once you have any kind of emotional connection through your physical contact, do whatever it takes to deepen it. When something strengthens your sense of connection, do more of it. Stop doing things that don't work even if (1) you or your partner want to do them or (2) you think they work for other couples. Maintaining a relationship involves self-control, and sex is no exception. When you and your partner can maintain a resilient emotional connection during sex, you can expand this to other behaviors in which you usually lose contact with each other.

Once Nancy and Carl had a sense of connection when touching each other's face, they knew what they were looking for. When Nancy touched Carl's chest and the back of his neck, that sense increased. When she played with his ears (which Carl didn't like), it went down. They started doing more of the former and less of the latter, and both Carl and Nancy became increasingly aroused.

Then they switched and used the same approach with Nancy. Carl usually touched Nancy's genitals sooner than she wanted, and she typically moved his hand away. This time she didn't stop him and let him feel for himself that this really didn't arouse her. Carl finally realized this didn't work, and he stopped doing it. Touching Nancy's breasts that particular time really turned up the heat. The next time it seemed to be the inside of her thighs. It helped them feel like they weren't stumbling blindly around for what to do. It was something they could both feel, and they were willing to respect it.

Optimize Your Thoughts, Feelings, and Emotions

You want your total stimulation as high as you can possibly get it. The more you exploit all levels of your sexual potential, the more likely you will achieve desired results. It's possible to raise your total stimulation far beyond what it takes to get erect or wet or have an orgasm. Optimizing your thoughts and feelings is a powerful way to do that.

Suggestion 11: Establish a More Collaborative Alliance with Your Partner, Both in and out of Bed

Put some effort into the nonsexual aspects of your relationship. Flowers and candy are nice, but daily things make the difference. Whether it's planting a garden together or going on family outings, there are lots of ways to create a shared sense of emotional investment. Carl started broadening his interactions with Nancy in areas that had nothing to do with sex. He signed them up for dance classes, which Nancy had always wanted to do. "Lack of time" turned out not to be the stumbling block Carl thought it would be. Nancy was more willing to confront her own sexual inertia when she saw Carl making efforts out of bed.

Collaboration often involves going through difficult moments together without becoming adversarial. Carl and Nancy persevered in their sexual encounters, whereas they probably would have stopped in the past. Kindness, patience, and consideration are some of the best sexual lubricants.

Suggestion 12: Explore New Dimensions and Depths of Your Sexual Connection

Expand your repertoire of sexual behaviors, "tones," styles, and meanings. Push yourself beyond your conventional sexual boundaries, and try a sexual behavior that feels like a stretch. This will increase your ability to express yourself through sex and increase times and ways you can engage your partner profoundly. It will also trigger your own struggles for self-development, a topic we will discuss throughout the rest of *Resurrecting Sex*.

For now, think of one behavior or style of sex that would help your relationship if you could grow to like it. It doesn't have to be one your partner has been pushing (unless you think your partner is on the right track). In your own judgment, what is one thing you could do in bed that would help your problem?

Consider expanding three dimensions of your sexual potential that people often avoid. These are your capacities for eroticism, sexual desire, and emotional union with your partner. If you want to increase your desire for sex, or desire for your partner, try mixing carnality and communion.

Eroticism. Eroticism is what turns you on, the part of sex that makes things *sexy*. Eroticism is very personal and self-revealing—that's why partners typically hide their eroticism from each other. It emerges in the styles and nuances of the sex you like. Think of eroticism as "the way you want to engage your partner" or "what really cranks your clock."

Desire, passion, and love. Desire, passion, and love contribute to your overall arousal because they are biologically wired in to your sexual response. That's why desire for your partner, deeply shared moments, and your ability to love all affect (and are affected by) your sexual function and satisfaction. Profoundly meaningful connection with your partner contributes to your total stimulation. When you're having incredibly arousing and deeply meaningful sex, sexual desire becomes a simple matter of good judgment. But you have to open your heart first and want that kind of sex *before* you have it, to have a prayer of getting it.

Emotional union. Profound emotional connection during sex can bring your stimulation to all-time highs. Nancy and Carl couldn't see this at first because they were so awkward and embarrassed with each other that, if anything, things felt too close. But Nancy was able to see how out of sync they were during sex. She found that the more positive emotional connection she and Carl developed, the better their sex became. However, this wasn't happening the way she had expected. She had thought if she felt more secure with Carl, her sexual anxieties would go away. But it turned out that the more they each controlled their own anxieties, the stronger their sexual union grew. Realizing they had gone about this backward for twenty years made it easier to understand why it took so long to turn things around.

Suggestion 13: Work Out Your Issues with Your Partner
End the wars. Deal with issues you and your partner have swept under the carpet. If you're going to bed angry, frustrated, or resentful, you're more likely to give your mate the *un*screwing of his or her life. Don't simply try to reduce negative feelings—go about this in ways that build collaboration and friendship. Just "straightening things out" won't give you the best shot you've got. Bring out the best in your relationship if you want to maximize your (and your partner's) arousal.

After twenty years of wondering how he could put up with Nancy, Carl was really starting to want her. And after decades of mind-wandering during tepid sporadic sex, Nancy started to pay attention. They were spending more time talking and looking at each other, and neither of them seemed bored.

Both Nancy and Carl became deeply engrossed in the dramas unfolding weekly in their bedroom. Whereas previously sex focused on Nancy trying to have an orgasm, they were starting to have sex the likes of which they had never had before. They noticed the rest of their relationship changing as well. They didn't seem as tense and defensive with each other. Arguments had less of a hard edge and didn't flare as quickly. Nancy and Carl found the process of resurrecting their sexual relationship was more like the birth of it.

Suggestion 14: Develop a Better Relationship with Yourself

Generally speaking, the more unresolved personal issues you are dodging, the more you have to tune out during sex and the more vulnerable you are to sexual problems. You might be able to get physically aroused and even reach orgasm, but your overall arousal is usually diminished.

Learn to soothe your own frustrations and disappointments. Anxiety can impair sexual function and satisfaction many ways. If you want more control over your sexual function and, likewise, better functioning in the rest of your life, improve your ability to regulate your anxiety. Starting in Part 2, we'll talk about this as "holding on to yourself." Holding on to yourself involves soothing your own anxieties, insecurities, and frustrations. This helps stabilize your relationship and keeps desire alive.

Rest assured that I understand the magnitude of this suggestion, like the previous ones and those that follow. We'll spend the rest of this book exploring exactly how to accomplish them.

Using Sex to Become the Person You Want to Be

You can do much more with your thoughts and feelings than just create lots of wonderful sexual arousal. You can use sex in a conscious and deliberate way to grow into who you want to be. This takes hard work rather than hyperbole.

Suggestion 15: Operate from the Best in You

Your efforts to resolve your sexual problems need to come from the best in you. How you go about this process and whether you're responding from the best or the worst in you makes a big difference in the results you achieve. It's all a matter of how you respond.

When you have a sexual problem it's easy to respond from the worst in you. You perceive your problem to mean you're screwed up, inadequate, damaged, or unfit for human consumption. In this case, you'll be ashamed of your situation and more likely to avoid problems as long as possible. Your efforts to change will be halfhearted and less effective, and you won't have much resilience if things don't improve immediately. When you approach the situation from the worst in you, the most you can hope for is proving you're not as defective or incompetent as you thought.

However, if you approach your sexual problem from the best in you, it can become a doorway to a new way of life. The best in you can hang in and keep trying, in spite of your fears and insecurities. Likewise, the best in you understands fair play and right from wrong when dealing with your partner. Approaching things from the best in you can accomplish far more than eradicating signs of "inadequacy." It can help you believe in yourself and increase your self-respect.

Suggestion 16: Don't Get Lost in Psychodynamic Interpretations

I've found that resolving sexual problems usually requires growth rather than repairing emotional problems. Forget pop psychology interpretations of your sexual difficulty, like "You hated your mother (or father)" or "You hate your partner." Lots of people who hate their spouse have no problem getting their genitals to work. Try not to drive yourself nuts over possible unconscious meanings of your sexual problems, and don't be enamored with symbolism. Sexual symptoms themselves have no inherent psychological meaning.

Don't start with jaundiced interpretations, like "Your sexual problem serves some purpose in your relationship (or life) that you don't want to give up." Maybe you *are* subtly withholding your love and commitment. Maybe you unconsciously *do* want to frustrate your partner. However, my experience says people with sexual problems go through elaborate mental gymnastics to keep from disappointing anyone—most of all themselves. My guess is, you are ready to be rid of your problem!

It's too easy to interpret sexual dysfunctions and desire problems as caused by an unconscious desire to deprive your partner of satisfaction. But don't overlook the obvious: Sexual dysfunctions and desire problems *do* deprive your partner. That's true whether you like it or not, whether you "caused" it or not, and whether you "unconsciously want" it or not. Avoid psychobabble and keep your eye on the central issue: Sexual problems *always* deprive your partner. At a certain point, what causes your sexual problem is beside the point. The only real questions are these:

- How do you feel about this?
- What are you going to do about it?

Suggestion 17: Don't Turn Yourself into a Stereotype

No personality traits or life experiences invariably create sexual problems. Common stereotypes about particular life experiences supposedly causing sexual problems aren't borne out by research. Religious sexual prohibitions, social class, family messages that sex is shameful, lack of education, and unpleasant prior sexual experiences don't invariably make a difference.

Don't jump to conclusions because of something in your past. Don't lump yourself into stereotypes or preconceived explanations. When the NHSLS study results were analyzed by religion, women who reported some religious affiliation were *more* likely to have orgasms than those who didn't.

Suggestion 18: Discover the Meaning of Your Sexual Problem

Many people are preoccupied with what their sexual problem means. Don't get sidetracked playing amateur psychoanalyst. Pay attention to your specific situation. Look at what is actually going on for you. That is where you'll find the real meaning of your sexual difficulties. The "meaning" isn't necessarily the cause of the problem, but rather, what arises as a *result*.

Yes, sex *always* has meaning. If you haven't had sex in years because of your partner's medical problem, of course that means something to you. Even if you don't doubt your own attractiveness or your partner's love, it still means you're probably frustrated, disappointed, and angry. *That* means you've probably had to decide whether to show your feelings. And if your partner has been coming to bed later to avoid possible sexual approaches from you, that probably means something to you too.

Earlier in their relationship, Carl's decision to come to bed after Nancy was asleep had great meaning to Nancy. This played a large role at the time she and Carl stopped having sex. Nancy heard Carl saying, "I give up" loud and clear. Nancy said, "I give up" back to Carl when

she started meeting her women friends for breakfast on Saturday morn-
ings—his preferred time to have sex.

Sex isn't empty when you're turned off or dissatisfied. Sex isn't empty
when it feels empty. The most frustrating and unpleasant sex still has
plenty of meaning: It expresses the people involved, and they draw lots
of meanings from it. For better or worse, your sex life embodies what is
(and isn't) happening between you and your partner.

Sex is an incredibly rich language. Everyone speaks the language of
sex by virtue of being born human. You and your partner communicate
through sex, even when you don't like the messages being sent. Both of
you exchange meanings (communicate) all the time, especially when
you're having sexual problems.

Some couples, like Carl and Nancy, become celibate in an attempt to
create silence. Even if neither partner says a word, unspoken dissatisfactions, frustrations, and disappointments during sex can be deafening.
Not having sex becomes one way they try to stop conveying these messages to each other. Unfortunately, there are no time-outs in marriage.

Couples have sex—and *avoid* sex—in ways that express what they
are feeling, who they are, and what's going on. Carl and Nancy's sex
typically consisted of a few brief kisses before Carl "went to work" on
Nancy. He then tried to make her climax by rubbing her clitoris with his
fingers. Nancy never had an orgasm during intercourse, so once Carl
inserted his penis in her vagina she knew it meant Carl had "given up."
Carl got the same message from Nancy whenever she said, "Just come
inside me." Carl heard Nancy giving up on herself, on him, and on their
relationship. Nancy got the same message when Carl came inside her.
What is more heartbreaking? Hearing "I give up" while you and your
partner start having intercourse? Or hearing "I give up" every night that
you don't touch at all?

Suggestion 19: See Yourself Through the Window of Your Sexual Relationship

Anything you do (and don't do) can be a window into yourself and your
relationship. Kissing is highly revealing and very intimate. (That's why
couples stop kissing even though they still have intercourse.) Even not
kissing says a lot. No two couples avoid kissing the same way.

First, think about how you and your partner have sex. Where are
your (or your partner's) hands? Do you gently touch each other's face?

There's nothing magic about face-touching. It's a matter of whether or not it happens, how it happens, and the meanings you make of this. The same holds true for holding hands, holding glands, and holding each other's gaze.

Then apply this to your sexual problem. How do you and your partner interact when your sexual problem occurs? Do you stop having sex altogether or do you continue? Do you carry on valiantly although your hearts are breaking, or do you genuinely shrug it off and keep a warm connection between you? What does the way you and your partner handle your sexual problem say about each of you and your relationship? Rather than speculating about causes of your problem, pay attention to what's going on.

Changing Any Sexual Relationship

Your reactions to my suggestions can range anywhere from "That sounds great!" to "Do I have to?" to "I can't do that!" You may be thinking, "I know I should do the things you mentioned, but how do I get myself (or my partner) to do them?" Or "You don't understand, my partner and I are not in a good place in our relationship." Or "Don't you have anything simpler or easier to suggest?!"

As I said, these suggestions are not easy to do and often require personal growth, which requires change. It's human nature to want to change things *a little* while keeping everything else the same. It's also human nature to think insight will set you free. Unfortunately, relationships have a way of demanding more of us at times than we're eager to do.

If resurrecting sex simply involved knowing what to do, we could end this book right here. I've given you loads of ideas about what's going on and suggestions on what to do about it. For most readers, however, our discussions are just beginning. Everything I've said up to now may make perfect sense, but we haven't really dealt with putting it into action. Information by itself doesn't help. Resolving sexual problems requires putting information to use. Nancy and Carl exemplify how it can take decades to be ready, willing, and able to do that.

Starting with Chapter 6, we'll deal with sexual problems as they occur in the real world. There's no point discussing what to do with your genitals if we don't acknowledge that they're attached to *you*. *Your* relationship provides the context and meanings in which you're trying to turn sex around. If we are really going to help you resurrect your sexual relationship, we have to seriously consider how you, your partner, and your relationship operate.

One thing I can pretty much guarantee: If you're going to resurrect or create an intimate sexual relationship, you'll have to change the relationship you have now. Doing this is no small thing. At the very least, three specific areas of change will probably be involved, as the next suggestions discuss.

Suggestion 20: Changing Your Relationship Involves Recognizing New Truths

Successfully changing your sexual relationship involves understanding what's already going on. Using sex to more accurately see yourself can confront you with truths you prefer to ignore. Sex is a sensitive topic, and issues often get distorted or buried in the name of harmony. It is easier to say "I don't like sex" than it is to say "I don't like sex with you."

Partners put on masks that can be difficult to take off. It's hard because both partners' pictures of reality get shaken in the process. If and when you let yourself be seen for who you really are, your partner may feel disillusioned, betrayed, and distrustful. (The irony is that you are becoming more honest, real, and trustworthy.) Exposing new or previously hidden sides of yourself can unsettle your partner's equilibrium, and challenge your ability to validate and accept who you are. That's why couples spend years pretending they don't really know what's going on. But it's a rare couple that really doesn't have a clue.

Suggestion 21: Changing Your Sexual Relationship Involves Deeper Emotional Connection

Changing your sexual relationship usually involves *tolerating* deeper connection, even if that's exactly what you want. Given that many couples never achieve much emotional union through sex, this can actually involve a lot. Even if you want your partner to know you better, that doesn't mean you are comfortable with it. Hesitancies about resurrecting sex are common, in part, because it involves greater intimacy than you are used to.

You can have sex with your partner year after year and be out of contact while you're doing it. When you don't want someone *feeling* you, it's not hard to block it while you're touching. (Think about hugging your least favorite parent or your spouse's lecherous friend.) Deep connection during sex requires a sensory and emotional bond with your partner. That involves more than just hesitantly "letting your partner in."

Suggestion 22: Changing Your Sexual Behavior Involves Changing Your Identity

It's easy to see why people get defensive about changing their sexual behavior. Your partner's request for change, no matter how sweetly stated, implies some dissatisfaction with the sexual status quo. If your adequacy and identity rest on doing certain sexual behaviors or going about sex in particular ways, it's hard not to feel threatened.

Resurrecting sex requires doing things differently. This always impacts both partners, even if only one acts differently. Common hesitancy to change stems, in part, from the fact that your sexual style is connected to who you are. Your sexual persona and your sense of self are intricately interconnected. When you change your sexual relationship, you're tampering with how you and your partner see yourselves and each other.

Tampering with your identity in this sense is not negative. Whenever you expand or change your sexual repertoire, your identity and your relationship shift (whether you have sexual problems or not). Changing what you do sexually changes who you are.

Sometimes the process reveals you and your partner not to be who you thought you were. And if (like most people) you're still struggling to figure out who you are, you've come to the right place! Sex in a committed relationship often teaches you more about yourself than you may have wanted to learn.

Conclusion

Resurrecting sex involves raising your total level of stimulation and a whole lot more. It often requires growing up, accepting new truths, getting closer, and changing yourself in the process. This is how the meaning of your sexual problem is finally determined. It comes from how your problem turns out, rather than what caused it.

You can simply try to make your sexual problems go away, or you can approach them in ways that bring out the best in you and your relationship. When sex is at its best, it is full of generosity. When you're having sexual problems, generosity is what your partner desperately needs. Helping your partner increase his or her total stimulation is generosity in action. This is more readily accomplished if your intent includes generosity toward your mate. So whether you lend your partner a helping hand—or improve how you use yours—compassion, friendship, and operating from the best in you are generally required.

If you and your partner are real people with sexual problems, your anxieties make it hard to be friendly or compassionate. Keeping your anxiety under control can be difficult. Overreactions may be frequent. You might be deadlocked in polarized positions and not feeling particularly generous toward each other. Resurrecting sex requires getting unstuck without taking out your frustrations on your partner (even when he or she deserves it).

How do you do this, particularly when your relationship may be in the pits? Does this sound like one tremendous leap of faith?

If it does, that's good, because that's exactly what Part 2 is all about!

PART II

How Sexual Relationships Work

6

Changing Is Often Difficult— and Worth It

Most of them lead lives of unquiet desperation, continually seeking, in sex they wish was love and in the love they suspect is only sex, a center for their worlds to turn on.

—David Dempsey (1958), describing characters in
Warren Miller's novel *The Way We Live Now*

Up to now we've looked at the mechanics of sexual function and dysfunction. We've addressed your relationship as a factor that contributes, for better and worse, to how sex works for you. In Part 2, we're going to approach things the other way around. We've going to look at how your sexual relationship works, and we'll approach your sexual functioning as an integral factor that shapes how it operates. One constant in our discussion will be the role of anxiety.

A Different View, a Different Approach

How do relationships *really* work? Traditional psychology approaches focus on your childhood, which makes sense on the surface. But by claiming that past idiosyncratic events and untoward experiences direct our lives in the present, they unwittingly embrace a view of relationships as being driven by partners' "pathology."

Here in Part 2, I'm going to show you a radically different view of what drives emotionally committed relationships. We're going to focus on the ways people try to regulate their anxiety and get their identity through their present relationships, rather than dwelling on childhood wounds and fears of abandonment from the past. We'll explore how your relationship is controlled by natural healthy growth processes, rather than by how you're screwed up. *The dominant patterns of your relationship are more likely caused by things that are going right than by things that are going wrong.*

I'm also going to show you an alternative to the ways Masters and Johnson dealt with anxiety when they developed modern sex therapy in the 1960s. Masters and Johnson limited their focus on anxiety to people's performance anxiety during sex, and their religious prohibitions (anxiety) about sex. Their overall treatment strategy involved reducing people's anxiety as much as possible in order to improve their sexual function. They approached anxiety as the sex destroyer, something to be avoided.

A decade ago my book *Constructing the Sexual Crucible* revolutionized sex therapy by taking a broader view of anxiety in sex and intimacy. It considered how couples handle anxiety in general. There's a lot more anxiety involved in turning sexual problems around than performance anxiety or guilt about sex. Couples frequently have anxieties about facing their relationship, or changing sexual behaviors, or being better known. The Passionate Marriage® and Sexual Crucible® approaches, on which *Resurrecting Sex* is based, address these realistic anxieties. Their broader focus leads to entirely different strategies from those of Masters and Johnson, ones that don't emphasize anxiety reduction above all else, because that's not the way relationships really work.

Resolving Sexual Problems in the Real World

Resurrecting sex involves more than knowing what makes your genitals function. You or your partner may be eager for things to be different, but it's not always easy to change. In reality, resolving sexual problems creates lots of anxiety in relationships. Like Peter and Judy, you could be scared and insecure at the outset.

Peter and Judy were arguing, which was unusual. Peter was usually ready to keep the peace at any cost. Judy typically deferred to her fears of what Peter and others thought about her. They were a typical conflict-avoidant couple who never argued (openly), but now they were bickering about sex. Was this the beginning of the end of their marriage?

Judy kept asking why Peter couldn't just forget about sex. This wasn't the most important part of their relationship. Sex had always been problematic, although their friends would never have believed it. People said Peter and Judy were the perfect couple. But Judy was uncomfortable about sex and often had difficulty getting aroused or reaching orgasm. She felt Peter should pay less attention to sex, if he appreciated how difficult it was for her. Often he did that for months on end. However, lately Peter was more insistent that they do something about their problem.

On the other hand, you could be like Alexia and Martin, angry and locked in polarized positions, battling over what to do and who should do it. Alexia and Martin used to have a satisfying sexual relationship, but years of arguments had taken their toll. Alexia thought Martin should make more sexual overtures. If Alexia wanted more sex, Martin countered, she should make the initiations. He thought Alexia should be less demanding and more considerate of his erection problems. Alexia responded by attacking his virility and competency as a lover. Martin replied that even if he had the world's best erection he wouldn't lift a finger (or anything else) to please Alexia.

Don't Take It Personally—It's Business as Usual

Although these two couples could not seem more different on the surface, they illustrate two major dynamics that shape emotionally committed relationships. One has to do with how partners regulate their anxiety through their relationship. The other involves how they derive their sense of identity and self-worth the same way. In this chapter, you'll learn how your and your partner's attempts to cope with your anxiety and identity issues shape your relationship.

People generally expect their partner and their relationship to make them feel safe, secure, wanted, and valued. When both partners act accordingly, this creates a dominant pattern in relationships. I call this the comfort-safety cycle. In the comfort-safety cycle there is little anxiety and upheaval in the relationship, and partners seem accommodating and compatible.

Relationships also have a second pattern I call the growth cycle. In the growth cycle, your anxiety is generally higher and the relationship feels less stable (because people are changing). Contrary to the way it feels in the moment, the growth cycle is a necessary part of long-term relationship stability.[1] It's what I've referred to as the people-growing processes of marriage. The growth cycle is built into all emotionally committed relationships—including yours—even if you and your partner seem thoroughly stuck.

You need to understand these two basic patterns, because we have to consider the state of your relationship when solving your sexual problems. You don't want to blow up your marriage in the process of working out your sexual difficulties. If you're going to disrupt powerful anxiety- and identity-regulating processes in your household—as is often required when resolving sexual problems—you have to be prepared to handle the predictable impacts.

I presume you don't want to ruin your relationship by doing something contrary to the way relationships work. Doing something out of the ordinary (i.e., anxiety-provoking), however, is not the same as doing something contrary to the way relationships operate. It's just a shift from one relationship pattern (the comfort-safety cycle) to another one (the growth cycle). Effective solutions to many things in life require tolerating more anxiety for a while.

Unfortunately, many couples, especially anxiety-avoidant ones like Peter and Judy, have different ideas about how relationships should work. They convince themselves that their relationship should always be in the comfort-safety cycle (where anxiety is low and they feel safe and secure). This is why they experience departures from the status quo (increases in anxiety) as "everything falling apart" and start looking for explanations about "what's going wrong."

However, disrupting business as usual is not the same as destroying your relationship. It just shifts your marriage from one smooth-running pattern (the comfort-safety cycle) to another reliable but anxiety-provoking pattern (the growth cycle) involving dormant natural growth processes embedded in your relationship.

There is nothing wrong with reducing your anxiety when you can, and it's understandable that you'll try. But this is what you're up against *any* time you try to change your sexual relationship. When you start having sexual problems, it becomes even harder. This is why sexual problems can be difficult to change, and it has nothing to do with you and your partner's "pathology." Reflecting on this will help you more than thinking that one of you is inhibited, defective, or screwed up.

If you lose sight of this (as couples tend to do), you'll be less likely to succeed and more likely to take this personally and feel terrible about yourself. That is why, besides understanding how *sex* works, you need to know how *sexual relationships* work. Developing this knowledge and putting it into action (kicking your relationship into the growth cycle) makes people say, in retrospect, that their sexual problem was a blessing in disguise.

I want you to have this kind of positive outlook as you go about changing your sexual relationship. Whether you are a conflict-avoidant couple like Peter and Judy, a high-conflict couple like Alexia and Martin, or somewhere in between, you probably could benefit from an optimistic way of seeing your situation.

Anxiety in Relationships

Now let's apply this to resolving your sexual problem. We're going to examine the intricate ways partners regulate their anxieties through their sexual relationship (the comfort-safety cycle).

People Have Sex in Ways That Keep Their Anxieties Down

Let's start with a simple premise: People have sex in ways that feel comfortable to them. You and your partner channel your sexual expression into behaviors and meanings to which you're accustomed. Understandably, you stick to familiar sexual routines because this makes you feel safe and secure (for the moment). This by itself creates a situation such that changing any sexual relationship (even making a good one better) generates anxiety. This particularly applies when you change your sexual relationship to cope with sexual problems.

The tendency to have sex in ways that don't create anxiety isn't wrong, because it's actually part of how sexual relationships work. But eventually you have to do something new, even if just to cope with sexual boredom. And this creates anxiety. Later on I'll show you how you can master this anxiety, and how this can help you, your partner, and your relationship grow. But for now, relax if you're anxious about changing your sexual relationship. It's part of the deal.

If you or your partner has sexual dysfunctions or low desire, you'll probably have to go about having sex differently. Whatever you're used to doing (or not doing) hasn't created the results you want. If what you are doing could resolve a problem you've had for some time, it usually would have happened by now. Things have to get a little uncomfortable and "business as usual" (the comfort-safety cycle) has to come to an end.

Using an Unfamiliar Sexual Behavior or Style Often Creates Anxiety
Anxieties about change commonly surface as arguments about sexual repertoire and preferred technique. It's easy to think your marriage is failing when, like Alexia and Martin, you have repeated arguments about "my way versus your way" and "What's the matter with me the way I am?!" These are actually arguments about whose anxieties, insecurities, and limitations will control the sexual interaction. (This is the antithesis of operating from the best in you.)

For example, Judy got anxious when Peter suggested they experiment with new ways of making love. She said that if Peter really loved her, he wouldn't ask her to do things that made her uncomfortable. Peter countered by saying if Judy really loved him she'd be more adventurous and do new things to make sex better. He was afraid their sex life would be as bad as his parents' was, and they'd get divorced like his folks did. Although it looked like Judy and Peter were taking opposite positions, they were both saying the same thing: "If you love me, accept my fears and accommodate to them."

Like Peter and Judy, you may interpret similar struggles as signs of sexual incompatibility. Ironically, it can be a sign your marriage is working. It is pressuring you to grow.

Conflicts about sex and intimacy stretch your ability to keep yourself on an even keel. Your ability to tolerate a little anxiety and calm yourself down determines whether doing something new feels exhilarating or frightening. That holds true in sex and other aspects of your relationship and your life. Although this involves the growth cycle of marriage, it is contrary to how couples like to run their relationships.

Anxiety Regulation Through Accommodation Is the Norm in Relationships

Regulating your (and your partner's) anxiety through accommodation is commonly known as "keeping the peace" and "not rocking the boat." It's done by adapting in ways that calm each other's anxiety and ease the immediate situation. It happens in the blink of an eye and at such an incredibly subtle level that you're usually not even aware it's going on. (When anxiety regulation through accommodation breaks down between you and your partner, however, it registers big-time.)

Didn't you think that anxiety regulation through accommodation is exactly what good partners do? Although it stabilizes you and your relationship for the moment, it's not the virtue it first appears. Perpetually adapting to each other's limitations and insecurities means the worst in both of you runs your relationship. Don't kid yourself that it's the best in you that's adapting. Typically, you or your partner is "caving in." More often than not, your anxiety (perhaps triggered by your partner's anxiety) makes you perpetually conform and adapt. As we'll discuss shortly, repeated anxiety regulation through accommodation leads to emotional gridlock.

Think back to Judy pressuring Peter to forget about sex. She was asking for accommodation. Peter wanted the same from Judy, pushing for sex to soothe his fears of repeating his parents' pattern.

It's a little harder to recognize anxiety regulation through accommodation in Alexia and Martin's case because they argued constantly. That's the point. Whereas Peter and Judy were upset by arguing openly, Alexia and Martin's bickering actually was anxiety-reducing. When either partner couldn't contain his or her anxiety, each engaged the other in a petty argument. Fault finding and bickering made them feel less alone. Hostile banter was actually a form of relatedness with which they felt fairly comfortable.

Understanding how anxiety regulation through accommodation operates in your sexual relationship allows you to account for interactions outside your bedroom as well. Look beyond common notions that your sexual relationship mirrors the rest of your relationship. More accurately, the ways anxiety shapes your sexual relationship also shapes your whole marriage.

Regulating Anxiety Through Accommodation Only Works When It Lowers *Both* Partners' Anxiety

All of this comes together in a way most couples never expect, due to a simple fact they never foresee: To expect accommodation from your partner when this will make him or her anxious is futile. Your partner has expectations similar to yours. You're not supposed to do things, or ask him or her to do things, that make him or her nervous. *You* are supposed to adapt in ways that reduce *his or her* anxiety. It doesn't matter if you accommodated your partner in the past or you say, "I do plenty for you, now you do this for me!" An entirely different set of rules applies when anxiety is involved, no matter how unfair you think this is.

However, you *will* expect your partner to accommodate you. If you've depended on his or her help regulating your anxiety all along, this isn't going to suddenly change. When you hit an issue on which accommodating each other doesn't reduce your respective anxieties, you and your partner will be emotionally gridlocked. This readily happens over sexual problems, because effective solutions generally make one or both partners a little nervous at first.

Therefore, don't expect your partner (or yourself) to be eager to change your relationship. As in Peter and Judy's case, your partner may be expecting you to accommodate to your sexual problem (or not talk about it) like you may have in the past. If you're a high-conflict couple, like Alexia and Martin, arguing so you don't have to go forward amounts to the same thing. This is the backdrop against which changing your sexual relationship often occurs.

Two-Choice Dilemmas

Lots of areas in marriage exist in which accommodation does not reduce both partners' anxieties. In all likelihood you and your partner have been stuck in other aspects of your marriage. If so, this contributes to difficulty changing your sexual relationship, because partners often don't feel generous or accommodating if they've been gridlocked for long.

Sex, money, kids, and in-laws tend to be couples' major problem areas for this exact reason: Decisions tend to involve choices between mutually exclusive outcomes. You can't have and not have sex, any more than you can have and not have a baby, or save and spend the same dollar. You can't agree to disagree about many things in marriage because someone's going to be nervous or unhappy. Normal expectations for anxiety regulation through accommodation create catch-22 dilemmas due to the realities of how relationships really work.

As if that weren't enough, many times we want more than one choice on an issue. Deciding to handle some situations any way we want still makes us nervous. That's because we're anxious about more than one outcome. We actually want to handle things *two* ways at once, even if that's impossible.

For instance, Judy was nervous having sex their usual way because it never really aroused her, but the thought of doing something unfamiliar also made her anxious. Peter felt pressured to interest Judy in sex, but she froze at the merest suggestion of anything novel. Likewise, Alexia didn't want the responsibility or vulnerability of initiating sex, but she didn't like Martin initiating only when *he* wanted to. Martin didn't like feeling pressured to perform when Alexia initiated sex, but he also didn't like initiating simply because she expected it.

Sounds perfectly understandable in each case, doesn't it? But look beyond each person's ambivalence and you'll see that what's going on here involves more than feelings. It involves a natural anxiety-provoking mechanism built into committed relationships. When I conceptualized this a decade ago, I labeled such situations *two-choice dilemmas* because you want two choices (at the same time) but you get only one. (Your partner also gets a choice, unless you "solve" your two-choice dilemma by stealing your partner's choice.)

Two-choice dilemmas are a major source of anxiety in committed relationships, and a primary reason why so many couples are grid-locked. Two-choice dilemmas invariably halt anxiety regulation through accommodation, because your partner can't accommodate you without raising his or her own anxiety.

Actually, two-choice dilemmas surface because everybody wants the choice nobody gets: the choice between being anxious or not. (Guess which way we want to decide that one?) Unfortunately, marriage (and parenthood) never lets you choose between being anxious or not. You only get your choice of anxieties. The difference between an adult and a child is that the adult accepts that the only real choice in life is between productive anxieties and useless ones.

The elegance of two-choice dilemmas is that they prod you to become an adult. Two-choice dilemmas push your relationship into the growth cycle because they are not resolvable in the comfort-safety cycle.

Selfhood and Validation

The same ways we expect our partner to accommodate and make us feel secure, we also expect him or her to make us feel good about ourselves. Our sense of identity and self-worth quickly comes to depend on how our partner feels about us. Once again, this has predictable consequences few of us anticipate.

Getting Your Identity and Self-Worth from Your Relationship Shapes Your Marriage

People often try to get their sense of self (identity and self-worth) from their partner or their relationship. This is called a *reflected sense of self,* meaning your identity and self-worth hinge on how your partner (and other people) views you and treats you. Judy felt crushed when Peter expressed the slightest displeasure with her. Peter felt destructive when Judy got upset, and he spent much of their marriage walking on eggshells. Alexia felt beautiful and charming when Martin wanted sex with her and ugly and unattractive when he didn't. Martin complained that Alexia knew how to drag him down, and, in truth, she frequently withheld the support and validation he wanted. Most of us greatly depend upon our partners to make us feel good about ourselves—and then we resent the control this gives them over our lives.[2]

To the degree that you rely on a reflected sense of self, feeling lovable, desirable, and adequate greatly pivots on your own and your partner's sexual function and satisfaction. That's why sexual dysfunctions, desire problems, and general sexual dissatisfactions can play havoc with your (and your partner's) adequacy and self-worth. They upset your identity, challenge your security, and raise your anxiety.

Dependence on Your Partner's Validation Inevitably Destroys Intimacy

There's nothing wrong with wanting validation and acceptance from the people you love, but things operate differently when you're dependent on it. Pretty soon you stop showing who you really are (*self-disclosure*) and present yourself in ways you anticipate your partner will like (*self-presentation*). Decisions you make and ways you act don't accurately reflect who you are or aspire to be. Getting your partner's validation and acceptance, and keeping yourself and your partner calm, become more important then "being real." Sex and intimacy suffer when your need for approval makes you downplay differences, dodge conflicts, and pretend to be someone you are not. This is why so many people feel out of touch with the significant people in their lives, whether it's their spouse, parents, children, close friends, or colleagues.

For instance, Judy was afraid Peter might leave if she openly stated she wasn't interested in improving sex. When she hid this, she felt more alienated and more fraudulent during sex. This increased her anxiety, decreased her sexual interest, and reinforced her problem. Similarly, Peter tried to act supportive and understanding when he was frustrated and fed up. If he didn't applaud and reinforce every little effort Judy made, she was less likely to have sex. At the same time, making her feel secure seemed to encourage her to avoid their problems. When Peter eventually did confront Judy, she quoted his own prior words of praise and encouragement and told him he was never satisfied.

Dependence on Your Partner's Validation Makes It Hard to Change Things

Validating each other is part of every relationship, and everyone wants affection, consideration, and caring. But you have to be prepared for the periodic indifference and invalidation that comes with the territory. Likewise, there are many times where your relationship depends on being able to stand alone. Resurrecting your sexual relationship is often one of them. That's hard to do if your stability hinges on an affectionate glance or kind word from your partner.[3]

When your identity and self-worth are based on a reflected sense of self, your relationship has to remain static (even if you espouse a desire for change and growth). If your relationship or your partner changes, your sense of self and personal value is threatened. When you or your partner tries to change your sexual routine, it will challenge your and your partner's self-image and adequacy. It happens even if upsetting each other is the last thing you want to do, and what you've specifically tried to avoid.

Mutual-validation pacts like Judy and Peter's fall apart when there's a sexual problem. Both partners need validation from each other and neither one has much to give. As the responses Judy and Peter so depended upon from each other began to diminish, their relationship gradually deteriorated—which made it harder to turn things around. If you depend on your partner's validation and accommodation, your relationship can spiral downward until one of you stabilizes your own feelings.

Martin's difficulty with erections got worse, for example. The problem wasn't simply that he couldn't function when Alexia didn't "applaud" by having an orgasm. It was that he desperately needed other people's applause both in and out of bed. In fact, the more Alexia complained that her needs for "communication" were unfulfilled, the more Martin lost interest in sex and intimacy. Actually, Alexia was complaining about missing the validation and acceptance she derived by talking. (It was the same validation she got by having sex.) What Martin and Alexia really wanted was for the other to validate, accept, and "bring out the best" in him or her. There was no way one partner could accommodate the other, given how much each depended on the other for his or her stability.

When One Partner Tries to Change the Relationship, the Other Is Not Likely to Applaud

From what we've said about common dependence on others to make us feel secure and worthwhile, you can develop a realistic expectation: Your partner probably isn't going to validate you when you shake up the status quo. Martin's picture of himself as a virile lover was shaken when Alexia suggested doing something new. Judy's image of herself as a loving wife crumbled when Peter suggested they have sex. Neither Martin nor Judy applauded their partner's efforts to change their relationship, even when Alexia and Peter said their efforts came from finding their mates desirable and attractive.

Judy wanted Peter to accommodate her (accept things as they were) to reduce her anxiety. She wasn't about to validate him if he didn't. Since Peter depended heavily on Judy's support and encouragement, he felt stuck. He didn't want to propose anything she might not like, and he backed down at the first sign of disagreement. Judy was no fool and she was accustomed to Peter's pattern. She pushed Peter for anxiety regulation through accommodation by challenging his sense of self-worth. Don't be surprised when your partner does that with you (or vice versa).

Couples Are Often Stuck in Gridlock

At first glance, this doesn't look like a very pretty picture. However, many couples come to appreciate this in an entirely different light. This is what the people-growing machinery looks like in its early stages. It brings the comfort-safety cycle in your relationship to an end and drives you and your partner into the growth cycle.

Gradually, you or your partner feel like you've sold yourselves out. One or both of you get tired of misrepresenting yourselves "for the good of the relationship." You stop respecting yourself and you start resenting your partner. One day the inevitable happens: You feel there's no room left for accommodation without selling yourself out or violating your integrity in some unacceptable way. You reach an inevitable point in all relationships: emotional gridlock.

Emotional gridlock is another predictable relationship pattern I identified a decade ago.[4] Emotional gridlock is the most common problem couples have, because of the normal ways couples attempt to deal with anxiety (the comfort-safety cycle). It occurs in all relationships, especially when it comes to anxiety-provoking topics like sex and intimacy.

Emotional gridlock may not seem like the best circumstance under which to try to resurrect your sexual relationship, but it certainly is a common one. This normal development in a relationship makes it hard to change you sex life. When you're used to steering your relationship according to you and your partner's anxieties and insecurities, it's hard to suddenly change course and sail off to uncharted waters. This is not specific to your particular sexual problem—it has to do with the nature of relationships per se. However, when changing your relationship in order to deal with sexual problems, you're tackling this preexisting system head-on.

We have to contend with the reality that your relationship may already be stuck, and you and your partner may be contentious and alienated from each other. Understanding this will help you unshackle from the emotional gridlock that controls couples' lives. This is what Alexia and Martin faced for years. Peter and Judy experienced emotional gridlock when Peter finally insisted that they do something about their problems.[5]

Gridlock involves more than stubbornness and accumulated resentments. It occurs when the position your partner wants to take on an issue blocks the position you want to take, and vice versa. It's just like a New York City traffic jam and feels about as good. Sometimes your positions are mutually exclusive (like whether or not you're going to have sex tonight). Other times you can't accommodate or validate each other *and* maintain your integrity or self-respect *and* keep your anxiety down.

Gridlock doesn't stem from communication problems, although it is often misinterpreted as such. More talk doesn't resolve gridlock because it isn't caused by lack of information. You are usually well aware of what your partner wants and how profoundly important this is to him or her. This doesn't change your situation, except perhaps to make it more poignant and anxiety-provoking.

Peter, for instance, reached the point he couldn't ignore that being patient and giving Judy more time wasn't improving their sex. When Peter didn't press the issue, Judy just let things slide. Being understanding of Judy was one thing, but lying to himself was another. Peter could no longer avoid confronting himself and Judy with the fact that they were getting nowhere. It was no longer an issue about sex. Now it was a matter of integrity and selfhood.

Here's another way couples create gridlock, this one less noble: Gridlock occurs when accommodating your partner would force you to confront yourself about a personal issue you've been avoiding. When you are not willing to confront yourself, you're going to confront your partner instead (i.e., push for accommodation). For instance, when Peter finally spoke up after months of no sex, Judy tried to silence him by declaring, "All you ever think about is sex!"

For another example, Alexia couldn't stop pushing for sex because she used sex to get a reflected sense of attractiveness and desirability. She wanted to accommodate Martin's feelings, but she couldn't handle the insecurities that surfaced when a partner didn't pursue her. Likewise, Martin didn't feel like he could have sex more frequently without feeling as if Alexia were controlling him. Both Alexia and Martin felt controlled by each other, but the problem was, they couldn't control themselves. Their gridlock surfaced in Alexia screaming, "The last three times we've had sex, you went soft!" and Martin retorting, "It's hard to keep a hard-on with a bitch like you!"

Is Your Relationship Gridlocked?

Gridlock manifests as relationship problems that won't go away and repeated arguments that go nowhere. You and your partner are often at each other's throats. For example, when high-conflict couples like Alexia and Martin are gridlocked, the volume of arguments and frequency of door slamming increase. For conflict-avoidant couples like Peter and Judy, it surfaces in more stony silences and emotional withdrawals. (They are still fighting nonetheless.)

Since gridlocked partners need each other's agreement and support, there often seems no possible resolution except divorce. Actually, gridlock is the point at which couples are most likely to divorce because they interpret it as "falling out of love," "growing apart," or "incompatibility," rather than a natural midpoint in all relationships. Gridlock is either an irresolvable impasse or a pivotal turning point, depending on how you deal with it.

When you are gridlocked, everything feels highly personal. You and your partner tend to overreact, bad faith abounds, and there are lots of hard feelings. Even if you're gridlocked over issues elsewhere in your relationship—like disciplining the kids, spending money, career moves, household responsibilities, your mother-in-law moving in, or your next vacation—the impact typically spills over into sex.

Gridlock strongly affects if and when you say, "Let's try something new and different in bed!" It also shapes whether your partner takes this as an invitation or an insult. If you're stuck in gridlock and feeling defensive, he or she is more likely to take it negatively. Martin, for instance, lit up when a woman at work expressed a slight sexual interest in him. The same interest from Alexia doused his ardor. It wasn't that he found the other woman more attractive than Alexia. It was that he wasn't gridlocked with his coworker.

If you and your partner are gridlocked, relax. Gridlock is predictable and the pattern is unmistakable (once you recognize it). Knowing a "map" exists makes your task feel less daunting. Other couples make it through gridlock, and you can too.

On the other hand, consider this: If you've been gridlocked for any length of time, you're at a place in which there are no easy solutions, and you can't count on your partner to make it easier of you. Moreover, you can't wait until things get better to do something. You probably will have to operate under conditions that seem less than ideal.

- You and your partner probably don't feel great about yourselves.

- You have hard feelings toward each other.

- You're afraid to let each other know what you really feel.

And yet, these are precisely the circumstances under which couples change their sex life. As you'll see, it's all part of the natural people-growing machinery of emotionally committed relationships. There is never a good time to change things. Going forward at the point of no return helps you grow in ways that stabilize your relationship and permit greater intimacy, desire, and passion. This is the growth cycle in action. (I understand this is not much consolation when you feel awkward and ill at ease in bed.)

Couples Are Emotionally Fused Rather Than "Out of Touch"
Now that you know about emotional gridlock, you can make another profound shift in how you view your situation. The problem for most couples is not that they are out of touch, it's that they are emotionally fused with each other. *Emotional fusion* is connection without separateness. Emotional fusion is another key feature of emotionally committed relationships.

Emotional fusion is a tenacious emotional link between people that allows anxiety to flow between them. It arises as the natural consequence of incomplete emotional development, wherein each partner relies on the other to support and supplant his or her functioning.[6] I'm not referring to some kind of unconscious feeling, but rather a tangible process by which people pass anxiety between them.

When I talk about establishing emotional connection with your partner during sex, I am referring to positive connection between partners who can regulate their own anxieties. When people can't regulate their own anxiety, this creates barriers to feeling while touching. Couples close down to each other's touch because they are *too* connected.[7] They try to *limit* the emotional connection between them, because they infuse each other with anxiety and impact each other's sense of self tremendously. This causes their partner's touch to feel noxious or empty.

Emotional fusion is far more the common state of human existence than is lack of connection and "attachment problems." Emotional fusion is what gave rise to Martin's difficulties with commitment. He already felt so overwhelmed by Alexia's emotional volatility that his gut reaction was to get away. Likewise, Alexia was so reactive to (i.e., connected to) Martin's hesitancies that she often stormed off in a huff.

Emotional fusion often diminishes people's functioning more than does "lack of support." Pete, for example, was much better at standing up for himself at work than he was at home. Being acutely aware of Jane's feelings, and feeling responsible for her happiness, made it harder for him to say what he really thought. Likewise, Jane didn't back away from challenges in the rest of her life like she did in her marriage. When she had to do things that made her nervous, she did them without too much problem. However, the more Pete treated her with kid gloves, the more vulnerable and fragile she seemed to become.

Recognizing emotional fusion can make the world look upside down. Most people think it's the absence rather than the presence of a connection that cripples emotional functioning and makes a marriage grind to a halt. But the picture of relationships we're developing depicts you and your partner enmeshed and entwined in gridlock.[8]

Your future efforts to help yourself will be guided by your understanding of what's happening to you. If you think you and your partner are too far apart you will do things to get closer together. When you realize you are probably more like Siamese twins—fused at the hip, passing anxiety, validation, identity, and self-worth back and forth between you—your efforts will go in the opposite direction. However, the solution isn't getting further away from your partner; it's regulating your own anxiety and developing your own sense of identity and self-worth. This allows you to get closer to your partner, in more pleasant ways than you are now: This is closeness *with* separateness.

Borrowed Functioning

Seeing how marital problems arise from emotional fusion lets you understand another powerful process in emotionally committed relationships: borrowed functioning.

Thus far we've described what happens when couples cannot successfully regulate each other's anxieties, identity, and self-worth. Borrowed functioning occurs to the degree that you and your partner are successful. But borrowed functioning is not as virtuous or as constructive as lending your partner a helping hand (true mutuality).

You probably never thought about what happens to partners who exchange anxiety regulation, selfhood, validation, and support, when they themselves are a "quart short" in these areas. Marriage takes its reliable shape because most of us don't have enough emotional resources to begin with. In the ongoing emotional transfusions, one partner or the other often comes out with less "self" than at the beginning. His or her functioning begins to decline and the partner starts to function better. In borrowed functioning, one partner looks stronger, more solid, or more independent than he or she really is, while the other's functioning is correspondingly suppressed.

For instance, Martin became calm and rational when Alexia ranted and raged, and Alexia looked interested in intimacy as long as Martin backed away from "committing to the relationship." When Alexia kept herself under control, Martin's fears of being controlled surfaced, just as Alexia started demanding commitments whenever Martin stopped apologizing for himself. Likewise, Judy looked like she didn't have a problem in the world as long as Peter basically gave up having sex. And Peter looked like he was the strong one in the relationship as long as Judy acted fragile to fend off his sexual overtures.

Other instances of borrowed functioning are more vampire-like, wherein the "donor" feels he or she is being eaten alive or sucked dry by the spouse. In many cases, the "recipient" acts needy or helpless. But one husband insisted on helping his wife, despite her objections. Being helpful helped him feel better, but interfered with her prerogatives and development. In this case, she was the "donor" and her husband the "recipient," although it looked the other way around.

Borrowed functioning is most obvious when it's finally over. As the donor develops greater self-mastery, the recipient starts to loose his or her grip on himself or herself. This frequently emerges in angry eruptions, sullen withdrawals, and extramarital affairs. People who scream that they don't feel "supported" are often demanding borrowed functioning.[9] Gridlock can exist for decades when partners won't give up the borrowed functioning in their emotional fusion. Emotional fusion is necessary for borrowed functioning to occur because it is the conduit for the "transfusion."

Spouses are usually equally matched in ability to regulate their anxiety and validate themselves. The result is that when one of you is about to "lose it," the other is often just a step behind. So what's going on when one seems much better able than the other to hold on to himself or herself? It usually reflects emotional fusion and borrowed functioning.

Unshackling from Anxiety

As long as your relationship remains gridlocked, and you and your partner remain emotionally fused, it's hard to resolve your sexual problem. Likewise, when you start doing new things that might resolve gridlock, you or your partner may get anxious because business as usual is coming to an end and your relationship feels unstable. Even though you may be on the right track, mounting anxiety can encourage you to duck back into the comfort-safety cycle. This usually takes the form of more promises to "try harder" and further brief attempts at accommodation— which lead you into the same old gridlock once again.

Here's the challenge you face when trying to resolve your sexual problems: *How do you change your relationship without creating (too much) anxiety?* How can you make a significant difference without triggering your partner (or yourself) to cling to the status quo? At first this may seem like an impossible task. That's why it requires a seemingly impossible solution: *All you have to do is create change while maintaining stability.* If you are asking yourself, "How am I supposed to do that? It's impossible!" you must realize partners try to create change while maintaining stability all the time.

Conflict-avoidant couples often try Peter and Judy's method: Peter tentatively proposed sex in a roundabout way. If and when Judy got nervous he backed off, telling himself perseverance was unwise. Peter stopped trying to change things for several months, convinced by his own efforts that progress was still not possible.

The Good and Bad News: Nothing's Going Wrong
This "test and fold" process doesn't signify that anything is wrong with a relationship. Peter thought he'd taken his best shot, done what he could do, and failed. However, this situation is the beginning of the change process. It's just the opening act in a rather lengthy and incredi-

ble drama. (If you think it's the end of the story, as many people do, you are more likely to give up and get divorced.)

High-conflict couples go through the same process, although their style is more "test and attack": When Alexia's hints and innuendos did not elicit sexual advances from Martin, she attacked his competency. Although Martin took this personally, Alexia was just trying to soothe herself because she felt humiliated and rejected. Such occurrences are daily events when you depend on your relationship to control your anxieties. But your partner better recognize your behavior as a failed attempt to create change while maintaining stability, or both of you could end up feeling like your situation is hopeless.

Yes, couples try all the time to create change while maintaining stability. That's what usually creates emotional gridlock. However, the problem isn't what they're trying to do. It's how they try to do it.

Creating Change

There *is* a way to change things that can revolutionize your relationship. The trick to creating change while maintaining stability involves shifting where your stability comes from: *Your anxiety regulation, identity, and self-worth have to come from you rather than depending on your partner.* Long-term sexual relationships teach you that this trick is both possible and necessary. Resolving gridlock stabilizes your relationship because the only way out of gridlock involves becoming more stable in yourself. That's why the midpoint of what eventually gives your relationship stability feels like tremendous upheaval.

What finally creates change? What could move you to do something that may sound scary, especially if you haven't been willing or able to do that up to now? What might prompt you to believe in yourself, hold on to yourself, take a stand, and risk changing your relationship? It usually takes something powerful. That "something" turns out to be a common development in committed relationships. The necessary motivation surfaces when

- You feel like your integrity is on the line

- Gridlock becomes intolerable

- What and who you love is at stake

- Your fear that things will stay the same exceeds your fear they will change

Empowering yourself to take action comes from a desperate fear of losing what you hold dear, whether that is your partner, your marriage, or your relationship with yourself. At that point, holding on to yourself and taking a stand is an act of self-preservation (that often preserves your relationship). Rather than be forever constrained by your partner's fears or your own self-rejection, you make a move in your relationship and you look to yourself for support. In that moment, gridlock no longer exists. And at least for that moment, you've done the seemingly impossible.

That fateful moment arrived for Peter and Judy one night as they lay in bed. Peter made a sexual approach to Judy, his first in several months. Judy said, "Can't we just lie in bed together without having to ruin it with sex!" The big event happened when Peter didn't look beaten down and mournful. He said in a very quiet voice, "I don't know how much longer I can go on like this." Peter wasn't pouting or acting as if he'd been slapped down. He just flatly stated the truth that was painfully obvious to him in that moment. Peter couldn't believe he said something so unguarded.

Thoughts of divorce filled Judy with fear! But she responded differently to this different Peter. She settled down and talked seriously about their options, rather than withdrawing to her side of the bed in tears. This didn't solve all their problems but it was the beginning of a solution.

Judy and Peter thought about their interaction for the next several days. When Judy initiated sex a few days later, they were both ready to be there. They were more present and focused during sex than in the past. And although there was less stability in their relationship than before, the sex actually seemed better. The change in Judy's presence was unmistakable to Peter. Judy herself wasn't sure why it seemed easier to get into sex this time. She found Peter more sexually interesting the way he was acting, although it scared her to think this.

The sex wasn't fabulous and Judy didn't have an orgasm, but Peter felt this was progress. He saw they could get somewhere if he didn't cave in, and he wasn't about to forget it.

You Have to Stand on Your Own Two Feet

A sexual relationship involves shared responsibilities, but it is not a 50–50 split. This kind of thinking leads to neither partner taking responsibility when gridlock sets in. Assigning equal responsibility and blame sounds fair, but that is not how relationships work best. Don't waste your time extracting commitments, exchanging promises, or making "no exit contracts" with your partner. These are just fancy ways of dressing up a 50–50 split that will keep you stuck.

Resolving gridlock in general, and sexual problems in particular, requires you and your partner to function independently. (It's not just a matter of "getting closer"—you need to resolve the emotional fusion.) That means taking 100 percent responsibility for *yourself*, 100 percent responsibility for things you haven't done and for things you can still do—regardless of what your partner has or hasn't done. Functioning independently is not the same as being uncaring, indifferent, or pursuing your self-interests elsewhere. Your ability to function independently is a crucial mainstay of your relationship.

Alexia and Martin learned this in the midst of one of their typical arguments. Martin was feeling sorry for himself because of problems at his office. Alexia made a sexual overture, and he responded with his typical sad-sack, "I'll have sex if you really need to." Alexia started criticizing his response, when she stopped in midsentence. She said, "My best friend has leukemia, my mother is getting old, and I'm such a bitch I can't stand myself! I'm not spending the rest of my life raging at you, even if you deserve it. You're worried about your work. Let's forget sex. You don't need a second job and I don't want to be serviced. I want a loving sexual relationship. If you are ever interested, you know where to find me." Instead of storming around the house as she normally did, Alexia was actually cordial and low-key after she spoke.

At first Martin thought this was just a fancier way of Alexia attacking him. But when he realized she was containing herself, Martin was both impressed and stunned. Breaking their usual pattern created an opening for something new. When Alexia came home the next night, their bedroom was lit with candles. There were fresh sheets on the bed. Martin said, "I know where to find you and I'm here, too. I'm sorry your friend is not doing well. I've been feeling so sorry for myself about my work I haven't paid much attention. Let's spend some time talking and making love." For the first time in a long time, Alexia and

Martin had a true cease-fire in which they relaxed and made contact during sex.

The shift to accepting, validating, and supporting yourself requires a real leap of faith. It usually comes at a time when, although you're filled with doubts, your integrity stands up in a life-changing way. This shift in individual functioning shifts your relationship from the comfort-safety cycle to the growth cycle. Even if only one partner does it, it completely changes how your relationship functions and impacts both of you.

Shouldering the Load

There are times when you or your mate has to stand up while the other "sags." Relationships depend on partners' abilities to function independently when one (or both) are not doing so well. Stepping forward at that moment is what partnership and collaboration are all about. This includes speaking up if your partner continually dodges issues, like sex or intimacy problems, that need to be addressed. Not allowing yourself to be controlled by your fears and insecurities—or those of your partner—makes your relationship (and both of you) blossom. (When your spouse or child becomes chronically ill or seriously injured, you learn this lesson the hard way.)

Independent functioning doesn't have to be adversarial. It usually isn't when it's driven by the best in you. Standing on your own two feet is not about selfishness or self-indulgence. It is the essence of commitment. Sometimes one partner or the other has to shoulder the load to keep your relationship afloat. Just don't confuse shouldering your rightful responsibility with constantly adapting to your partner's weaknesses, limitations, and immaturities. In some situations, like Peter's, collaboration requires refusing to continue the accommodation and anxiety regulation you've been doing up to this point.

An Accurate Picture of Relationships Really Helps

Real patterns of normal sexual relationships differ markedly from what most couples expect. They don't realize that hard times can be purposeful and productive too. Couples with ongoing sexual problems often feel defeated, despondent, and insecure. It's hard to believe this is a good time to change the rules. It will help you (as it does my clients) to see there is an underlying rhyme and reason to how your relationship is operating.

"Best Thing That Ever Happened to Us"

Even highly troubled couples can put their sexual problems to use. Clients like Judy and Peter often say they might have limped along forever with so-so sex if their problems had not become severe enough to demand attention. Their sexual problem turned out to be one of the best things that ever happened to them (although they didn't think so at the time).

Going through their problem gave Judy and Peter more capacity for intimacy, desire, passion, and eroticism than they ever had before. Neither one was ever deeply involved when they had sex, and sex never really became profoundly intimate. But Peter showed himself that he had more integrity than he thought he did, and he was less dependent on Judy's validation thereafter. This made him more willing and able to let Judy get close to him. And although this was not Judy's first choice, she found it to be a better one for her. She had more respect for Peter, and she became more willing to confront her reluctance to have sex.

Perhaps the biggest reason people say good things come from their sexual problem lies in watching the best in themselves come forward. This involves more than expressing feelings and opinions. Resolving your sexual problems commonly requires holding on to yourself and taking a position: developing a solution strategy and implementing it in the real world. Sometimes this requires making the first move to change the ways you have sex. Other times you may have to say, "Let's give our marriage another try" when your partner is ready to give up (or already has). By holding on to yourself in the face of your anxiety, you actively create the world you want to live in.

What makes us so afraid to do this? In Alexia's case it wasn't just fear that they might fail. Alexia harbored another fear that scared her even more: If she functioned better but Martin didn't, *she might have to choose* what was most important to her and act accordingly. This fear immobilized her more than breaking up by mutual agreement. Alexia was terrified about making a bad decision and regretting it for the rest of her life. She turned the tide only when she stopped giving in to her own fears. Only then did the best in Martin finally stand up.[10]

Implications for Sexually Troubled Couples

If your relationship is troubled, these are the kinds of things you need to confront. You'll do best if you handle yourself like an adult. My clients find the straight unvarnished truth surprisingly soothing.

- You can't hold back to protect yourself, because this doesn't offer protection. Holding back, although understandable, creates more problems.

- Don't expect your partner to make the first move to change. Or the second move, or the third. Not if you want to get out of gridlock.

- Change in any relationship is usually introduced unilaterally (by one partner) rather than by consensus. Earlier we approached this point from a different perspective: We said people stick to familiar ways of having sex to keep their anxiety low. You'll probably have to unilaterally introduce something new into your relationship if you want it to change.

- Don't expect your partner to make you feel secure. Your own expectation makes you vulnerable whether your partner soothes you or not.

- You have to tolerate some anxiety before your anxiety goes down. You can't get comfortable doing something new until you do it repeatedly, and that involves being uncomfortable for a time. This makes perfect sense, but most of us aren't logical when we're anxious.

- Safety, security, and comfort come after you've had new sexual interactions and incorporated them into your relationship. A "stretch now, be comfortable later" strategy isn't as crazy as it might first seem.

- People grow by mastering themselves in the face of their anxiety. In our current context this might involve new styles of sex, speaking up in your relationship, or allowing yourself to be held.

- Gridlock exists only as long as you let your anxieties limit your options. When you can better soothe your anxieties, totally new forms of resolution become possible. Not only can you finally think, you are more reasonable and adaptable (from the best in you).

- If you are nervous about changing your relationship, take heart. It's not only normal, it's part of the deal. It helps if you think of this as Creation's methodology for developing your capacity to love.

Looking Ahead

Breaking free of gridlock requires confronting and validating yourself rather than counting on your partner for support. That's the path to becoming an adult who can lend a hand instead of demanding you receive one. Gridlock teaches you that real caring requires standing on your own two feet.

In the next chapter we'll explore effective ways to create change while maintaining stability. You'll discover this involves four things: holding on to yourself in the face of your anxiety, staying clear about yourself when people you love pressure you to conform, remaining nonreactive to your partner's anxieties and overreactions, and mobilizing yourself to do things you might otherwise avoid.

You will find doing these four things will dramatically change your relationship and your life. They are crucial to creating the future you want. You may even find they change how you look at your past.

7

Hold On to Yourself!

No man knows who the wife of his bosom is until he has gone with her through the fiery trials of this world.

—Washington Irving, *The Sketchbook of Geoffrey Crayon* (1819)

A husband is what is left of the lover after the nerve is extracted.

—Helen Rowland

What determines whether or not you make progress with your problems? I've worked with lots of hard cases who considered themselves hopeless causes, and this is what I've found: It's not the size of your problem. It's not how long your problem has existed. And it's not how bad things have gotten. *The critical factor in making progress is your ability to hold on to yourself and do what needs to be done.* Clients who have had sexual problems for decades have done amazing things in a few weeks, or days, or even overnight. It always hinges on someone doing something previously ruled out as too scary, vulnerable, or difficult. In practical terms, here are three recommendations:

Take a giant step. The longer your problem has existed, the more you need to do something that announces, "This is no longer business as usual." This usually requires doing something you have felt is beyond you. The need for this leap of faith is built into every relationship.

Don't limit your efforts to what's easy and comfortable. The more you and your partner tolerate temporary discomfort, the quicker you can get to the feel-good part of sex and intimacy. The bottom line in moving forward in any tough situation involves doing what it takes until the job is done.

Create hope. Seeing yourself (or your partner) do something out of the ordinary to help things creates *realistic* hope. It's not easy, but that's how you and your partner earn your own (and each other's) respect. This is vital for many couples. I don't advocate a baby-step approach, because taking significant action is key to resolving sexual problems. Bravery counts—and bravery requires anxiety.

Holding On to Yourself Helps You Reach Out to Your Partner

Perhaps you are asking yourself, "How on earth am I ever going to do that?" Here's the one-sentence answer that will take this whole chapter to flesh out: You need to hold on to yourself. Holding on to yourself is crucial to changing your sexual relationship and your life. Holding on to yourself involves four basic activities:

- Staying clear about who you are (staying honest with yourself and true to your values) when challenged by your partner or situation

- Calming yourself down, soothing your own anxieties, and licking your emotional bruises

- Remaining nonreactive when your partner becomes anxious, reactive, or provocative

- Tolerating discomfort so you can grow and move forward

Let me tell you about the first of several couples who discovered how important holding on to yourself can be: Kelly dominated her fifteen-year marriage to Donald with her temper and tirades. Donald caved in to Kelly, who prevailed in every argument on every point. Kelly grabbed the moral high ground in their squabbles, which fit well with Donald's self-effacing style. In this respect, you might say Kelly and Donald were well suited to each other. However, it made for a perpetual disaster in bed.

Kelly hated having sex with someone who clearly feared her. At the same time, Kelly was insecure and she acted like an avenging angel when she was threatened. Donald just wanted Kelly to accept and love him, and he took whatever she dished out. The picture of Kelly reflected in Donald's meekness was enough to make her take another crack at him.

Not surprisingly, Kelly had difficulty reaching orgasm and Donald had intermittent problems maintaining erections. He often tasted her wrath when their sexual problems coincided. When Donald finally stopped getting defensive whenever Kelly attacked, their lives turned around. He learned, as partners do, that you can't count on your partner to make this easier.

Resurrecting sex requires holding on to yourself and not giving in, giving up, or blowing out. You and your partner need time *during* sex (and outside the bedroom) to get yourselves settled down. Kelly, for instance, would storm out of bed in a huff when she couldn't reach orgasm. She said she was trying to calm herself down, but Donald felt like she was punishing both of them. Kelly would sit in a chair in the dark, repeatedly asking, "What's the matter with me?" Half the time it sounded to Donald like Kelly meant, "What's the matter with *you?*" If he stayed away from Kelly when she was upset, she accused him of not caring. Reaching out to her elicited a cutting "Leave me *alone!*"

It was hard for Donald to stay clear about who he was and what he was doing. When he looked at himself through Kelly's eyes he was a cold, ineffectual man who bothered his wife. Ever ready to believe the worst in himself, and always looking to others for acceptance, Donald spent years defending himself whenever he approached Kelly. It took more than a decade for him to stay clear and calm enough about himself to finally see what was happening.

Hold On to the Best in Yourself

Lots of us become tenacious when we are at our worst. Kelly, for example, felt like a pushover unless she got angry. She identified her "strong" side as the best in her, and her inability to set limits with others as her "weak" side. When Kelly was soft, gentle, and considerate of others (the true best in her), she felt like she couldn't say no to anything. When she felt used, getting angry helped her set limits. At those moments, Kelly latched on to the worst in her, thinking it was her best because she was standing up for herself.

Likewise, Donald thought the best in him was being understanding and patient with Kelly. That changed when he realized how scared and inadequate he felt to deal with her. The best in him was the part that allowed him to see this painful truth.

The next time Kelly couldn't reach orgasm and berated herself and him, Donald said, "I'm not participating in this anymore. If you can't have compassion for yourself, at least have some for me. I'm tired of scurrying around like a scared little mouse whenever you get angry."

Self-Confrontation Is Part of Your Relationship with Yourself

How do you know you're holding on to the best in yourself? That's where confronting yourself comes in. Holding on to yourself doesn't involve standing up to other people. If anything, holding on to yourself is more like standing up to yourself, because it requires confronting who you are.

When Kelly finally confronted herself, she saw how she demanded Donald accept her tongue-lashings as long as she abused herself as well. For her efforts, Kelly got a painful look at herself, new insights about her mother, and a new way of living. Kelly grew up thinking her mother hated her because her mother raged on for hours, castigating herself and Kelly in the process. Kelly secretly feared that she didn't love Donald because she did the same to him.

When Kelly stopped dodging her own destructive behavior, she discovered a new understanding of it. When Kelly couldn't soothe her own anxieties, insecurities, and hopelessness, she raged at Donald. People who are drowning in their own feelings sometimes verbally abuse others in their attempts to stay afloat.[1] Kelly realized her mother's raging, like her own, didn't have to involve hatred.

Confronting the worst in herself helped Kelly realize that she was capable of loving and that she really did love Donald. This calmed her down and her rages declined. Kelly began to believe that her mother might have loved her too, in spite of the way she acted.

Donald went through an equally difficult time. His statement about being a scared little mouse didn't come out of nowhere. He knew he often scurried around, ducking Kelly's wrath, but what finally made him confront himself was watching coworkers treat him disrespectfully and presume he would tolerate it. Later that evening, when Kelly berated him because she couldn't reach orgasm, Donald simply spoke his mind. He wasn't confronting Kelly as much as he was openly confronting himself. For days afterward, Donald wasn't sure he had done the right thing by speaking up.

Holding on to yourself involves doing what you think is right, even when you are doubtful. Doubt is very important, *because holding on to yourself does not guarantee that what you're doing is right*. It makes a big difference, however, where your doubt springs from. When it comes from the worst in you, doubt will consume you. When the best in you has doubt, your actions become more accurate and appropriate because you are heedful of your impact and learn from your mistakes.

Holding on to yourself doesn't guarantee success, but it's your best shot. It pays to keep confronting yourself—to double-check that you're acting wisely. Without self-confrontation, validating yourself is very dangerous. You could be validating yourself about doing something totally misguided.

When you confront yourself, do it from the best in you. The purpose of all helpful confrontation is to prod you to stand up rather than to beat you down. The latter happens when you confront yourself from the worst in you. It shows up as self-flagellation and self-castigation, which immobilizes you or prompts you to act impulsively.

You especially need to keep an eye on yourself when you confront your partner. Given the choice between confronting our partner and confronting ourselves, lots of us confront our partner straightaway. It's not the best in us doing it, either.

Maintain a Clear and Accurate Sense of Yourself

Now let's consider the four main aspects of holding on to yourself. The first involves staying clear about who and what you are, when the people you love pressure you to accommodate. It's hard enough to perceive yourself clearly and accurately, and even harder when the people you love tamper with your perceptions.

Instead of reflexively confronting your partner, or always giving in, focus on developing a stable and accurate sense of yourself. If you misrepresent yourself to assure positive feedback, you destroy the possibility of intimacy or building a solid relationship. You can't build on your partner's positive feedback (if you get it) because you know he or she doesn't know the real you. This affects your thoughts and feelings during sex, which limits your total level of stimulation. This, in turn, decreases the likelihood of resolving your sexual problem.

On the other hand, successfully confronting these kinds of issues can turn your sex life and your relationship around. Let me tell you about another couple who went through this process.

Linda had faked orgasms ever since she was an adolescent, including when she and Charles got together in their late twenties. Linda never felt good enough, smart enough, pretty enough, or sexy enough for anyone to really love her. When her possessiveness and insecurities destroyed her relationships, this reinforced Linda's sense of inadequacy. Once she began faking orgasms with Charles, she wasn't about to change the picture she presented. She was as ashamed of not having orgasms as she was about lying about them. She also thought Charles would be crushed if she told him the truth. He needed her to have orgasms to feel he was an adequate lover, the same way Linda felt she needed them to be an adequate woman.

This pattern continued for almost twenty years. Then, when Linda was in her midforties, she detected a lump in her breast. With the exams, fears of cancer, and then surgery, Linda wasn't interested in sex. Charles and Linda's sexual relationship plummeted during this time. Although Charles was understanding and supportive, he began having difficulty with erections.

After her mastectomy, Linda's health returned but she went through another six months of depression. The surgery triggered her long-standing feelings of inadequacy and inferiority. Linda emerged from her experience more willing to face up to who she was (and wasn't), and that included no longer faking orgasms.

Linda knew being honest with Charles about faking orgasms (holding on to herself) would shake his perceptions of her, himself, and their relationship. Linda felt pressure to continue misrepresenting herself from twenty years of marriage, several prior relationships, and forty years of media brainwashing. It was hard to maintain a clear sense of purpose, stay calm, and be honest when she and Charles had sex. But Linda drew on the strength she had discovered in herself going through her medical problems.

When Linda fessed up, she learned a lot about tolerating pain for growth. She couldn't count on Charles to validate and soothe her, and she braced for his reaction. Ever the gallant gentleman, Charles said he was glad Linda had finally told him the truth. However, his erection problems got worse.

Sexual Problems Challenge Your Sense of Self

Charles and Linda discovered the truth behind the saying, "When sex is good it's 10 percent of the relationship, and when it's bad it's 90 percent." It's hard to hold on to yourself when sex deteriorates. If you depend on a reflected sense of self, you begin to question your attractiveness and desirability, and your anxieties run wild. You and your partner become more dependent upon each other's affirmations. You look to each other for reassurance, which neither of you believes. You operate from the worst in yourself, and bring out the worst in each other. Then you take each other's bad behavior personally.

Linda's disclosure was a step in the right direction, but it didn't improve things immediately. Charles felt diminished by Linda's deception, and by the fact that he'd been clueless. It made him question their two decades together, doubt his own adequacy, and his continuing problems with erections further diminished his self-esteem. On top of this, Charles was unsure how to deal with Linda's growth, especially since he wasn't driving her wild sexually, as he had thought.

Charles didn't say much about Linda faking orgasms, but he started picking on her other shortcomings. When Linda was right about something, Charles could no longer acknowledge it. When she was wrong, he couldn't let it go. Without realizing it, Charles was pushing Linda to become more deferential in order to reduce his anxiety. This threatened Linda's tenuous good feelings about herself—which was intuitively what Charles was trying to do. However, his efforts didn't produce the reaction he wanted. Linda started telling Charles about his own limitations and petty wrongdoings. At that point, Linda and Charles were gridlocked.

The more accurately Charles and Linda critiqued each other, the worse things got, because neither one wanted their flaws revealed. When their views of each other were distorted and inaccurate (as happens when people are anxious), things got worse because neither could trust the other's judgment. The point is, things *often* get worse when you're dependent on each other's validation and acceptance.

Why Is Having a Clear and Solid Sense of Self Important?

A solid sense of self is the opposite of a reflected sense of self. You know who you are without needing your partner to tell you. A clearer sense of yourself emerges from facing real-life challenges and confronting yourself. For example, Linda's mastectomy forced her to confront the feelings of inadequacy she harbored all her life, and also provided the framework in which she finally resolved them. Coming clean about faking orgasms was a further step in defining herself.

Likewise, a solid sense of self does not mean you're rigid or walled off. You can let your partner be important to you. You can accept your partner's input and you can care about what he or she thinks. You don't overreact when your partner is wrong about something, and you acknowledge when she or he is right.

Emotionally fused couples don't enjoy these benefits. Often, for the worst reasons, your partner accurately sees the worst in you. When he or she focuses on your faults to deflect attention from his or her own limitations, acknowledging your shortcomings can feel like you're saying your partner is completely right and you are totally wrong. At such moments, your ability to hold on to yourself determines whether your relationship goes forward or stays gridlocked. Holding on to yourself involves

- Listening to your partner's feedback because it won't totally destroy your picture of who you are.

- Making personal acknowledgments and positive contributions to resolving your sexual problem.

- Not ranting and raving about needing to be "understood," "heard," or "seen." (This is the psychobabble way of demanding accommodation and a positive reflected sense of self.)

Are You Running Scared or Developing a Solid Sense of Self?

Many people depend on their partner's validation because they have an even worse relationship with themselves. The first challenge in resurrecting sex involves going forward believing in yourself, rather than running scared. Running scared means desperately pursuing better sexual performance to prove you're not inadequate or defective. You can be running scared when trying to get aroused or have an orgasm. You can be running scared using new biomedical technologies to enhance your sexual performance. In other words, you can do something from the worst in you that would otherwise be progress.

When Charles ran scared and pushed himself to get an erection, he was disappointed whether he got one or not. Even if he got an erection one time, he had to prove himself again the next time. The same thing happened when Linda faked orgasms to prove her (and Charles') adequacy. Seeking better performance to prop up your reflected sense of self accomplishes little, even if you resolve your sexual problem. Seize this opportunity for emotional emancipation. *How* you go forward, and not simply *if* you go forward, determines where you end up in the future. Don't run scared for a solution.

Calm Yourself Down and Lick Your Own Bruises

The second part of holding on to yourself involves calming yourself when you are anxious and soothing your own disappointments. Two problems with intimate relationships make self-soothing important. They are not intimate all the time, and tolerating intimacy is itself often difficult. Your marriage will become more stable (and more sexually interesting) when you and your partner calm your own anxieties and lick your own wounds.

Manage your own anxieties when your partner is unavailable or disinclined to manage them for you. Likewise, hold on to yourself when your partner wants to manage *you*. In committed relationships, your partner is usually a major source of your anxiety. Think back to our opening story of two frogs climbing on each other in their frantic fear of drowning. There's often a frantic frog lying next to you in bed.

This is one of the crucibles of marriage: the more you really need your partner to soothe, support, or motivate you, the less likely your partner will be able to provide this. Since partners usually have about equal ability to hold on to themselves, the more desperately you need your partner

to soothe you, the more he or she will be busy trying to keep himself or
herself together. If you can't function effectively on your own, you're
going to stay stuck and you're going to hurt until you learn to take better care of yourself. If you want this to happen sooner rather than later,
here are four things that can help.

- When you start to lose your grip on yourself, stop talking and
  focus on your breathing. Lower your volume, unclench your
  teeth, and talk in a softer tone of voice.

- Try not to take your partner's behavior (or lack of change)
  personally. This is another "opportunity" to let go of your
  reflected sense of self.

- If you can't regulate your emotions, control your behavior.
  Don't shoot your mouth off or make things worse. When you
  start saying, "Maybe I shouldn't say this, but . . ." take your
  own advice.

- Stop your negative mental tapes. Stop telling yourself, "I can't
  believe this!"

Some Forms of Self-Soothing Work Better Than Others
The most effective forms of self-soothing involve calming yourself while
maintaining positive emotional and physical connection with your partner. However, sometimes self-soothing involves breaking contact with
your partner. In the best scenarios, you and your partner briefly disen-
gage so that you can get back together on a more positive note. However, if you have more difficulty holding on to yourselves, getting away
from each other becomes an end in itself. Time apart minimizes contact
with no intent to make things better.

This pattern shows up even within the space of your bed. When your
problem first develops, perhaps you can calm yourself during sex and
maintain positive emotional connection with your partner. As your problem continues you may stop when it occurs during sex and withdraw to
opposite sides of the bed. Perhaps you "repair" yourself in the silence
and reach out to your partner, making a second attempt to make contact.
If this fails, you might avoid contact with your partner altogether—like
getting out of bed to smoke a cigarette or having a drink to calm down.

Ideally, you want to calm yourself down while maintaining good contact with your partner. When things start to go wrong during sex, calm down and talk with your partner about what is happening. Jumping out of bed, pulling on your clothes, and driving off into the night is not good self-soothing. Neither is standing in the doorway, barring your partner's way when he or she indicates the strong need to be alone. Ineffective self-soothing often triggers domestic violence.

The same increased distancing that can occur within sexual encounters can happen in your overall relationship. If your difficulty self-soothing continues, you may move to separate beds or bedrooms just to be able to sleep. Some people start an extramarital affair, a highly ineffective form of self-soothing.

Here's the bottom line. You and your partner will create as much physical space between you as is required to calm yourselves down. The more emotionally fused you are, the more time and distance you need to accomplish this. It helps if you don't dally. Offer to schedule time to reconnect in order to demonstrate your good intent. Show up on time.

Use your time apart effectively. Take care and replenish yourself: exercise, relax, read a good book, or do something productive. Friends, hobbies, and outside interests can soothe and refuel you, depending on how you use them. Reflexively distancing from your partner doesn't increase your ability to self-soothe, nor does bad-mouthing your spouse to your close friends. Self-soothing is not self-indulgence, like bingeing on food, clothes, drugs, or alcohol.

If your partner needs physical distance from you to calm down, try not to take it personally. It often has more to do with difficulty holding on to himself or herself than with lack of love for you. (The more you love someone, the *harder* it is to soothe yourself.) Unfortunately, the more your partner needs to do this, the more likely you are to react negatively to it. Intimate relationships teach you that compassion is only possible when partners can soothe themselves. Your best shot at a loving and compassionate relationship, as well as at resurrecting sex, lies in getting good at soothing your own heart.

Give Your Dilemma Meaning

Giving your dilemma meaning is one of the most powerful ways humans soothe themselves. For instance, when you see your struggles as part of the natural growth processes of intimate relationships, you are more likely to try to calm yourself, so you can go through your situation productively. Stupid useless pain is much harder to bare than pain with purpose. When you see larger meanings and potential benefits to your situation, you are more likely to hold on to yourself and persevere. This makes you less likely to get divorced and more likely to get more married.[2]

For Linda and Charles the path to success was difficult and prolonged. Even when Linda made a move from the best in her and told the truth, things didn't magically turn around on the spot. Linda had to hold on to herself while Charles went through his own set of reactions. Between his erection problem and their shifting roles, Charles was nasty and unkind for weeks on end. Over a month went by before they could make use of the groundwork Linda laid down by finally telling the truth.

Linda and Charles' Solution
Self-confrontation, self-disclosure, self-soothing, tolerating anxiety, and unilateral action all came together in an exquisite way for Charles and Linda. This happens all the time for couples, because these are the drive wheels of intimate relationships. In Charles and Linda's case, it happened when Linda proposed they change how they had sex.

Linda suggested Charles stop trying to "pleasure" her, and instead stretch out next to her so that she could hold him. Looking beyond Charles' anger and distrust of her, she could see the man she loved in pain and needing to be comforted. When she said this, Linda knew that Charles wasn't likely to agree. Chivalry was at the core of his sense of masculinity. This meant that when they had sex, he had to be the "doer" and Linda's role was to receive. Learning the truth about faked orgasms made it even harder for him to accept the comforting from Linda that he needed more than ever. But the best in Linda reached out openly with compassion to the person she had hurt.

This produced an intense two-choice dilemma for Charles. Ever the gentleman, he felt obligated to respond graciously to Linda's immensely important gesture. At the same time, here was Linda wanting him to do things entirely differently again! He felt incredibly inadequate just doing what they used to do!

Charles was torn. He was as embarrassed by his treatment of Linda as he was by his poor sexual performance. He wanted to be stubborn. He wanted to pull back and overreact. He wanted to give in to his anger at Linda for deceiving him. But with his whole life seemingly eroding, Charles held on to some vestige of what he believed in. Charles could not slap Linda down when the best in her was reaching out to him. He gave up the form his beliefs had taken, and he held on to their substance. Charles lay down beside Linda and they held each other.

Charles and Linda's abilities to soothe themselves were stretched beyond their prior limits. Charles stretched to accept his limitations as well as Linda's strengths. He let Linda get emotionally closer than they'd ever been before, at a time when he never felt more vulnerable in his life. Letting himself be held could have made Charles feel more inadequate. But by responding to Linda from the best in himself, it was easier to handle these feelings. As it turned out, Charles' sense of pride and a good stable erection arrived at just about the same time.

In the months that followed, Linda was able to reach orgasm with Charles. Reduced anxiety, increased positive emotional contact, and the increased meaningfulness of their sex helped Linda have orgasms for the first time in her life. The same conditions returned Charles' erections to their prior reliable nature. Linda stopped "faking" in all aspects of her life. Charles stopped hiding behind a facade of gentility and became stronger and gentler. They became more resilient in the face of life's trials and tribulations.

Human Resilience

One of humankind's most outstanding characteristics is our remarkable emotional resilience. Infants are not as helpless as we imagined—and neither are adults. Children obviously seek soothing from their parents, but just as parental neglect stunts children's development, so does constant comfort and reassurance. Frustration, uncertainty, and anxiety are necessary during infancy, because they start developing our capacity to self-soothe. There's more than enough frustration, uncertainty, and anxiety in marriage to finish the job.

The hallmark of being human is not dependence or fears of abandonment. It is our indomitable urge to chart our own lives, to persevere through difficult times and keep going. The basis of human resilience is not mule-like stubbornness but, rather, self-soothing. Self-soothing is so dominant in humans that we show some rudimentary ability by the time we're six months old.[3] Yes, we have frailties. But the best in us can desire our partner in ways that don't stem from neediness and fears. *That's* the part you want driving your marriage.

Don't Overreact to Your Partner's Overreactions

The third part of holding on to yourself involves not reacting to provocations from your partner. When you're irritated, hurt, or anxious, you are more likely to overreact to things your partner does (or doesn't do). When you can't soothe yourself, compassion recedes. Withdrawing into yourself and repeating through clenched teeth, "I'm *not* going to let you get to me!" is not a good example of soothing yourself and not overreacting.

On the other hand, you don't want to be insensitive to your partner. It is not in your best interest to ride roughshod over your mate in the name of improving your relationship. This sometimes happens because people often try to reduce their reactivity by disinvesting or becoming indifferent. Remaining nonreactive but invested and sensitive is much harder.

Are You or Your Partner Indifferent or Insensitive?
People frequently complain that their partners are insensitive to their needs and desires. When you try changing your sexual relationship, charges of insensitivity may arise. Oftentimes the real problem is exactly the opposite: partners are *too sensitive* to each other's needs and feelings.

Men, in particular, are frequently positioned in conventional marital therapy as being insensitive, which encourages them to drop out of treatment. In reality, many men are sensitive guys who can't stand their sensitivity. If they were truly insensitive, they wouldn't need to continually defend themselves or act deaf. For all their appearance of putting up walls or being emotionally dead, "wall-builders" are vulnerable people who are very much alive and alert on the inside. This was the case with John and Phyllis.

John, 58 years old, had been having increasing difficulty getting and keeping an erection. He had high blood pressure and was taking medication. He also had a long history of alcohol abuse, although he denied this was a problem. John was the proverbial good ol' boy, affable and social in public, hard-drinking with the guys, a staunch supporter of traditional values—and a lousy relationship with his wife. There were many possible sources for his erection problems, including medications, neurological damage from alcohol abuse, and his long-troubled marriage.

Phyllis and John married thirty years ago when their respective first marriages ended. John's wife left because of his drinking and abusive manner. Phyllis's marriage ended when she discovered her husband was having an affair. She was determined to make her second marriage survive at almost any cost.

John often became verbally abusive when they disagreed, especially if he had been drinking. After years of terrible scenes, Phyllis didn't speak up like she had in the past. John stopped drinking because his body couldn't handle it, and that was good enough for Phyllis to stay in the marriage. However, it wasn't enough to keep her sexual desire alive. Phyllis settled for going along with John's sexual needs. Sometimes she had an orgasm, sometimes she didn't, and most times it didn't matter to her either way.

Phyllis found John's bullheaded reactivity unattractive. She didn't know that behind his seeming dismissal of everyone's opinion but his own, John was extremely insecure. At the first sign of contention, John became anxious and verbally annihilated the opposition. It was John's acute sensitivity—coupled with his inability to soothe himself—that made him look so insensitive.

Now let me tell you about another couple, in which the man also fit the stereotype of a typical "insensitive" guy. Andrew and Gwen had sexual problems for most of their thirty-year marriage. When they first met, Gwen had never had an orgasm. Eventually she had orgasms with oral sex (which they did rarely) and with a vibrator. Andrew frequently struggled with premature orgasms, and he was threatened by Gwen's ability to have orgasms by herself. He thought he should bring her to orgasm during intercourse, and she did too. But like many other aspects of their relationship, they never discussed this.

Andrew was a hardworking corporate executive who devoted his life to his career. Gwen made a life for herself with her hobbies and friends. In the last several years their kids left for college and Andrew's retirement was now in sight—and so was the prospect of future decades of cold silence together. Watching their friends become infirm and die made it increasingly difficult for Gwen to sit by and watch her life drift away.

Andrew was a perfect example of how apparent indifference and insensitivity sometimes masks caring and vulnerability. One partner can attempt to minimize the tremendous impact of the other partner by acting indifferent. Couples with sexual problems try to avoid feeling each other's dissatisfaction and displeasure. If you depend on your partner's validation, it's hard not to react negatively to his or her frustrations and disappointments. How you deal with your reactivity and emotional sensitivities shapes the course of your relationship.

Staying Nonreactive to Your Partner

Remaining nonreactive is the exact opposite of being insensitive and indifferent. Remaining nonreactive allows you to be sensitive and responsive in productive ways. If you want to stay close, peaceful, and happy, you can't constantly overreact to things your partner does (and doesn't do). Overreactivity surfaces in trying to argue your partner out of his or her point of view, or "trumping" your partner's list of dissatisfactions with a bigger list of your own.

John was like a bull in a china shop once he lost his grip on himself. He found fault with every move Phyllis made and belittled her. Once John became defensive, as he often did, everything Phyllis did was wrong, and what she wasn't doing was wrong too.

Andrew handled his sensitivity and reactivity somewhat differently. Andrew's style was to turn a deaf ear to Gwen. She referred to this as "the deep freeze." He was civil, even polite, but completely unavailable. Gwen had learned it was best to leave Andrew alone until he was ready to interact. Trying to talk with him when he pulled back was like cornering a fox, which will bite when trapped.

It was hard for Gwen when Andrew walled her out. Sometimes this went on for months, and she carried resentment about this. She found solace in close friendships, teaching signing to the deaf, and taking care of her children. Life with Andrew involved lots of time alone, and Gwen tried to use it as best she could.

Phyllis, on the other hand, was emotionally exhausted by her constant interaction with John. When he would "lose it," he'd tell her she was stupid. He would assault her intelligence and reduce her to tears and apologies. John and Phyllis illustrate a pattern that leads many couples to divorce.[4]

Don't Be a Reptile

People become reptiles when they get really anxious. The reptilian part of our brain takes over and the worst in us comes forward, lashing out to protect ourselves and snapping at whatever we deem threatening. And when we're "reptilian," everything looks threatening. There's nothing wrong with being a reptile, and reptiles do have sex. However, they don't make love. If we want to make love, we need *human* sexuality. To have that, we must soothe our anxiety so the thinking part of our brain (our neocortex) can run the show.

What kinds of anxieties turn people into reptiles? Consider the typical gauntlet of provocations facing couples with sexual problems.

- "If someone's to blame here, it isn't me!"

- "I'm not changing!"

- "There's nothing wrong with me the way I am! You're the one who's the problem!"

- "Just give things more time as they are. Be patient!"

- "I don't have time for this!"

- "You know I'm sensitive about this. If you love me, you won't make me deal with it."

- "You had this problem before me. Take care of it by yourself."

Anxiety-provoking, accusatory, and defensive responses frequently surface when couples start addressing their sexual problems. Some partners raise their voices, some bludgeon with tears, and some call names. I don't suggest you tolerate being abused, but harsh words often pass between partners when they feel anxious and pressured. If you're serious about solving your problem, you have to hang in long enough for your partner to realize that you're not going to give up or ignore your situation. He or she may not see you as being loving or considerate, but it has everything to do with partnership.

Tolerating Discomfort for Growth

The fourth and final aspect of holding on to yourself is crucial to resurrecting sex. Tolerating discomfort for growth is as important to making progress in your relationship as it is in the rest of your life. The good and bad news about marriage is that it invariably provides lessons in self-soothing and tolerating discomfort for growth. Your only choice is whether or not you learn from them.

A long-term intimate relationship is inherently discomforting. John, however, wasn't interested in more discomfort. He wanted to keep the status quo, except for how his penis functioned. He thought Phyllis should make him feel like the king of his own castle. Intellectually John accepted anxiety as a fact of life, but he became a reptile when forced to live it out. The natural processes of committed relationships were completely off his map of romance and love.

Moreover, Phyllis wasn't interested in tolerating discomfort for growth any longer. She simply tried to weather John's emotional storms and keep things as pleasant as possible. She tried to keep her marriage together, but it no longer came from the best in her. She didn't want to start a new life for herself or face her family if she divorced. The last thing she wanted to do was confront John about his shortcomings.

Handling Confrontations with Your Partner

In the same way self-confrontation drives your marriage into the growth cycle, confronting your partner when necessary does too. Bringing up discussions he or she wants to avoid is not adversarial (even though your partner may respond as if it is), but you need a clear and solid sense of yourself to pull this off.

Confrontations are part of *healthy* relationships. Effective confrontation is a form of collaboration and partnership that says, "I see you, you see me seeing you, and in this moment we are both revealed." When used productively, confrontation builds better relationships, stronger people, and greater intimacy.

Confronting your partner doesn't involve threats or ultimatums. The best (and safest) way to confront your partner is to first confront *yourself*. When you confront yourself, your partner is confronted (through your relationship) because his or her emotional stability is so intertwined with yours. If your partner's emotional equilibrium depends on your accommodation, when you hold on to yourself he or she will feel the "tug." It's a productive way to use (and end) emotional fusion.[5]

But what should you do when your partner confronts you? What if he or she really nails you where you feel most vulnerable? What if it doesn't feel collaborative or doesn't come from the best in your partner? If you're willing to tolerate some discomfort for growth, here are two things you *shouldn't* do:

- *Don't make your partner say it perfectly kindly.* Don't expect him or her to do it sweetly or gently. Lots of emotional steam can build up over time, and it generally comes out with the truth.

- *Don't make your partner be perfectly accurate.* If your partner is in the ballpark, help him or her fill in the picture rather than disputing the inaccuracies. In other words, nail yourself.[6]

These two points mark the difference between our couples. Andrew and Gwen were willing to confront themselves when it seemed unavoidable. And to that degree they tolerated being confronted by each other. John, on the other hand, acted as if he were defending the Alamo—and only the American version of the story was permitted. If Phyllis was 99 percent accurate about him, he'd pick at the 1 percent she was off.

Likewise, Andrew and Gwen were better at keeping their interaction from developing a hard edge. Andrew defused difficult discussions with a touch of humor, and Gwen didn't corner him on issues he wasn't ready to discuss. John's eruptions, in contrast, epitomized hard confrontations. He confronted Phyllis belligerently to avoid confronting himself. Phyllis, in turn, caved in rather than look at herself and John.

Establish a Collaborative Alliance

When you repeatedly act in ways that promote partnership, it helps your partner realize your confrontations are part of your attempts to establish a more collaborative alliance. This invariably requires tolerating discomfort for growth. Working together for your mutual and individual benefits challenges and strengthens your ability to hold on to yourself.

Many of us have no successful experience maintaining a tractable alliance with those we love. Some of us learn to regulate our anxieties by getting away from the important people in our lives. Andrew learned early on it was best not to count on others and just handle things by himself. So, while it made good intellectual sense that he and Gwen should work together as a team, it did not compute for him emotionally.

Like Andrew, you may feel the best way to deal with anxiety is to go off on your own, handle what you can, and try to ignore the rest. While this response may have sufficed in your life until now, it doesn't work well for resolving sex and intimacy problems. Expanding your coping style so your situation can go forward obviously requires tolerating some discomfort.

Sometimes this requires confronting the darker side of marriage. Acknowledging things going on beneath your interactions is another form of tolerating pain for growth.

Partners torture each other all the time through their sexual relationship. Feigning ignorance about what the other wants. Withholding passion, or intimacy, or sex. Engaging in demeaning interactions with disrespectful attitudes. Making your husband beg for sex. Making your wife smile when she wants to brain you for losing your erection just before she's about to reach orgasm. Sex is one of the more convenient ways to tear out your partner's heart.

I call this *normal marital sadism*—lying to inflict pain, manipulating information to control your partner, withholding the sweetness of sex, and enjoying your partner's unhappiness. This is normal because it's a fact of life when people cannot hold on to themselves. Normal marital sadism runs rampant when normal couples have sexual problems.

I did impromptu research at my workshop on normal marital sadism at the Family Therapy Networker Symposium in 2000. Eighty-seven percent of 120 therapists in my audience reported they engaged in normal marital sadism. They estimated that the same percentage of their clients did too. Accepting these realities is part of tolerating discomfort for growth. It's hard accepting that you and your partner deliberately do things to hurt each other, even though you love each other.

Andrew and Gwen and John and Phyllis faced these kinds of issues, as all couples do, but they differed in how they dealt with them. Andrew and Gwen were able to establish a collaborative alliance and hold on to themselves when things got tough. John and Phyllis's alliance fell apart whenever John was threatened, and his verbal attacks returned.

John wasn't about to acknowledge his sadism because he couldn't validate himself to begin with. Phyllis was not a total martyr either. She knew what a good screw was, and John wasn't going to get that from her. Phyllis wasn't about to see this in herself, for the same reason that John was blind. She couldn't validate herself enough to accept that a part of her knew how to hate.

Gwen and Andrew hated (and loved) each other as long-term partners often do. The difference was that they could accept it better. Gwen eventually sat down with Andrew and told him she wasn't looking forward to his retirement. Andrew sat stunned, not knowing whether to withdraw, as he usually did, or not. Gwen said she knew this was hurtful to hear, but it was better that he hear it from her mouth than read it in her behavior. She spoke of her anger about the years they had wasted and said she didn't want to lose the life she'd created in his absence. She acknowledged a part of her wanted Andrew to hurt when he heard this. Gwen offered him the respect of saying it to him directly.

Andrew was badly shaken, but he didn't attack or leave, even as his picture of retirement evaporated before his eyes. He was quiet, but his silence wasn't icy. Gwen saw he was taking in what she said, and he simply did not know what to do. Andrew knew Gwen was angry with him, but he never thought it would come to this. He said, "I'll get back to you," and left the room sadly and slowly.

Make Repair Attempts

Making repair attempts to your partner is a form of tolerating discomfort for growth that becomes especially important when your relationship deteriorates and you're feeling alienated. A repair attempt isn't about giving in or avoiding difficult subjects or subjugating or humbling yourself. It involves the best in you standing up.

A repair attempt can be anything that helps fix things with your partner. In general terms, think of it as turning toward your partner rather than turning away. It often boils down to making the first move to get something positive going after unpleasant interactions have occurred. This could involve

- Reaching out to your partner "in the moment" when your sexual problem occurs

- Making conciliatory overtures while your partner is pouting

- Referring to prior good moments or meaningful hard times you have been through together

- Easing the tension with humor when conversations become contentious

- Forthrightly apologizing when you lose your grip on yourself, without your partner having to force it out of you

Here's why tolerating discomfort for growth and self-soothing are critical factors in your repair attempts: You have to make about six repair attempts before one is successful (meaning, your partner responds positively). If you've been at each other's throats or engaged in a cold war, you can double that. When your relationship becomes warm and friendly, the necessary ratio goes lower. Making one or two repair attempts and then giving up is tantamount to doing nothing at all.

John could make one or two repair attempts at best, before he blew up if Phyllis didn't respond. And Phyllis was slower to respond to John's attempts at reconciliation as time wore on. It was increasingly hard for her to believe things would ever be different. Phyllis made few repair attempts, John made almost none, and he often rebuked the approaches she made.

Andrew was not great at reaching out, but he could do it when necessary. Gwen was less willing to always make the first approach, but she could do it when she wanted to. Andrew and Gwen could reach out to each other a few days after an argument. John and Phyllis went weeks or months before one or the other tried to make amends. It wasn't that John and Phyllis were less needy and dependent than Andrew and Gwen—in fact, just the opposite.

As John and Phyllis's relationship deteriorated further, John started drinking again and stopped going to Alcoholics Anonymous. One night on the way home from carousing with his buddies, John sideswiped a car driven by a mother with two young children. He was arrested for driving while intoxicated.

This was the final straw for Phyllis. She was worn out and her integrity demanded she leave the marriage. Her fears of condemnation from her family paled in comparison. Within a week she moved out and filed for legal separation. A year later they were divorced.

What makes people eventually take a leap of faith and tolerate the ensuing discomfort? It's not when they stop being fearful, vulnerable, or insecure. They go forward when their fear of violating their own integrity exceeds their other anxieties. Or their goals become more important than their discomforts. Either one can surface many ways in the process of resurrecting sex. (If you completely avoid self-confrontation because you won't tolerate pain for growth, neither of these two things can happen, and the best in you may never stand up.)

Were John and Phyllis doomed from the first? Did they have everything going against them? I think not. I've seen couples like John and Phyllis hold on to themselves and turn their lives around, just like I've watched couples like Andrew and Gwen completely fall apart. It was not John and Phyllis's particular problems or contributing factors that made the difference. It was their *response* to their problems.

Would things have turned out differently if John didn't have erection problems? Again, I think the answer is no. Reliable erections might have made John less likely to have tirades, but so many other things triggered them that his sexual performance anxiety was the least of it. Better sexual function doesn't always help; in fact, it can bring relationship issues to a head. In Part 3 I'll show you exactly how this happens.

What Does Success Look Like?

The difference between our couples lies in their ability to hold on to themselves in times of trouble. This often determines whether your marriage survives or not. The stability of your relationship depends more on soothing your feelings than on expressing them. Don't make the mistake of presuming emotional expression is the key. The core process is *regulating* your emotions effectively. For John, that meant controlling his outbursts. For Andrew, it meant not putting his feelings on ice.

Andrew got back to Gwen, as he said he would. His first impulse was to punish her for frightening him. He wanted to march in and restate his position that he worked hard to provide a great lifestyle for Gwen and their children. However, Gwen clearly preferred less money and more of a life together, while he pursued his career for himself. Andrew's life was playing out before his eyes: He saw how a banker's son could grow up with everything and have nothing.

Andrew was flooded with anxiety. He held on to himself, however, and didn't give in to his habitual reaction to withdraw. He kept himself calm enough to stick to business. If he had waited a month to get back to Gwen, their dealings would have been different than they were 24 hours later.

The next day Andrew sat down with Gwen and told her he wasn't going to withdraw. He was willing to do what he could to have a new life together. He said he wouldn't pressure her to give up her activities, but he wanted to have more of a place in her life than she described. His bottom line was that he didn't want a "gilded-mausoleum marriage" like his parents'.

Gwen was taken aback by Andrew's openness. She knew he had it in him, but she'd given up hope that this would ever happen. However, Gwen had no intention of being swept up in an emotional moment. She told Andrew she appreciated what he said and how he said it, but they'd have to see what happened as time went on. She wasn't cutting Andrew off, or telling him it couldn't happen, but she also wasn't running in to support him either. Gwen wanted to see what Andrew would do if left to his own devices.

Gwen saw that Andrew kept himself on track. They started spending more time together, although things at first were a little tense. Gradually they realized they really did enjoy each other's company, and things became more relaxed. Gwen now had the best of both worlds, an exciting life and a romance with her husband that she never thought she'd have. And Andrew started relaxing during sex in ways he never had.

Had Andrew felt threatened and demanded that Gwen give up her activities to be with him, they probably would have ended up in a very different place. Actually, Andrew found Gwen's independence sexually attractive. Being more self-revealing was awkward for him at first, but he certainly liked the results. Gwen seemed to find him more sexually interesting too.

For the first time in his life, Andrew stopped having rapid orgasms. Had he responded from the worst in him, the same anxieties and circumstances might have led to the exact opposite. Instead, Gwen got to watch "the iceman" thaw out. She saw it in their bedroom and noticed it between Andrew and their children.

As things progressed, Gwen and Andrew experimented with what adult sex offers. Once when they were totally engrossed in their encounter, time seemed to stop. There was not a sound. The world dropped away and nothing existed but the two of them. Their union was solid and profound. There was so much presence in the moment, Andrew thought the air was shimmering. He had never experienced anything like that in his life. The next day Andrew came over to Gwen several times to hold her and stand together in warm silence.

You can move toward similar goals by applying the four points of holding on to yourself and setting your marriage into motion. Here are some suggestions to help you.

- Stop approaching your sexual problem as if you're eradicating a disease.

- Take a closer look at yourself. Start singing Michael Jackson's song "I'm Starting with the Man in the Mirror."

- Stop thinking, "Why do *I* have to go through this?" Remind yourself that many couples find this to be an extremely meaningful process, sometimes almost spiritual. You won't experience this by repeating the mantra, "Oh, God, why me?"

- Don't expect your partner to act like an angel while you're having a devil of a time. Change your view of your partner being there for you. The Dalai Lama talks of this as approaching your adversary as your teacher. He suggests the fallback position of reminding yourself that your partner is a sentient being, trying to avoid suffering just like you. So either realize that your partner is not some monster reptile, or tell yourself that Godzilla and Rodan had their lessons to teach, and they needed love, too.

- Don't count on miracles overnight. Be prepared for the long haul.

Given how we demand immediate improvement (without effort), it's easy to see why sexual solutions like pills, rub-on creams, vacuum pumps, and surgery are ever popular. But even when you are chemically stabilized, anesthetized, and disinhibited, you still have to make contact with your partner. We'll learn about drugs, sexual devices, and bionic solutions in the next three chapters, but your local pharmacy likely won't serve up what Andrew and Gwen tasted (at least not anytime soon). Viagra may take some of the worry out of being close, but it won't remove your fears of being intimate or known.

So what does the brave new world of sexual medicine really have to offer? That will be the focus of our attention in Part 3.

PART III

Medical Options

8

Sex Devices and Surgical Procedures

To the mind of the modern girl, legs, like busts, are power points which she has been taught to tailor, but as parts of her success kit rather than erotically or sensuously.

—Marshall McLuhan, *The Mechanical Bride* (1951)

In the next few chapters we're going to consider mechanical, pharmacological, and surgical aids for resurrecting sex. At first you might think of these as medical or nonrelationship solutions that eliminate the need for everything we've discussed in Part 2. But medical or physical solutions to sexual problems always have a relationship component, too.

Anytime sex changes it impacts you, your partner, and your relationship. When that change occurs rapidly, as with surgery or medication (or illness and injury), the impact can be dramatic. Just the fact that somebody did something to change things makes things different. This fact alone can be delightful or disquieting. When you contemplate the technological marvels we'll discuss, remember that you and your relationship largely determine their benefits and impacts.

Are You Addressing or Avoiding Your Problem?

Crude sexual devices and (bogus) aphrodisiacs document how couples have sought relief from sexual problems since the dawn of recorded history. Desperation has inspired laughable, ingenious, painful, or dangerous solutions. But today you have available safer and more effective options than any preceding generation. Together with greater freedom to openly consider your options, today's medical alternatives offer unprecedented opportunities for couples wanting to improve their sexual functioning and their marriage.

Sex devices and potions have also long offered the prospect of enhancing performance regardless of one's partner, situation, or relationship. Bionic solutions are particularly attractive to those who hope technology might allow them to ignore their marriage. Clients hoping to bypass their emotional life ask me, "Doc, isn't there a shot you can give me or a pill I can take?" Some want a solution they can implement without involving (or alerting) their partner.[1] They don't just want a quick fix, they want it impersonal, too.

Using medical options doesn't have to involve attempts to avoid intimacy. However, if I just described you, it would be trite and disrespectful to tell you not to pursue this route. I'd rather talk realistically with you about what motivates people to pursue medical solutions for nonmedical problems. Perhaps you won't have to deal with your relationship to improve your sexual function. What you'll read here will let you judge if medication or surgery will help you avoid this.

If you plan on using *any* device, drug, or surgical option during sex with your partner, you'll still need to hold on to yourself. The dandiest device and the most powerful drug won't get used much, and they won't be as useful, if you can't hold on to yourself. At the very least, you'll have to soothe yourself and not overreact.

The growth you derive, and how clear you become about who you are, is entirely up to you. How much self-confrontation are you willing to do? To what degree are you running scared for a solution? The more you operate out of the best in you, the more sexual aids can help you and your relationship.

Sexual Devices

Pharmaceutical companies, card shops, confectioneries, florists, and your local adult bookstore are well aware that sex enhancement is big business. And there's no secret about the purpose of Victoria's Secret. A dazzling array of lubricants, vibrators, dildos, and penis vacuum pumps are on the market. So what can they do, and which one is for you?

Lubricants

Perhaps it's the John Wayne in every guy coming out, but a surprising number of men need to be told to use lubrication when they masturbate. It never dawns on them that solo sex doesn't have to hurt. Even women, who know that masturbation is better if it's wetter, suffer through painful intercourse because they think augmenting their natural lubrication is cheating.

It's easier for a woman to relax and enjoy sex if her introitus (the opening to her vagina) is wet. It's also easier to stroke a flaccid penis to erection when there's some glide between the shaft and your hand. Technically your erogenous zones are mucous membranes, like your mouth, which generally feel best when moist.

Women are prime users of sexual lubricants. Vaginal dryness can have many causes. It can be anything from lack of arousal, taking antihistamines or medications, a good long session of lusty intercourse, or a partner who has delayed orgasms. Some causes are easily corrected, and some require more than loading on the lube.

If you're not familiar with commercially prepared sexual lubricants, here are three things you should know.

Saliva is the most popular sexual lubricant. It's always available and the price is right. Many men and women lick their hands and transfer saliva to their genitals to ease the initial moments of intercourse or manual stimulation. Unfortunately, saliva evaporates quickly. If the woman's own lubrication response doesn't kick in rapidly, intercourse can become dry and painful. This, in turn, can create other sexual problems like low sexual desire (and, eventually, vaginismus).

Don't use petroleum jelly. Petroleum products are not friendly to vaginas. They also damage condoms and inhibit oral sex. Your local drugstore carries several *water-based* "personal lubricants." Some are pleasant to feel, smell, and taste. Try several until you find one you like.

Don't use lubricants to compensate for (or cover over) what may be missing in your connection with your partner. If your vagina *and* your relationship are both dry, you won't find your solution in a bottle. Painful intercourse is emotionally detached sex because (1) your mind is elsewhere (focusing on your pain), and (2) you don't want your partner to know you're in pain. Connection at that moment is not your top priority.

Using lubricants when you need them can help you relax and get back with your partner. Some couples find using lubricants both considerate and erotic. The actual process of using the lubricant can be a positive emotional experience. It becomes a signal for playfulness, investment in your partner's (or your own) pleasure, and an invitation to "really get it on!" The difference between a good and bad experience comes from what's in your head and heart, not what's in the tube or bottle.

Some women endure dry, painful sex for years because they or their partner believe "artificial" lubricant shouldn't be necessary. It's not hard to understand why they do this, once you realize they are dependent on a reflected sense of self. Some women, like Jaclyn, are fully aware of store-bought lubricants—Jaclyn had a bottle next to her bed, which she used while masturbating. Using it with a partner was a different thing. Jaclyn didn't want to hurt her partner's reflected sense of self by reaching for the bottle on her nightstand. Instead, she chose to accommodate her partner, assuage both his and her anxieties, and tolerate the pain.[2]

Many women tolerate painful sex rather than do something about it. Jaclyn was a sophisticated single woman to all outward appearances, but still timid and shy about sex. She was more afraid of the rejection she anticipated (for using lubricant) than the vaginal pain she felt in the moment. Jaclyn's solution involved holding on to herself and speaking up.

Deborah was more than willing to stop and add lubricant, but whenever she did, her partner, Daniel, would stop having sex on the spot. Daniel took it as a negative reflection on his sexual abilities and stormed out of their bedroom. Deborah tried inserting lubrication before sex until Daniel began to "check her" to see if she was "cheating." Deborah's ability to hold on to herself couldn't weather Daniel's temper tantrums. Eventually she acquiesced to his terms and lost all desire for sex.

Daniel illustrates how people with a reflected sense of self invariably squeeze the life out of the people around them, whether or not this is their intention. Usually they are married to someone with a tenuous sense of self, like Deborah, who is all too ready to give herself or himself up as soon as he or she is "squeezed." Sexual pain is often the end result of borrowed functioning in emotionally fused relationships.

When you are too emotionally fused to your partner to use lubricant that you need, you lose any sense of positive emotional connection during sex. This is no different from what happens when you misrepresent yourself in nonsexual intimacies. Standing on your own two feet—while you're lying down in bed—helps you get closer to your partner.

Lingerie

Couples' passions and pathos play out in sexy lingerie. Many women hope new teddies will turn their Freddies into Fernandos. Some hope new outfits will transform them into the desirable and lovable women they don't believe themselves to be. Others won't put on anything for fear of looking pathetic and inadequate. Men, like women, put on (or fear wearing) provocative G-strings for both the best and worst of reasons.

Some women, like Kim, dress up for themselves. Her partner, Lloyd, was just the secondary beneficiary. Kim personified Shania Twain's song: "Men's shirts. Short skirts. Man, I feel like a *woman!*" As Kim prepared for sex, she wasn't just enjoying her anticipation of Lloyd's response. She was *hot* at that moment, all by herself. Kim got a kick out of pushing Lloyd's comfort level, daring him to dress up and play as an equal. When Kim let herself cut lose with undergarments, she was wet before Lloyd walked in the room.

As sexual enhancements go, lingerie is quick, inexpensive, and instantly reversible if you don't like the results. If you feel good about the way you look, it can enhance your performance. However, if you lay on lace to cover up rather than to entice, it can have the opposite effect.

Lucy, for instance, went ballistic when Lester bought her what he thought was a dynamite sexy outfit. He was shocked when she accused him of not loving her for who she was and disliking her body. His gift triggered Lucy's feelings about her own body and stretched her beyond the themes and styles of sex with which she was comfortable.

Similarly, not all men respond positively to boudoir clothing. One man, married to a woman like Kim, refused to have sex with her whenever she dressed for sex. He called her a slut and berated her for her stockings and garter belts. Over the years she went from being highly interested in sex and having multiple orgasms to having problems with sexual arousal and desire.

Here's the rule: the more you depend on a reflected sense of self and accommodation from your partner, the less flexibility you have about using (or not using) lingerie. The more solid your sense of self, the more you can put on different images without feeling anxious or phony. As we have seen, a solid sense of self is a *flexible* self that lets you accept influence from your partner.

Vibrators and Dildos

If you can think of a size, shape, color, or texture for a vibrator or dildo, it's available. Vibrators come in four different forms. Some look like a long-handled wand with a vibrating head (e.g., the Hitachi Magic Wand, the Wahl Magic Fingers, and the Panasonic Panabrator). Another popular style looks like a small handheld electric mixer with massage attachments that stick out at a 90-degree angle (e.g., the Prelude III).

A third group of vibrators are penis-shaped devices called dildos. (Not all dildos vibrate.) Contrary to men's fantasies and fears, many women don't insert dildo-shaped vibrators into their vaginas. They put the tip or shaft against their clitoris. Other women use dildos exactly as men imagine. A fourth category of vibrators are egg-shaped for insertion inside an orifice.

Women who have difficulty having orgasms often find a vibrator helpful. Those looking for their first orgasms are likely to have them this way. Some women find directing a stream of water on their clitoris works just as well. Men who have difficulty reaching orgasm sometimes find a vibrator helpful; others find it is a distraction.

Vibrators and dildos, like lubricants, require holding on to yourself in two ways. First, vibrators sometimes bring up issues about whether masturbation is okay. More often than not, these turn out to be struggles of self-ownership rather than moral dilemmas. Second, when you introduce a vibrator into your relationship, holding on to yourself is critically important. Some men feel awkward when a vibrator is introduced because their reflected sense of self is threatened.

Rolando was less concerned about challenges to his masculinity than about Rosa's assertion of her independence. By introducing a vibrator, Rosa was making clear the kind of relationship she wanted with Rolando. She was less willing then her mother to walk three steps behind her man and always stay in his shadow.

As is true for every couple we've discussed thus far, how Rolando handled himself determined whether his situation (the vibrator) threatened his adequacy or demonstrated it. Even though there was no point competing with a machine, it was understandable that Rolando felt threatened. Men raised in machismo cultures often think they're supposed to be sexual Rambos with the staying power of the Energizer Bunny.

Rolando got a grip on himself because he didn't want to lose Rosa. Fingers, tongues, and penises can't move nearly as fast or as long as mechanical toys. They do, however, offer greater sensitivity, finesse, and caring. It's hard enough to *feel* your partner when you're using your hands, mouth, or genitals. It's even harder doing that through a vibrating "magic wand." Rather than compete with her vibrator, Rolando put his fingertips on Rosa's genitals and touched the vibrator to the back of his hand. He used himself, not the machine, to turn Rosa on.

If you experiment with a vibrator by yourself, use this approach to dampen the intensity if the stimulation is too strong. A towel placed between you and the vibrator will accomplish the same thing. Some vibrators have built-in variable speed control, unlike many partners.

Don't bother with vibrators that run on replaceable batteries. They're noisy, too weak to be effective, and cost a fortune to run. Electric-powered vibrators are best (some rechargeable cordless models are powerful and convenient). They are available in appliance and kitchenware sections of major department stores and drugstores.

Occasionally I'm consulted by women who fear becoming "vibrator-dependent." Diane enjoyed her vibrator, but worried because this was the only way she could reach orgasm. Rather than seeing her as hooked on her vibrator, I helped her broaden her ability to reach orgasm by pairing it with other forms of stimulation (e.g., intercourse). The two forms of stimulation become a reliable orgasm trigger, and in some cases the second one becomes sufficient in itself. Diane joked that she started liking housework once she realized that she never met a vibrating appliance she didn't like!

Condoms, Sleeves, and French Ticklers

Given that erections are the currency of men's sexual adequacy, mechanical devices have for centuries helped men "go for the gold." Most methods are more ingenious than effective. Throughout history men have constructed crude splintlike devises, much like collar stays for the penis. Generally speaking, these are the least sophisticated erection aids available.

French ticklers are condom-like latex devices that add a little length and girth to a man's erection and greatly reduce his sensation. French ticklers come with fanciful bumps on the sides or faces on the tip, for instance, a man sticking out his tongue. Supposedly these protrusions provide your partner additional stimulation and greater pleasure. Although some women get off on these things, many find them interesting only as an occasional novelty (if at all). Men's fantasies and fears about women, and their concerns about penis size, keep these devices in production.

However, you *can* enhance sex by reducing risks of unwanted pregnancy and communicable diseases. Particularly for new sexual relationships, condoms help reasonable people relax. When you're just getting to know each other—and especially if you're having sexual problems—relaxing in bed together is important. (Partners in long-term *monogamous* relationships don't need condoms to reduce the threat of AIDS, herpes, syphilis, and gonorrhea.)

If you are a man having difficulty with erections or reaching orgasm, you may not be eager to use a condom. You may think you need all the stimulation you can get. However, you are probably better off wearing the condom, calming down, making contact with your partner, and having her do unimaginably wonderful things to you because you have touched her heart.

Conversely, guys who struggle with premature orgasms may insist on using a condom. They use condoms for the very reason most men hate them: It reduces their sensitivity and stimulation. In Chapter 13 I'll describe an entirely different solution for rapid orgasms that gives better ejaculatory control *and* greater stimulation. For now consider this: You have to stop trying to reduce your sensitivity (by using a condom). This works against eventually having better control when you receive *good* stimulation. You can't get there by killing your pleasure from the outset.

Some couples use condoms because they haven't made peace with male ejaculate (or female lubrication). If this is you, you have much to gain by putting your rubbers away. Your discomfort with sexual fluids separates you and your partner by far more than the thickness of a condom.[3]

Changing the rules on condoms raises the challenges of holding on to yourself that lubricants and vibrators do. They kick the "people-growing machinery" into gear. For instance, culture strongly influences men's willingness to use condoms. Couples often have to choose between the anxiety of deviating from cultural norms and the anxiety of the life-threatening health risks of AIDS. The solution to this two-choice dilemma is just like all others. You have to hold on to what's most important to you and validate your own adequacy. Even in a one-night stand, you have to hold on to yourself if you're going to insist on safe sex.

Constriction and Vacuum Devices

In contrast to mechanical devices, cock rings and vacuum devices work hydraulically. They try to draw more blood into the penis or prevent blood in the penis from leaving. Cock rings go around the base of the penis as well as the scrotum and restrict normal blood flow from leaving the penis. Cock rings come in several basic styles: solid hard (metal or rubber) bands, elastic bands, and leather with snaps or Velcro.

As with vacuum devices, cock rings can create permanent penis damage if erections are maintained for several hours (priapism). Leather cock rings with fasteners are safer since they can be removed at will. Some men have had to have the rings cut off in order to save their penises. Remember, the man places his penis *and* his testicles inside the cock ring before he gets an erection. That means he's got to have a fairly flaccid penis before he can get it off—unless he can unfasten it. That's the advantage of Velcro or snap closures.

Vacuum pumps go cock rings one better, by first drawing blood into the penis before an elastic band is placed around the base of it. The man inserts his penis into a hard plastic sleeve, with a hand- or battery-operated pump on the end. By pumping, the man creates a vacuum in the sleeve, which draws blood into his penis and produces an erection. He then rolls a band, sitting on the mouth of the sleeve, down to the base of his penis before withdrawing it from the device. The restricting band keeps his penis engorged and erect.

Vacuum devices have been around for years, but they recently received FDA approval as a legitimate erection aid. Clinical studies show that 60 to 80 percent of men get erections with these devices. Many men drop out due to pain, numbness, bruising of the penis, and problems with ejaculation. Don't forget, vacuum devices create a condition that can permanently damage a penis if the band is left on for several hours.

If you're wondering how someone could not take care of that, meet Matt. Matt's idea of a good time was to take lots of drugs, pump up with a vacuum device, and "party hard" at group sex gatherings. One time, Matt passed out in a chemical stupor and awoke with a grossly enlarged penis. He had his metal cock ring cut off in the emergency room of the local hospital.

Similar things happen more than you imagine. Emergency room physicians trade stories of men coming in because their penis "happened" to get stuck in the vacuum cleaner hose while doing housework in the nude. And with vacuum pump advertisements promising prodigious penis size, some men tend to overdo things. However, FDA-approved vacuum devices are a legitimate option for erection problems.

Buying Sexual Paraphernalia

If you pursue any of the enhancements we've covered, the experience will remind you of buying your first tampons or condoms. Making a purchase in a store means you have to validate your sexuality in front of the cashier and other shoppers. You can get around this by ordering on the Web, but I don't recommend it. You have much to gain by tolerating a little discomfort for growth. If you're going to fold in the face of people whom you don't even know or care about, what are you going to do when your spouse pressures you to conform?

Think of it this way. You can get a vibrator or lubricant and practice self-soothing all in one trip. Pick up your purchase, calm your pumping heart, and walk to the checkout counter. Tolerate a little discomfort, so you can get what you want (in more ways than one).

Surgically Enhanced Sexual Response

Now we shift from lighthearted times to the no-fooling-around versions of sex enhancements. To date, surgical attempts to enhance sexual response have mainly focused on erection problems. Women's genitals neither require nor lend themselves to the kinds of surgical procedures that have been developed for men. In past decades surgery was often performed as a general solution for erection problems, regardless of their cause. Now that Viagra and similar drugs provide more convenient and effective options (Chapter 9), surgical solutions are appropriate only where specifically indicated.

Vascular Surgery and Penile Implants

Vascular erection problems can be caused by (or coincide with) heart disease, tumors, cancers, and some forms of diabetes. At risk are the arteries that conduct blood to the genitals and the veins that carry it away. All these (and a lot more) must be intact and operating properly.

Surgical solutions center around (1) enhancing blood flow into the penis and decreasing blood flow out or (2) inflating the penis by some artificial means. The options run along two different lines: fluid hydraulics or mechanical engineering—meaning vascular surgery or penile implants.

Some men have vascular problems that limit blood flow to their penises. Sometimes surgery can correct congenital vascular anomalies or traumatic injuries to arteries in relatively young men. A few decades back, vascular surgery to tie off small blood vessels of the penis became popular. This is not a common procedure today and should not be performed without direct evidence of vascular leakage.

By current standards, surgical solutions seem unbelievably crude. Studying erections on the level of neurochemical transmitters and receptor sites within the penis was fanciful thinking thirty years ago. The possibility that John Q. Public could play with that process at will by the turn of the century (with Viagra) was beyond imagination. Thousands of men opted for vascular surgery and penile implants in prior decades. Some are happy with the results; many are not. Some had the procedures because these were their best options at the time.

Rigid implants. Modern penile implants first appeared in the 1960s, in the form of rigid silicon rods inserted within the penis. Implant surgery replaces (or hollows out) the corpus cavernosa, two spongelike cigar-shaped bodies in the fleshy underside of the penis. Normally these cavities expand when engorged with blood, producing rigidity for an erection. Surgery produces a constant erection with silicon rods, which extend from the base to the head of the penis. When not in use, this permanent erection is strapped to the man's leg in order to keep him from inadvertently clearing the table or scaring other guys at the gym.

Semirigid implants. Hinged (semirigid) implants, which soon followed the rigid type, produce a more manageable erection. These are similar, except the rods flex like hinged soda straws, bending near the base of the penis. Men can thus aim their permanent erection up or down, depending on intent. Couples who make a game out of aiming it are usually most pleased with this implant. Their attitude, not their aim, makes the difference.

Inflatable implants. In the mid-1970s, an entirely different technology emerged. Inflatable implants consist of narrow hydraulic cylinders (instead of silicon rods) inserted into the penis. These inflatable tubes mimic and replace the man's corpus cavernosa. They are connected to a fluid reservoir located in the man's scrotum (like a third testicle). This reservoir contains its own pump and valve system, which operates by squeezing it repeatedly (inside the scrotum). Men who have one, and who like it, say it works better than it sounds. The inflation process becomes a shared (rather than a hidden) activity for couples who adapt well to it.

Penile implants are appropriate and helpful when a diagnosed vascular or neurological problem exists. Typical candidates are men who've had radical prostatectomy, or heart bypass surgery in which a portion of their saphenous artery (near the groin) was harvested. Implant procedures can now be performed in 1 or 2 hours, sometimes as outpatient or day surgery. It generally takes 4 to 6 weeks to heal sufficiently for intercourse. With oral and insertable erection-enhancing medications now available, implants have become far more rare.

Potential Complications

Rigid and semirigid implants are more likely to cause men physical discomfort or erode or poke through the head of the penis and require removal. Sometimes partners of men with silicon rod implants have pain during intercourse because the penis is so unbending. This is usually correctable by modifying sexual positions. Sufficient lubrication during intercourse is important for all involved.

Hydraulic implants are more prone to mechanical problems than the semirigid type, but the failure rate is relatively low (10 percent). There can be fluid leakage from the cylinders and connecting tubing or mechanical failure in the pump. Inflatable implants are considerably more expensive.

After implantation, the head of the penis often feels cooler, and some partners do not respond favorably. These issues are worth considering because *penile implants are not reversible*. Additional surgery can be performed to remove the implant or reinsert another one, but the man will never get a "natural" erection because the corpus cavernosa in his penis have been destroyed. Implants are *not* the approach of choice when you're not sure what's causing your problem—or you know but don't want to deal with it.

Issues That Determine Satisfaction

Nowadays complete physiological testing, as well as psychological screening and counseling, are commonplace prior to surgery. If you are considering an implant, be sure you *and your partner* participate in the evaluation.

Your partner's acceptance is pivotal. Research indicates that your partner's reactions pretty much determine subsequent satisfaction and adjustment. Her feelings about your new improved penis have a big impact on whether or not you get to use it with her. This comes as a rude awakening to men, like Karl, who think a stiff penis—by whatever means—will cure their estranged relationship.

Excluding your partner from your plans from the outset is just asking for trouble. However, Karl preferred facing a surgeon's scalpel to asking Melissa to help him with his erections—and that's exactly what he did. Melissa didn't find out Karl had implant surgery scheduled until the hospital nurse called to confirm his admission date.

Karl illustrates how the anxiety and reflected sense of self that makes some men eager for penile implants also makes them high risks for disappointing outcomes. Melissa was so undone by not being included in

Karl's plans that she refused to have sex with him. Whereas before they had sex infrequently, after surgery they became celibate. Karl's relationship certainly didn't proceed the way he envisioned.

Other Surgical Procedures

The diffuse vascular processes that occur in a woman's vagina don't lend themselves to surgery as readily as does a man's corpus cavernosa. That's probably a good thing, given the surgical alternatives that have been available to (read: forced on) women. Involuntary surgery has been conducted on women for years, supposedly to enhance their sexual response. One procedure, called a partial clitorectomy, involves removal of the clitoral "hood." Similar procedures are sometimes performed for the exact opposite rationale.[4]

Any improvement in sexual function from cosmetic surgery is indirect. Breast reductions for overendowed women are as much a matter of physical comfort as they are about appearance. After surgery, women may be friskier during sex (and the rest of the day) because they feel more comfortable and like the way they look. Likewise, some women pursue breast augmentation because their clothes fit better and they feel better about their appearance. Silicon breast implants were more popular until their complications became a cause for class-action lawsuits.

Lots of us *are* better in bed when we feel good about ourselves. However, you're headed for trouble if your self-esteem hinges on your appearance or sexual approaches from others. For some, elective cosmetic surgeries like face-lifts, eye tucks, vagina tucks, liposuction, lipoinsertion, pigment implantation, tattooing, and body piercing are motivated by dependence on a reflected sense of self. For others, they are acts of emancipation and self-validation. When you appreciate how hungry some of us are to feel accepted and wanted, repeated surgeries become understandable.

Conclusion

In this chapter, we've considered things you can do to enhance your sexual stimulation and physical responsiveness. Some can be bought at your neighborhood mall; others must be installed by your surgeon. In each case, we arrived at the same point we've encountered in prior chapters. We'll see it again next chapter, when we consider drug-based sexual enhancements like Viagra. It's not the lubricant, vibrator, surgery, or drug that determines how things turn out—it's the people. No bionic enhancement replaces compassion and consideration in your relationship. Medical solutions are most likely to deliver good results when the best in you pursues them.

9

Sex Drugs: Better Loving Through Chemistry?

Is it not strange that desire should so many years outlive performance?

—Shakespeare, *Henry IV* (1597)

Throughout history, men and women have taken potions and elixirs to enhance sexual performance. Most were ineffective, and some were dangerous. You, however, have access to some truly effective medications. But which ones really work, and just how much can they do? What side effects do they have? Is one of them best for you?

Some people fear sexual performance-enhancing drugs will make sex more bionic and less human. Whether this happens or not is determined more by your agenda than by your medication. As we explore the brave new world of sexual pharmacology, I suggest the following mind-set: Don't dichotomize your mind and body, or read this chapter like you're a collection of nerves and blood vessels. Don't shift your frame of reference from relationships to test tubes. Instead of converting your boudoir into a chemistry laboratory, consider whether or not to move your medicine cabinet into your bedroom.

The Quantum Model (Chapter 2) can help you understand how sexual medications work their magic. Viagra and other drugs attempt to lower your body's response thresholds and amplify your body's response to sexual stimulation. Available medications, by themselves, do not directly increase your total level of stimulation or your pleasure or satisfaction. This would require a drug that affected your brain. Today's drugs aim at your genitals.

Future sexual performance-enhancing drugs may be more effective, but current medications don't differ much in terms of how many users report improvement. The big differences among them lie in their method of delivery. They are all more convenient and more reversible than surgery but differ among themselves in ease, speed, and comfort. If current sales are any indication, ease of use means a lot to people.

Injectable Drugs

Before Viagra appeared, penile injection therapy was the most common medical treatment for erection problems, because it was effective with a wide range of causes. In this therapy, medication is injected into the corpus cavernosa, the two fleshy chambers in the underside of the man's penis.

Various brand-name drugs offer different combinations of papaverine, phentolamine (Regitine), and prostaglandin E1. Penile injection therapy attempts to directly increase blood pooling in the penis (vasocongestion) in order to produce an erection. It is not recommended for men with sickle-cell disease because they are already at high risk for priapism (a potential problem with injection therapy).

Injection therapies have high dropout rates. In rare cases (2 percent), it causes tissue scarring at the injection site. Prolonged painful erection after ejaculation (priapism) is a rare but serious complication, requiring prompt medical attention to prevent permanent damage. The main problems with injection therapy are timing and method of delivery: injections have to be administered shortly before (or during) sex. Few people find syringes their preferred sex toys, and injections leave many folks sexually uninspired.

On the other hand, physicians and therapists are besieged by men requesting "hormone shots" to boost erections and pep up sexual desire. Testosterone replacement therapy for men has been around for years, similar to estrogen and progesterone replacement therapy for women. Generally, results are similar. If you are hormone-deficient, getting up to normal levels helps your body respond to sexual stimulation. If you already have normal hormone levels, more doesn't improve performance. Moreover, research indicates no clear correlation between men's and women's hormone levels and their sexual functioning or satisfaction.[1]

Insertable Drugs

Recently, drugs developed for injection therapy have been repackaged in more convenient form. MUSE is a new delivery system for Alprostadil (prostaglandin E1). A pellet is inserted into the tip of a man's penis, into the urinary duct (urethra). In one clinical study 65 percent of men with medically related erection problems responded to Alprostadil. MUSE's efficacy is lower than injection therapy with the same drug because the new method's absorption rate is lower. Some men report burning sensations in their penis with MUSE insertion. Sitting, standing, or walking for 10 minutes after insertion increases blood flow and helps absorption.

Recreational Drugs

In today's drug culture, many people think swallowing drugs to enhance sex is the way to go. Recreational pharmacology ("better loving through chemistry") became a big thing in the 1960s. Today, drug counselors say Ecstasy, amphetamines, LSD, and Viagra are common mixtures taken at all-night raves (nonstop dances for young adults). Even people who remember Frank Sinatra have their preferred chemical appetizers: alcohol, marijuana, mescaline, cocaine, quaaludes, sedatives, heroin, and others. I'll briefly mention a few of the most common ones before turning to oral medications like Viagra.

Many people use *alcohol* to calm their anxiety so they can have sex. Initially, alcohol reduces sexual inhibitions, but too much dulls the sensations and anesthetizes you. Alcohol suppresses your body's ability to respond and increases the likelihood of sexual dysfunction. Intoxicated men and women find it harder to become aroused or reach orgasm. There's nothing wrong with a glass of wine to relax before sex, but lots of people have to sedate themselves to let somebody get that close to them. Excessive alcohol can cause temporary sexual dysfunction, and chronic alcohol abuse can cause irreversible damage to the genitals. (If you are one of the millions of people with a drinking problem, pay attention.)

Gynecological problems are three times more common among alcoholic women. One study found 70 to 80 percent of alcoholic women receiving psychotherapy had difficulty reaching orgasm, and another 15 percent had never had one.[2] Alcohol abuse is even more damaging to men's testicles than to women's ovaries. Irreversible damage to gonads and brain cells is a common cause of erection problems among alcoholic men. Heavy drinking reduces testosterone, as well as testosterone-related hormones that control masculine appearance.

What does it mean if sex is better with alcohol? Low doses of alcohol can have a mild stimulant affect. However, possibly you are anesthetizing a fair amount of anxiety. A better strategy involves dealing directly with whatever makes you anxious, and learning how to crank up your eroticism without alcohol.

Aging hippies know why ancient Eastern sex texts refer to *marijuana*. It produces relaxation, heightens sensory awareness, and increases sexual receptivity. Stressed-out, career-driven couples find this enhances their experience. Others find pot turns sex into "focusing on sensations" and blotting out (lack of) connection with your partner. The most upscale weed won't stem arguments that "It's not me, it's the drug that's turning you on!" A few widely publicized studies reported chronic marijuana usage reduces testosterone levels. These findings have not been replicated in subsequent research.[3]

Cocaine enjoys a reputation as a powerful sexual stimulant. While some men and women report cocaine increases their sex drive, it can also impair orgasms and interfere with erection or lubrication. Size differences between dosages that enhance or diminish sex can be small.

LSD, Ecstasy, mescaline, and peyote are popular *hallucinogens*. These drugs have no direct impact on sexual function, but in moderate dosages they can reduce inhibitions, increase sexual experimentation, and enhance sexual experiences by heightening sensory awareness. Larger doses and bad trips can cause frightening or disorienting experiences that destroy sexual interest and fry your brain.

Amphetamines stimulate sexual interest in some people but not others. Long-term amphetamine abuse reduces your desire and responsiveness and increases your belligerence and hostility (which doesn't encourage sex). Ecstasy promises you'll always make love with a friend—no matter who he or she is. (Real partnership comes from your relationship with yourself, not your relationship with your dealer.)

Young male heroin users may enjoy the drug's orgasm-inhibiting impacts for a while, but heroin and other *opiates* eventually reduce sexual responsiveness and create sexual dysfunctions. Opiate abuse generally reduces men's testosterone level and diminishes their erections. It also interferes with orgasms and sexual desire in both men and women. Methadone is known to cause similar problems.

At best, widespread use of recreational drugs to enhance sex reflects our quest for great sex and acceptance of sex as fun. In large measure, it underscores the unhappy empty sexual relationships in many people's lives. At worst, it illustrates how adding sex to an existing drug abuse problem only makes things worse.

Viagra

Pharmaceutical companies offer safer and far more effective drugs to enhance your genital function. Blind luck and follow-up research produced a new medication unlike any other we've discussed. Viagra (sildenafil citrate), the fastest-selling new medication ever (exceeding even Prozac), was actually an accidental discovery: Although Viagra was ineffective as a heart medicine, men participating in the clinical trials didn't want to return their supplies at the end of the study!

Pfizer released Viagra in March 1998 after spending $500 million in development. Ounce for ounce, Viagra sells at fifteen times the price of gold. When it was first released, physicians wrote an estimated 15,000 to 40,000 Viagra prescriptions a day. By its second quarter on the market, Viagra sales hit $411 million. By the third quarter, sales dropped to "only" $141 million.

Why Viagra Made Such a Splash

Other oral medications, such as yohimbine (and ginseng and herbs, if you include homeopathic medicine), preceded Viagra, but none begin to approach Viagra's effectiveness at improving erections. This wasn't the only reason why Viagra made headlines, however.

Viagra received unprecedented news coverage, in part, because it thrust the average couple's bedroom into center stage. It happened at a point in history when people were ready for the truth to come out about widespread male sexual problems. Viagra news coverage, appealing to both legitimate and prurient sexual interest, considered the topic openly.

Viagra brought out of the closet what sex therapists have known for decades. Sexual dysfunction and dissatisfaction are more widespread than ever-present sex themes in the media would lead you to believe. Millions of couples assume, "It must be just us." A large group of people think they are alone.

Viagra won't have as much impact as women's oral contraceptives did, but it will leave its mark. The Pill changed the workforce, the workplace, and the bedroom, and created dual-income families and latchkey kids. Viagra manages to spark public debates about insurance policy coverage and the value society places on couples' sex lives.

Consider an August 6, 1998, memorandum from the office of the Assistant Secretary of Defense to the Surgeon Generals of the Army, Navy, and Air Force, entitled "Practice Guidelines for the Evaluation of Patients Requesting Sildenafil (Viagra) for the Treatment of Male Impotence." It stated, "Only 6 tablets per month (in accordance with established clinical guidelines) may be dispensed. 'Lost,' 'stolen,' or 'destroyed' tablets will not be replaced." Does this keep the world's mightiest military force well supplied?

Potential Markets

Viagra may become the best-selling drug in history, in part, because it is a godsend for couples with medically related erection problems such as heart disease, diabetes, high blood pressure, and a host of other ills. Other groups also fuel Viagra sales.

As we have discussed, men's erections decline earlier and more rapidly than society has acknowledged. Many men notice subtle changes in their erections and orgasms (some by their midthirties), and lots of them will find Viagra helpful. A full erection produces different sensations for a man than does a less rigid one. Likewise, a full erection permits different hip movements during intercourse than a semierect penis, so sensations for both partners may be enhanced several ways.

Viagra appeals to older men trying to bypass the inevitability of aging. Today, 75 million baby boomers are getting acquainted with the physical realities of growing older. Viagra is a natural for the Woodstock generation.

As the later years of life increasingly become ones of activity, vigor, exploration, and growth, many couples want their sex lives to follow suit. Not all the older people who take Viagra are married. Older men often have sexual difficulties when reentering the dating scene after widowhood or divorce. Some have not been with a new sexual partner in fifty years, and they are as concerned about their sexual performance as they are about their morals.

However, Viagra doesn't improve performance in men with normal functioning. Viagra does not generally keep them hard once they ejaculate (although some report otherwise). Men who have premature orgasms will find their erections generally last no longer on the Big Blue Pill.

Taking Viagra

Viagra is available in doses of 25, 50, and 100 milligrams. A typical first-time dosage is 50 milligrams on an empty stomach, taken an hour before you intend to have intercourse. If this doesn't work, dosage is usually increased to 100 milligrams. Viagra begins to be effective within 30 minutes; absorption peaks at 1 hour, and the effects last about 4 hours.

Some factors affect the amount of Viagra reaching your bloodstream: age over 65, liver problems (such as cirrhosis), severe kidney problems, and some medications (such as ketoconazole, itraconazole, erythromycin, and squinavir). In these cases, the recommended starting dosage is 25 milligrams.

How Viagra works

Understanding how Viagra works reveals the biochemistry of erections. Nitric oxide, a neurotransmitter, is released inside a man's penis when sexual stimulation occurs. Nitric oxide synthesis creates a cascade of events that lead to production of cGMP (cyclic guanosine monophosphate, another chemical normally found in the penis), which causes smooth muscles to relax and allows the spongy chambers (corpus cavernosa) to fill with blood. That's how erections occur, but it's just the beginning of Viagra's story.

Another enzyme, phosphodiesterase type 5, is usually released in the penis, which breaks down cGMP. This is what makes an erection eventually subside. Viagra acts by blocking the action of this enzyme, causing cGMP to collect and remain in the penis. This facilitates getting an erection and somewhat extends its duration. (Viagra is the first of a new group of drugs known as phosphodiesterase inhibitors.)

In other words, Viagra does not produce an erection directly. It has no direct effect on the penis, unlike injection therapy and insertable drugs. Viagra works indirectly, enhancing the effects of nitric oxide by inhibiting phosphodiesterase type 5, which normally removes the cGMP that facilitates erection.

In practical terms, you need less stimulation for your body to respond sexually when Viagra is involved. Pfizer just says Viagra requires "effective stimulation" to work its magic. As you've seen, there's a lot more to effective stimulation than physical technique.

Viagra doesn't bypass your feelings, thoughts, or the situation. Stress and anxiety (read: adrenaline) reduce Viagra's effectiveness.[4] So keep in mind our discussions about modulating your anxiety by holding on to yourself. This can increase the benefits you derive from Viagra (especially if your relationship is highly anxious and contentious).

Clinical Research

Clinical trials of Viagra's effectiveness involved twenty-one different studies of more than 3,000 men ages 19 to 87 over periods lasting up to 6 months.[5] The men had erection problems from various causes, for an average duration of five years. Subjects demonstrated significant improvement in all twenty-one studies. Effectiveness was measured via self-report questionnaires covering firmness of erections, frequency, success and enjoyment of intercourse, level of desire, and overall relationship satisfaction. Overall, 64 to 72 percent of the men who took Viagra got an erection, compared to 23 percent of men who took a placebo.

These results demonstrate two things. First, Viagra is effective with erection problems arising from a wide range of causes. Anything that helps more than two-thirds of people who take it is pretty darn good. Second, the fact that almost a quarter of the men showed improvement with a placebo says men's picture of reality has a whopping impact on their ability to function sexually. As we've noted from the outset, your outlook and expectations play an important role in the sex you end up having. Viagra research demonstrates the power of sexual pharmacology and the powerful role emotions and perceptions *always* play in sex.

Among the twenty-one research studies, Viagra helped men with erection problems from diabetes mellitus, spinal cord injury, coronary artery disease, hypertension, depression, heart bypass grafts, radical prostatectomy, trans-urethral resection of the prostate (TURP), and those taking antidepressants, antipsychotics, and antihypertensive/diuretic medications.

Viagra works with erection problems stemming from vascular diseases, drugs, and emotional causes. Erection problems due to thoughts and feelings and spinal cord injuries showed the highest rate of response (80 percent), whereas less than half of men with chronic diabetes and radical prostatectomy showed improvement. If you are getting older, take heart in the fact that men over 65 showed similar responsiveness to the drug as did younger men.

While this is impressive, let's put it in perspective. Viagra isn't much more effective than prior erectile dysfunction treatments. As with papaverine, phentolamine, and Regitine (injection therapy), Viagra improves genital response for about 70 percent of the people who take it. What makes Viagra unique is its method of delivery and mechanism of action.

Side Effects

Thus far, most of Viagra's side effects appear to be brief and mild.[6] About 15 percent of subjects in the clinical studies reported headaches; another 10 percent reported upset stomach and flushing; and 4 percent experienced nasal congestion and mild transient color vision changes (a blue-green tint). Side effects increase with dosage level. Single doses of up to 800 milligrams were given to healthy volunteers, causing increased frequency of side effects already mentioned but no serious illnesses or deaths.

Viagra does not have the same high risk of priapism (prolonged painful erection) associated with injection therapies. Pfizer advises that Viagra be used "with caution" by men having an "anatomically deformed penis" (such as angulation, Peyronies disease, and penis fibrosis from injection therapy), and other medical conditions that predispose them to priapism (e.g., sickle-cell anemia, multiple myeloma, or leukemia).

On perspective, Viagra is remarkably free of side effects compared to other widely used medications. Prior to Viagra's release, 550 patients were treated for over a year. However, the real impact of a drug isn't known until it is in general distribution. Only then can the drug be assessed with sicker people (taking lots of medications) not typically included in clinical tests. Whether due to drug interactions or medical complications unknown at the time, probably every major drug in use today caused some fatalities when it was first released. When this occurred with Viagra, it made front-page headlines because it involved sex.[7]

In November 1998, the FDA issued new guidelines cautioning doctors about prescribing Viagra for men who had a heart attack, stroke, or serious heart arrhythmia in the prior six months. Doctors were also cautioned about patients with histories of low blood pressure (below 90/50 BP), high blood pressure (above 170/100 BP), cardiac failure, angina, and the eye disease retinitis pigmentosa (which sometimes coincides with the genetic disorder retinal phosphodiesterase). More recent studies indicate no increased death rate among older men with medical problems who take Viagra.

What can we conclude? Confirmed Viagra-related deaths cluster around older men with cardiovascular disease and nitroglycerin or nitrate drugs. Nitrate-based medications (such as nitroglycerin for heart angina) are commonly used to treat coronary disease. Combining nitrate-based drugs with Viagra can create a precipitous drop in blood pressure (hypotension). *Don't use Viagra if you're taking nitrate-based drugs.* Viagra does not have this effect when paired with nonnitrate heart medications.

Using nitrate inhalants (e.g., amyl nitrite, "poppers") while taking Viagra is also not recommended. People who use poppers to enhance their orgasm are also likely to be attracted to Viagra. If this is you, don't mix the two. Amyl nitrite belongs to the family of nitrate drugs associated with the original Viagra-related deaths. *DO NOT use amyl nitrite with Viagra.*

Risks of "Death in the Saddle"

Long before Goldie Hawn opened one of her movies with her "husband" dying in the midst of intercourse, people have feared having a heart attack or stroke during sex. Some causes of erection problems, such as high blood pressure and cardiovascular disease, are themselves linked to strokes and heart attacks. And given that people with these diseases tend to live sedentary lives, they are more prone to heart attack when they exert themselves—as with unaccustomed sexual athletics.

This is not the first time fears of "sudden death in the saddle" have surfaced. Studies of heart attacks during sex were conducted back in the 1960s, when heart bypass surgery was blossoming and more heart attack patients were surviving. Research revealed such cases were rare, but they had striking similarities when they occurred. The typical pattern involved an older man putting on the (last) performance of his life with a younger woman who was not his steady partner. The encounter was often preceded by lots of food and alcohol.

A word to the wise: This pattern can kill you no matter what drug you're taking. If you are thinking of going from Couch Potato to Potency Man with one swallow of Viagra, spend a few weeks in the gym beforehand.

Women and Sex-Enhancing Drugs

What can Viagra do for women? Technically, Viagra is FDA-approved only for treating men's erection problems. However, some women sampled their husbands' supply or got it from doctors who prescribed Viagra off-label (for other than FDA-approved uses). Anecdotal reports suggest some women experience increased lubrication, subjective arousal, and satisfaction, just as you might expect.

Men's and Women's Genitals Are Similar—and Different
Initially, experts anticipated that Viagra would improve women's genital responsiveness, given that men's and women's genital anatomy are remarkably similar in terms of nerves, blood vessels, and muscles. A clitoris has the same number of nerve endings as a penis (focused in a smaller area), and both become engorged with blood and swell during sex. A penis and a clitoris develop from the same embryonic tissue, taking different shape due to differences in hormones present during pregnancy. A man's scrotum is equivalent to a woman's vagina, his testicles equivalent to her ovaries.

A clitoris holds two corpus cavernosa made of the same erectile tissue found in a man's penis.[8] Some structures of the clitoris extend back into the vagina, being much larger than it appears and more similar to a penis than people realize. (This may be why many women find "shallow thrusting" focused in the outer third of their vagina triggers orgasms.)

Given that a vagina is such an incredible vasocongestive structure, the impact of Viagra (and similar drugs) on women might be more extensive. And more delicious. Since tissue in the vagina is more permeable than in a penis, women may be able to use a Viagra-laced cream, which might not work for men. Scientists, pharmaceutical companies, and many women are interested in such possibilities.

Initial Research Isn't Encouraging
A study of nineteen spinal cord–injured women who took Viagra demonstrated more subjective arousal, and barely measurable physical differences, compared to control subjects who took a placebo.[9] This is surprising, because men with spinal cord injuries obtained some of the best results with Viagra of all medical problems researched.[10]

In another study, women with no sexual problems who took Viagra showed measurably increased vaginal response. However, they had no change in subjective arousal.[11] Two other studies found no difference in subjective arousal reported by women taking Viagra and those taking a placebo.

What accounts for these disappointing findings? It turns out that a woman's genitals have much less capacity for nitric oxide synthesis than does a man's penis (ceasing altogether after menopause); this would reduce Viagra's impact. Moreover, many things besides blood flow are involved in women's subjective sexual response and satisfaction. The relationship between vaginal blood flow and women's subjective arousal and desire is quite variable. Lots of women have one without the other, so a drug that engorges your vagina doesn't necessarily make you feel aroused.

Needless to say, Viagra has sparked new interest in women's sexual problems. Prostaglandin E1 (used in penile injection therapy) is being developed by several pharmaceutical companies as creams and gels for women. Another penile injection therapy drug, phentolamine, is being developed as a vaginal suppository. A small study found that women with arousal problems who took phentolamine had improved blood flow to their genitals when they watched erotic movies. The women reported tingling genital sensations and more lubrication.

New Solutions on the Horizon

More medical marvels are on the horizon. Release of Vasomax and Vasofem, blood flow–enhancing medications for men and women (phentolamine) currently awaiting final FDA approval, have been put on hold pending further research. While likely to be less potent and have more side effects than Viagra, they are the next wave. Other phosphodiesterase inhibitors (like Viagra) are being developed that may operate even more efficiently and effectively.

Viagra works on the "excitement" side of the erection process. Researchers are looking into alpha blockers that control detumescence, seeking to slow the process down and keep men harder longer. Likewise, scientists have identified specific portions of the central nervous system that are involved in erections. Oral tablets of apomorphine, a dopamine agonist that stimulates erection-triggering mechanisms in the spine, may soon receive FDA approval. Some experts think it may help women's sexual dysfunctions.

Look forward to designer drugs with slick methods of delivery. The next wave of sex drugs will offer combinations of existing medications or new ways of taking them. How about one pill containing Viagra *and* phentolamine? Nasal sprays are on their way, because speed and ease make sprays attractive. Don't have an hour for your Viagra pill to take effect? Just grab a snort when sex is imminent, and you'll be ready in no time.

Scientists can (theoretically) use DNA–altering procedures to create human cells that release proportionately more nitric oxide. The cells can then be inserted into your genitals, delivered by a specially designed virus. When you take Viagra, you would have more response to the drug. A decade ago this would be science fiction. Today it's on the drawing boards at major pharmaceutical companies.

Think of Viagra as the forerunner of a new generation of medications specifically designed to slow the effects of aging. Now that the human genome is mapped, pharmaceutical companies hope to reset your metabolism and remove fat, stop degeneration of your eyes and bones, and keep you looking and feeling vigorous. Future drugs targeting your sexual desire may aim higher than your genitals, trying to directly influence your brain.

Then, as now, sex-enhancing medications will benefit countless people struggling with sexual problems. No doubt we'll confront new relationship issues, social problems, and ethical and moral dilemmas as sex becomes increasingly bionic. (We'll consider some in our next chapter.) To preserve humanity in your sexuality just keep asking yourself this question: Does this make sex more intimate, gratifying, or loving?

10

Can Medical Options Improve Your Marriage?

Women, as they grow older, rely more and more on cosmetics. Men, as they grow older, rely more and more on a sense of humor.

—George Jean Nathan, "Cosmetics vs. Humor" (July 1925)

Anthropologists and sociologists say technological advances have changed relationships between men and women throughout history. Look at what happened when vulcanized rubber made reliable latex condoms widely available. Consider the industrial revolution, mechanized farming, the birth control pill, and the computer revolution. New technologies confront us with barely imaginable issues about relationships, social values, and national priorities.

The issue is not what Viagra and other performance-enhancing drugs will do to us. Rather, it is how we will learn to use them. When such drugs are used by the best in us, and our expectations are realistic, these products will be extremely beneficial. When the worst in us drives our usage (or avoidance) of sexual enhancements and our expectations are unrealistic, we are more likely to bring unhappiness upon ourselves.

It is up to you and your partner to use these drugs to increase the *humanness* of your sex and intimacy, rather than pursuing robotic reliability and impressive performance in the hope of being loved. The more your fears, insecurities, and narcissism motivate your usage, the less likely you'll be happy when you try them.

Impacts on Your Relationship

The approach offered in *Resurrecting Sex* can help you find peace and emotional connection through your lovemaking. You don't need Viagra to do that, and in fact there's no guarantee Viagra will do that for you.

However, reliable sexual performance can allow you to relax during sex in ways you've not been able to. Freed from constant anxieties about performance, some couples make contact like they've never done before. Viagra doesn't have to be about hard pumping and bumping. It can also bring peace. Let me tell you about two different couples who illustrate this point.

Help Turning Things Around
If anxiety in your relationship is due to performance anxiety about sexual function, then Viagra may reduce your anxiety and break the negative cycle you and your partner have created. Jordan and Helen were a couple whom Viagra helped in this way. Jordan found he could look beyond his anxieties about getting an erection and be with Helen. Helen was reluctant to have Jordan use Viagra because she thought he was just trying to prove himself. She wanted to know that *she* was turning Jordan on, not some drug.

Jordan showed Helen his intent to be with her by how they went about having sex. Rather than have intercourse as soon as he got an erection, Jordan relaxed and looked at her. Helen saw a different look on Jordan's face than she had seen before. (I'll explain more about "eyes-open sex" in Chapter 13.) Jordan could feel Helen relaxing, too, so he relaxed more and deepened his emotional connection with her.

Before long Jordan had no difficulty getting and maintaining erections. Eventually he had to face the inevitable anxiety of having sex without Viagra, if for no other reason than to show himself he didn't "need" it. His erection wasn't as rigid those times, but he and Helen held on to themselves and everything turned out fine. Once past that hurdle, Jordan and Helen knew they had accomplished something that could keep sex and intimacy growing.

Jordan continued using Viagra intermittently because he liked the firmer erections it provided. Helen knew he used it as an asset rather than to make up for something lacking in either one of them. Helen had an entirely different reaction now when Jordan reached for his Viagra. She started thinking sexy thoughts that helped her get aroused. So in a manner of speaking, when Jordan took Viagra, Helen got a dose too!

Depend on Yourself, Not on Viagra

Keep in mind that you don't need Viagra to accomplish this. I see couples go through the pattern I just described without Viagra. They go through this when either partner has difficultly getting aroused or reaching orgasm. Tense situations around sexual problems frequently resolve themselves when one or both partners refuse to humble or reject themselves any longer. Ultimately, this is what you need to do to resurrect sex and change your life.

Viagra is not a solution—it is a tool. The solution lies in what the *person* taking Viagra does (not what his genitals do). This is why Viagra can create impacts other than the rosy one I just described. It can reinforce mistaken beliefs. For example: "Erections are the measure of men's masculinity" or "Men *have* to get an erection" or "Intercourse is the *real* way to have sex."

Viagra is no panacea. Let's consider three potentially negative impacts: decreased intimacy and increased performance pressure, Viagra "deception," and psychological dependence.

Harder and Stiffer Isn't Necessarily More Intimate

Medical enhancements will bring some couples closer and reveal to others that they are far apart. It will enhance sexual intimacy for some, but not those taking it to hide their feelings of inadequacy. The difference between one outcome and the other depends on your motivation rather than how much of the drug you take. The medication, vibrator, or surgical wonder one couple uses to increase intimacy can be used by another to avoid it.

The more that medical enhancements can increase your sexual performance independent of what you're feeling, the easier they can be misused to *bypass* what you're feeling. People who maintain a facade during sex (or throughout their lives) are more likely to abuse performance-enhancing solutions.

From this perspective, trying to enhance your appearance and performance is absolutely understandable and completely strange: all this effort to be noticed, at the same time you are trying not to be truly seen. When you try to validate (and avoid) yourself through your attractiveness to others, there's not much peace no matter how your body looks or functions.

In this way, drugs, implants, liposuction, tucks, lifts, dermabrasion, peels, and wraps can *interfere* with exploring your sexual potential. Sexual potential is not the same as looking youthful, enhancing your genital response, or having more or better orgasms. Sometimes it's the opposite: What do you do when your penis *doesn't* stand up or you can't reach a climax? Do *you* "stand up" (i.e., hold on to yourself) when your genitals don't? Or do you run scared, feel humiliated, or blame your partner? When you can stay present with your partner in the midst of your sexual problems, you've come further as a human being, and you're closer to having the relationship you seek, than if you could lubricate or ejaculate with machine-like precision.

Viagra "Deception"
Both newly forming couples and well-established ones face the problem of Viagra deception. Viagra deception makes it clear how you could use a sex-enhancing drug to break contact with your partner, and focus instead on good performance. Marty used Viagra without informing his partner, Heather, because

- He didn't want her to know he was having trouble with erections.

- He wanted Heather to see him as "better" than he was.

- He needed to think she saw him as a "big man."

Ironically, all this made Marty's Viagra deception very much Heather's business.

Deciding whether to tell your partner is a basic relationship issue, rather than something specific to Viagra. Single men with erection problems face this question with new partners. Some will be young adults groping through their first relationships. Some will be widowers hoping to satisfy new partners.

Understandably, you may not want your partner to know. You could be having casual sex, or perhaps you've been dating steadily only for a while. Maybe you don't think it's "necessary" that your partner know. Maybe you don't want to entrust her with such personal information. ("After all, we're only having sex, for crying out loud!")

On the other hand, it's usually best to start a new relationship on the same basis you want it to operate, particularly if you are looking for something long-lasting. When you use sex-enhancing drugs because you are afraid of rejection, for example, you are less likely to tell the truth when your relationship and your partner become more important to you.

Marty and Heather illustrate how Viagra deception can be an issue in long-term relationships too. You may not have the kind of intimacy, consideration, or partnership that facilitates honesty and full disclosure from the outset. You could be afraid your partner will monitor you like a science experiment during sex. And, yes, maybe you'd be sparing your spouse disappointment if the drug doesn't work, but if you're trying to duck for cover in case things don't go well, you're heading down the wrong path to begin with.

Whether your relationship is new or well-worn, ultimately you face disclosure decisions. It will have an impact if you reveal it later, and it will have an impact if you don't. Deception is far more corrosive to intimate relationships than loss of an erection or difficulty lubricating. Sexual enhancements don't stop two-choice dilemmas.

Psychological Dependence

Viagra is not physically habit-forming: increasing doses are not required to produce the same effect. But you can become psychologically dependent on Viagra, in the sense that you don't want to have sex without it.

Some new users become preoccupied with Viagra for a while. Murray became enamored with his newfound genital performance. He started having sex with his partner, Tina, like he was making up for lost time. For a while Viagra was all Murray could talk about. Given Murray's relief that his sex life wasn't over, this was understandable. However, Murray found himself progressively preoccupied with Viagra prior to or during sex. There were times when he put off Tina's sexual overtures because he hadn't taken Viagra beforehand. Just as Tina was settling in for some warm and passionate kissing, Murray was thinking, "How do

I call a time-out so I can get my stuff?" Although Viagra helped his erections, Murray was actually distracted by it.

Viagra's Impact on Different Couples

Sex-enhancing products are not for everyone. There are lots of couples for whom Viagra is unimportant. I've met many wonderful couples with medically related sexual problems, like spinal cord injury, cancer, and chronic illness, who are satisfied with tenderness and intimacy that doesn't include genital sex. Some haven't had sex for a decade or more, but they hold each other every night. Others do everything but intercourse, like one couple in which the husband awaited a kidney transplant. "Takes too much energy," he said. "We'd rather do oral sex. We'll live longer."

Somerset Maugham wrote that people marry because they don't want to be bothered about sex anymore. Some of us have a deep, loving, comfortable partnership without a lot of passion. A lot of us don't have either one. For some, sex and intimacy died a long time ago and a medical illness becomes a convenient tombstone under which to bury it. Not everyone wants to renew sex and intimacy with their partner.

If you are tired at the end of most days and you want to go to bed, you don't want your partner saying, "I just took my pill—let's party!" On the other hand, sales figures indicate that Viagra is impacting millions of people in one way or another. You can categorize these impacts into four different groups of couples.

It Works Again and That's Enough

The first group consists of couples who try Viagra and find it works as advertised. Millions of couples are delighted with Viagra's "Lazarus effect" and they are content to leave things at that. For instance, Chet and Eve were in their sixties and had been married since their twenties. Sex was never a big part of their relationship. However, they had an active sex life until five years ago, when Chet began having trouble with erections. Asking the doctor for Viagra was a big thing for them, because they weren't used to being open about sex. Chet took his pill and it worked fine. He hadn't had an erection that good in years. Eve liked the effects too. Sometimes Chet took Viagra, and often he didn't. As nice as it was, Viagra by itself wasn't going to change how or how often they had sex.

Making the Most of a Second Chance

The next group of couples is similar, except they want to make the most of their second chance at sex. Viagra is their ticket to pursuing their potential for eroticism and intimacy, and they want to "go for the gusto." As baby boomers enter their fifties, this group will grow over the next decade. Some lucky couples say they are like a couple of teenagers, although they are much better at sex and intimacy than they were back then. One older man wrote: "I'm seventy-one and still interested in making love. Now we have Viagra. All I can say is, Wow!! Sex for me is like I was thirty. Not a teenager but still mighty good. I buy my pills through AARP Pharmacy. I sure wish they had this pill twenty years ago."

The Unlucky 30 Percent

About 70 percent of men get better erections with Viagra, but it doesn't work for everyone. About a third of those who try it receive no benefit. Once this easy medical solution is eliminated, couples can suddenly be thrust into examining possible causes and solutions they may not have anticipated at the outset.

Harry and Patty, for example, found unexpected questions and feelings surfaced when Viagra didn't improve his erections. Why didn't Viagra help? If Harry had an undiagnosed medical problem, would Patty stick with him? Was the answer another drug, or surgery, or the counseling Patty refused to consider? If you end up in this category, what you are learning about holding on to yourself can help. You need to remain coolheaded while looking for answers, especially if you hope to make good use of your difficulties.

Attend to what we've said about anxiety and self-soothing (Part 2). It increases your chances of being among the lucky 70 percent of users for whom Viagra works. Relax with your partner and get more comfortable being personal and intimate.

Viagra is not a tranquilizer, a sedative, or a mood enhancer (although success can create these effects). Viagra doesn't bypass your anxieties about sexual performance or your partner's lack of interest. It does not produce surefire results. All it does is enhance a cascade of nitric oxide–related events in your genitals. The rest is in your head—and the rest of your body. If you're highly anxious and pumping adrenaline, Viagra is less likely to produce the results you want.

Harry and Patty were very anxious, and had been that way for so long that they took it for granted and didn't see it. Patty wanted to keep the lid on their relationship problems *and* have Harry get erections. She thought, "If I can tune out our lousy relationship and have orgasms, why can't he?" Patty wasn't interested in tolerating discomfort to make things better. Harry knew this, and it made him more nervous when they were in bed. Patty subtly pushed Harry to get better at tuning her out and having sex, just as she did with him.

The Truth Comes Out

Viagra reveals dark secrets among the fourth group of Viagra users. Sometimes enhanced sexual functioning destabilizes a marriage's status quo, instead of propping it up. This is the same as when women upset the power balance in their relationship by starting to have orgasms or becoming more erotic.

Lots of people are ready to forget about sex altogether. If this is you, you won't applaud when your partner takes Viagra and thinks his new erections are just the ticket to resurrect sex. You might be very overweight and avoiding sex, for example, because it feels physically or emotionally awkward. When your partner gives his penis a Viagra picker-upper, it can be a painful reminder about how you feel about yourself.

Moreover, some of us misrepresent ourselves as more interested in sex than we are, using our partner's sexual difficulty as our excuse to get ourselves off the hook. Charlotte, for instance, blamed her sexual passivity and disinterest on Marcus's problem penis. His erection problem became her explanation for refusing to have sex. Charlotte told Marcus she would resume sex when he could assure her he wouldn't have difficulty with erections. She was eventually confronted by a Viagra-enhanced Marcus who was ready to call her bluff. Without realizing it, his newfound erection destabilized their status quo.

Previously, Marcus took what he could get in their sexual relationship, because of his erection problems throughout their marriage. Charlotte feared he might push for more frequency, passion, or playfulness. "Now that Marcus has erections with Viagra," she wondered, "will his sexual expectations of me change? I'll probably have to have sex with him now that my old excuse is gone."

In Part 2 you learned that people have sex up to their level of personal development, and going beyond that creates anxiety. When this happens suddenly, because of a pill—especially in the absence of goodwill—the resulting sparks can be hot but not sexy. This is not unique to Viagra.

People misrepresent themselves when they are afraid or unwilling to face secrets in their relationship. Lots of inaccurate pictures get deliberately constructed to mask the truth. Having reality suddenly set straight because your penis stands up (or doesn't) may not be what you're anticipating when you take Viagra. For Marcus and Charlotte, this occurred when he got better erections, but the sex and intimacy he thought would follow didn't.

The destabilizing impacts of enhanced sexual function show up differently in different couples. Some men who get good erections with Viagra won't refill their prescriptions. Their long-frustrated wives are outraged by their refusal to use something they know works. If you tolerated years of lousy sex because your husband was unwilling to try psychotherapy, surgery, or injections, how would *you* feel if he wouldn't take a simple and effective medication that could solve the problem?

There are many reasons why men don't renew their Viagra prescriptions. This refusal is common among those who feel overpowered by their partners. Some guys say they don't want to face their physician or druggist. Sometimes the truth is they don't want to face, or have sex with, their wives.

Viagra can force hidden issues to the surface simply by delivering reliable erections. It makes it harder to keep telling your partner "I can't" when the truth is "I don't want to." If this happens to you, everything you've learned about holding on to yourself will come in handy.

Combat or Compassion?

Viagra doesn't present unique challenges to a relationship. At best, it presents a specific instance of the ways relationships operate. People who try to ignore sex altogether feel pressured by their partner's renewed interest in sex, whether this interest comes from personal growth or taking Viagra.

This was the case for Charlotte and Marcus. For years Charlotte offered Marcus "mercy sex." She was passive during intercourse and let him bring himself to orgasm inside her. Marcus had to get an erection pretty much on his own, and this was always a problem for him. Charlotte made it clear she felt burdened by Marcus's interest in sex, and he was not to take too long "doing his business." Charlotte had sex "just to make him happy." (This did not make Marcus happy.)

It wasn't always like this between them, but for the last ten years Marcus functioned under these circumstances more or less. However, now that he was getting older, Marcus needed more stimulation to get and maintain an erection. Eventually Marcus could hardly keep an erection long enough to reach orgasm during intercourse.

For a year Charlotte thought they had laid sex to rest. She wasn't overjoyed when Marcus started talking about Viagra. Now their long-dormant issues were surfacing because of some damn pill!

Charlotte was afraid that if Marcus tried Viagra, he'd get erections regardless of how passive or withholding she was, or no matter how she pressured him to finish quickly. She knew she would have to make good on her promise to have sex with Marcus if he could guarantee an erection, but she was at a time in her life when she didn't want sex. Charlotte was so mad at Marcus that she wanted sex to drop off the face of the earth.

In the past Charlotte had more sexual desire than Marcus. She'd given up in frustration when Marcus refused to seek marital therapy early in their marriage. They had real problems getting along, both in and out of bed. Marcus was more eager to take a pill now than he had been to dump his emotions in a therapist's office several decades ago—a perfectly understandable stance on his part, but not one that made Charlotte want to reopen her heart or her legs. Charlotte thought he had some nerve taking Viagra and deciding sex was his new hobby!

For a while after Marcus came home with Viagra, it looked as though no solution existed to their gridlock. Charlotte consented to sex intermittently and begrudgingly, but it was unpleasant for both of them. Marcus started getting angry that Charlotte lay there like a cold fish at a time when they had a chance for a new start. Eventually Marcus decided he didn't want sex with Charlotte when she "tolerated" him.

This led to a state of affairs that Charlotte had not anticipated. She never realized that the very reason she could punish Marcus sexually was because she knew he'd take it. When Marcus said he didn't want sex, suddenly it wasn't safe for Charlotte to continue because she didn't want a divorce. In this commonplace turn of events, Charlotte strangely found herself wanting Marcus to want sex.

From what looked to be an unstable situation came a long overdue reconciliation. With Marcus's more reliable erections, sex didn't have to be as frustrating for Charlotte as it was in the past. Now there was no way for Charlotte to punish Marcus without further depriving herself. Charlotte was vindictive, but she wasn't self-destructive. She owned up to how she was deliberately trying to sabotage Marcus's sexual interest. And Marcus apologized for being too embarrassed in their early years to get the help he needed.

Charlotte and Marcus stopped dancing around the truth, and started talking more openly. Along the way, there were moments where they feared their relationship might spin out of control. They calmed themselves down and licked their emotional bruises, which were pretty extensive. You don't have decades of a marriage like theirs without developing some pretty deep hatreds.

On the other hand, Charlotte and Marcus were actually each other's best friend, and there had been good times in their frustrating prior years. The way they addressed their current situation made Charlotte more willing to work things out. Perhaps they wouldn't have renovated their relationship if Viagra had not appeared on the scene. However, they seized the opportunity (read: calamity) and put it to good advantage. What first looked like the trip to divorce court turned out to be a path through the growth cycle to better sex and a more intimate relationship.

It Isn't Always the Wife Who's Afraid of Viagra
Don't presume it's always men who are ready to have sex and women who are unwilling. Some wives endure their husbands' sexual problems for years, believing nothing could help their situations. Now with Viagra on the scene, their husbands' excuses take on different meaning. They are shocked and dismayed when "can't" turns out to mean "won't." Here's what one woman, desperate for new solutions, wrote.

> I have been in a marriage for forty years. Thirty of them there has been no sex. My husband goes to the doctor and gets shots and pills and never uses them. He does not want a divorce, but it is driving me crazy. We stayed married because of a family business and children and family illnesses. We are college-educated people. I don't even know why I am writing this. Maybe it will make me feel better.

Actually, this woman may have been married to someone like Herman, a seventy-year-old man who established a relationship with a woman whose company he enjoyed. She was seventy-five, still active, and very interested in sex. At first Herman was attracted to her, but he soon became sexually disinterested. He had no difficulty getting erections, but he was afraid she would end their relationship if they never had sex. He wanted to know if Viagra or hormones might be helpful.

From Herman's description, medication was not the solution because he was dodging a common two-choice dilemma: Herman didn't want to have sex with this woman (which she wanted), and he didn't want to give her up. Herman wanted a drug to avoid having an open and honest conversation, because he feared such intimacy and partnership would end their relationship.

Herman needed to confront himself about the purpose of his relationship. Ostensibly it was about sharing friendship. Herman faced a choice: manipulate his girlfriend into a nonsexual relationship (which she didn't want), or treat her with compassion and be honest about how he felt.

Turning Instability into Growth
While enhanced sexual function due to Viagra or other medical solutions can destabilize a relationship, it is also true that this destabilization can be wonderfully productive if handled well.

The destabilizing effect that Viagra can have may turn out to be its greatest benefit, for couples who recognize it can raise more than erections. Viagra is simply another invitation to develop the personal integrity and resilience so vital to marriage. What Viagra triggers—and how you handle it—is more determined by how well you can hold on to yourselves, rather than by nitric oxide, cGMP, and phosphodiesterase type 5.

Realistic Expectations for Enhancing Your Sex Life

In this age of instant response we tend to expect immediate results. Wouldn't you like a pill that could resurrect your sex life—not to mention your marriage, your self-esteem, and your youth? Giddy with the dawning "golden age of pharmacology," some physicians claim sexual function and sexual desire will soon be reducible to chemical processes. I hope you now see why this won't happen any time soon.

Even when your penis stands up, you still have to grow up. Getting an erection doesn't necessarily resolve gridlock, and can actually intensify it. Drugs can enhance your genital function, but holding on to yourself enhances eroticism and passion.

So before you come to bed with your medicine chest, remember this: If you were lousy in bed before you had erection problems, Viagra can make you a man with an erection who's still lousy in bed. (When I said this on *Good Morning America*, I got smiles and nods from the stage crew.)

Dealing with Your Partner's Reaction

Don't presume handy-dandy drugs and devices can solve your relationship problems. No earthshaking orgasm can forestall divorce. No erection is hard enough or long enough to bridge the gulf between emotionally alienated partners.

On the other hand, medical solutions may help you get your first real taste of peace in bed. Lots of people are afraid to simply relax and be with their partner. That's why they focus on their sexual performance instead. Reduced fears of performance (through medication) clear the way for normal and necessary struggles of self-acceptance, intimacy, and love.

Sometimes these struggles surface in accusations like "You've changed everything!" Here are some common variations on this theme.

- "You wanted me when you couldn't function, so you probably won't want me now!"

- "Sex just doesn't feel spontaneous when we use a lubricant (or vibrator, condom, Viagra, penile implant)."

- "You don't need me to turn you on. Now you can do it all by yourself!"

- "Now I bet you'll want to do it all the time. Knowing you, I'll bet you'll want to do it with everyone."

- "So now you're fixed, and it's my turn to be the defective or inadequate one."

- "We won't enjoy sex as much if we do it more often. Let's save it for special occasions."

If and when you hear any of the above, hold on to yourself. When your brain screams, "You said you wanted me when I couldn't do it, and now I can and you don't want to!" you are in the process of tolerating discomfort for growth. Calm yourself down and take a hard look at the truths confronting you. The most important instructions for using Viagra won't be written on the prescription bottle.

Some couples who use injection therapy routinely have the spouse administer the shot. Other wives maintain contact with their husbands when he injects himself in bed. In the worst cases, the man injects himself in the bathroom "behind the scenes" so his partner won't know or won't see. These men have sex in totally different realities than those in the first two groups, although they may all use the same drug.

Conclusion

If men can be assured of reliable and durable erections, will their partners feel more pressure to have orgasms during intercourse? Will women's performance pressures increase if Viagra is available to them too? No doubt some will feel more obligated to lubricate or have orgasms than before.

What does all this mean, given that women and men develop low sexual desire when their partners expect sex on demand. Are men more likely to feel they've lost sole custody of their penis, now that Viagra makes erection on demand seem possible?

Many men feel pressured by their wives' larger sexual appetite and greater eroticism to begin with. No doubt some will fear being overwhelmed by their drug-enhanced Wonder Woman and fear she may take her sexual marathons elsewhere. Will men feel pressured to use drugs to keep up?

As is true of sex in general, Viagra and future sex-enhancing drugs can help us see what and who we really are. To do that, we have to appreciate and go through the natural processes of intimate relationships, rather than use drugs to circumvent them.

If better loving through chemistry ever occurs, it happens in the alchemy of emotionally committed relationships. Humanity and compassion are the essence of what making love is about. It will be produced by Jordan and Helen, Murray and Tina, and Marcus and Charlotte a lot sooner than by Lilly, Merck, and Pfizer.

PART IV

Couples in Search of Solutions

Solutions for Arousal Disorders

More belongs to marriage than four legs in a bed.

—Thomas Fuller, *Gnomologia* (1792)

When you first started reading *Resurrecting Sex*, did you imagine so much could be involved in "doing what comes naturally"? In Part 4 we have the task of assembling the many things we've covered into an organized plan for you. You'll also get to see couples successfully putting what we've said into gear.

This chapter focuses on arousal problems, the next two cover orgasm difficulties, and the final chapter addresses putting your plan into action. We'll follow the same holistic approach to sex we've used all along. You'll find that things discussed in this chapter in regard to arousal difficulties, such as medications and drugs, apply to orgasm problems as well. Likewise, illnesses and injuries discussed in Chapter 13 also apply to arousal problems. Things you'll discover about anxiety throughout Part 4 can help with any number of sexual difficulties.

Take a Goal-Directed Stepwise Incremental Approach

Regardless of whether your sexual problem involves difficulty with arousal, orgasm, or desire, you'll want to use the same strategy. You need to *do* things to resurrect sex. Reading this book is a start. I've seen many couples with lifelong sexual problems make wonderful changes. Other couples, many with (seemingly) fewer difficulties, didn't make much progress at all. The important thing that predicts success involves doing something effective to change your problem.

You want to approach what you do in a thoughtful way. First you should identify your problem and its causes. Then you should develop and implement a treatment plan. With both diagnosis and treatment, start with your least invasive and most reversible options first. For example, consider medications before you undergo surgery. Take oral medications before opting for injections. Try counseling *long* before you have elective surgery.

Don't overlook your general health and fitness. This has tremendous impact on your mood, appearance, endurance, and overall sense of well-being. Get yourself in good physical shape. Lose the extra weight. Do what you can with what you've got. You and your partner will find sex with each other more enjoyable.

Don't Just Fix Your Dysfunction—Pursue Your Sexual Potential

In some instances, it is possible to raise your total stimulation to your arousal or orgasm threshold by improving one dimension of the problem. This might involve better touching or different medications or making peace with your partner.

However, you are more likely to succeed (and enjoy it more) if you try to optimize sex and intimacy as much as you can. You want to improve the physical stimulation you receive, *and* address physical factors affecting your body's ability to respond, *and* change the meaning frameworks (your emotions, thoughts, and feelings about yourself, your partner, your relationship, and your life) that exist during sex.

Optimize Your Body's Ability to Respond

Anything that interferes with your body's ability to recognize and transmit stimulation can slow you down sexually. This means everything, starting from where you're being touched, to your nervous system, to your spine and brain, and then back to your genitals. You need to rule out the negative impact of disease, injuries, and prescription and recreational drugs. For instance, vascular, neurologic, and hormonal problems resulting from other medical illnesses (e.g., diabetes, multiple sclerosis, renal failure, alcoholism) can have an impact. Lists of possible medications and physical conditions that require evaluation appear in the appendixes at the end of this book.

Medical Checkup
For many people, especially men like Bernie, getting a medical checkup is no small thing. It was hard for Bernie to be straight with his physician from the outset, but he didn't dance around the purpose of his visit. Bernie gave himself the full benefit of his physician's ability to evaluate possible medical causes of his erection problems. He found the clean bill of health he received was worth every cent. Besides giving him peace of mind, it allowed him to focus his own efforts where they'd be most effective.

Physical Measurement of Genital Response
Although research laboratory methods can assess women's physical arousal, these are not readily available to the average physician. In contrast, elaborate evaluation procedures for erection problems have become commonplace. Bernie's physician had him undergo nocturnal penile tumescence (NPT) testing, a painless procedure conducted in a sleep lab or at home with a portable electronic monitor. A recording device monitored Bernie's brain for signs of REM (the deepest stage of sleep) and his penis for signs of life. (Lack of erections during REM sleep suggests that medical problems may be involved.) Bernie also underwent ultrasound testing, another noninvasive procedure that produced a picture of blood flow inside his penis. It turned out Bernie had good REM-sleep erections and no abnormalities in his ultrasound results. This allowed Bernie and his wife, Ellen, to concentrate on what

was happening between them during sex without worrying about what disease Bernie might be incubating.

Had there been need to look further, the physician could have arranged for another procedure, cavernosography, which produces X-ray photographs after dye is injected into the penis. Another option involves testing the speed of electric impulses transmitted through the nerves in the penis (nerve conductivity testing). There is also the stamp test: The shaft of the penis is banded with a roll of postage stamps before going to sleep. If the stamps aren't broken in the morning, there may be a medical problem. Results are unreliable and not worth the cost of the postage.

Medication Review

Medications can reduce your sexual responsiveness and sexual desire and diminish your perception of your own arousal. Lots of commonly prescribed drugs directly interfere with arousal and orgasm. These effects occur in men and women alike.

Antihypertensives. Over 40 million people have high blood pressure. Most antihypertensive drugs, especially early versions, can impair erection, lubrication, and desire. People taking hypertension medication are often prone to sexual difficulties from other disease-related problems (e.g., arterial narrowing).

Antipsychotics. Nearly all psychotropic medications (used in treating emotional problems) can diminish arousal, orgasm, and desire. Conventional antipsychotics (Haldol, Mellaril, Thorazine, Prolixin) can cause erection and orgasm problems and reduced desire. Atypical antipsychotics (Clozaril, Risperdal, Zyprexa) have somewhat fewer side effects.

Antidepressants. Almost all antidepressants interfere with sexual functioning in 40 to 75 percent of people who take them. Antianxiety drugs, known as benzodiazepines (Valium, Librium, Xanax, Ativan, Klonopin), also take their toll. Tricyclic antidepressants (Tofranil, Elavil, Norpramin, Pamelor) and MAO inhibitors (Nardil, Parnate) can create problems with subjective arousal, erection and lubrication, and orgasm. The most commonly used antidepressants are SSRI antidepressants (Prozac, Paxil, Zoloft). These are the most sexually problematic, and orgasm problems are especially common. (Remember that depression itself can reduce desire and arousal too.)

Newer non-SSRI antidepressants (Wellbutrin, Serzone, Remeron, Celexa, Zyban, and Desyrel) have far fewer sexual side effects. In one study, Wellbutrin was used to treat low sexual desire and sexual dysfunctions in sixty nondepressed men and women. Fully 60 percent of people who took it reported benefit (compared to 10 percent of those who took a placebo). If you could take an antidepressant that doesn't create many sexual problems, and helps sexual problems in people who aren't depressed, wouldn't that be your first choice?

If you currently take any medications, consult your physician about possible sexual side effects.[1] Don't forget to mention over-the-counter medications. Ask about alternative prescriptions. (Some medications within a drug type interfere with arousal and orgasm more than others.) Also ask if your medication can be reduced while maintaining therapeutic dosage. (Many side effects are dosage-dependent.) Brief "medication holidays" can also improve SSRI side effects. Some people find taking Periactin or Cimetidine before sex reduces their antidepressant medications' sexual side effects. One small study found Viagra improved antidepressant-based sexual dysfunctions in nine women.

Hormone Replacement Treatment
Both illness and aging can create the need for hormone replacement therapy. Women and men have identical hormones, but they differ in quantity and response. People even affect each other's hormones through their interactions.[2] Hormones operate within an elegant mutually self-regulating relationship. When this intricate hormonal balance goes off, your body immediately starts to react. Sometimes the effects show up in your emotions, thoughts, and feelings before they show up in your genitals.

Estrogen
Menopausal women, like Tammy, often need to augment the estrogen, progesterone, or testosterone their bodies produce. Tammy started having pain during intercourse, increased difficulty getting aroused, and other menopausal symptoms. Treatment often improves vaginal atrophy

and dryness, as well as hot flashes, headaches, insomnia, and memory loss. Estrogen can improve arousal, reduce risk of bone loss (osteoporosis), and stimulate oxytocin production (a "pair-bonding" hormone that may further help arousal, enhance relaxation, and increase sensitivity to touch). Feeling better does a lot to improve sexual interest. Research is equivocal as to possible increased or decreased risks of cancer.

Women's responses to taking estrogen vary. Tammy eventually found oral estrogen (Premarin, Progens, Estratest, Estratab, Estrovis) did the trick once it was augmented with testosterone.[3] However, some women report decreased desire and arousal when taking estrogen (with or without progesterone). Birth control pills (which contain estrogen) also reduce some women's arousability.

Progesterone

Progesterone is a female hormone that works in conjunction with estrogen. Progesterone replacement therapy restores desire in some women and decreases it in others. Because progesterone strongly affects menstruation and conception, it is used medically for contraception and treating menopause, endometriosis, and irregular vaginal bleeding. Progesterone is available combined with estrogen in both oral form (Prempro) and vaginal cream (Crinone).

Progesterone readily suppresses sexual desire.[4] First-generation birth control pills contained too much progesterone and reduced sexual desire in lots of women. Modern versions do this less. Progesterone-based contraceptives can exacerbate PMS symptoms, especially irritability and depression.[5] If you have problems with one brand of birth control pills, you may have none with another.

Testosterone in Women

When a woman's ovaries are removed as part of a hysterectomy (oophorectomy), she undergoes a marked reduction in testosterone. This is more abrupt than in natural menopause and symptoms are more severe. Some women report low sexual desire, depression, hot flashes, urinary problems, fatigue, headaches, insomnia, and dizziness.

Low-dose testosterone therapy for women is controversial but becoming more common. Women produce testosterone naturally. Whereas estrogen seems to control their sexual receptivity, testosterone affects sexual aggressiveness and interest in genital sex and orgasms.

Testosterone-deprived women commonly complain of reduced spontaneous sexual desire and increased difficulty becoming aroused when touched. (Some women who experience reduced desire from oral contraceptives do so because it lowers their testosterone.)

Sometimes estrogen therapy is ineffective until combined with testosterone.[6] Tammy's initial course of estrogen replacement treatment proved unsuccessful, but adding testosterone increased her physical and emotional responsiveness. Since she was seriously testosterone-deprived, she augmented treatment with a vaginal testosterone cream.

If you have gone (or are going) through menopause or had a hysterectomy, have your progesterone, total and free testosterone, estradiol, prolactin, and luteinizing hormone levels checked. Testosterone replacement can return a woman's sexual desire, but this does not necessarily lead to increased sex with her partner. Some studies find it increases only masturbation. You can't use hormones to bypass relationship issues if you truly want to resurrect sex.[7]

Testosterone in Men

Low testosterone levels in men are associated with depression, low sexual desire, decreased initiations, reduced nocturnal erections, and hypersensitivity to general (nonsexual) touch. These symptoms sometimes improve with hormone replacement. Erections do not hinge on testosterone, however. For example, men who are testosterone-depleted by hypogonadal disease still get normal erections watching erotic films or having sex with their partners. However, they have slower and smaller erections from their own fantasies. Testosterone therapy improves their fantasies and the erections they get from them.[8] In other words, testosterone has a bigger impact on men's brains than on their penises.

Testosterone levels gradually decrease in men until about age 60, after which the decline accelerates to different degrees for different men. Some reported symptoms of "male menopause" are weakness, lack of energy, listlessness, diminished productivity, irritability, poor concentration and memory, hypersensitivity to touch, decreased bone and muscle tissue, erection problems, and decreased sexual desire. However, no conclusive evidence exists for a male menopause occurring for men in their forties and fifties.[9]

If a man is testosterone-deficient, getting back to normal levels through hormone replacement therapy can create dramatic improvements. But if a man has normal levels of testosterone, more doesn't increase sexual function or desire. There are health risks in taking testosterone, so this is not something to do lightly.

Taking Testosterone

The manner in which men and women take testosterone makes some difference. All forms of testosterone encourage hair growth, masculinization, cancer, cardiovascular disease, and increased cholesterol and triglycerides. Oral testosterone (Halotestin, Testrin, Virilon) may damage your liver and is not recommended for long-term replacement therapy. Testosterone implants and injections don't do this, but pellet implants (lasting three to six months) are not yet FDA-approved.

Proviron (mesterolone) and testosterone undecanoate are widely available in Europe in both oral and injectable forms, but are not approved for use in the United States.[10] Injections of Delatesteryl, Depotest, or Depo-Testosterone are often used when men cannot metabolize oral testosterone into "free" testosterone. (Testosterone is found in the body in two forms: free and bound. The active form of testosterone is free, so both free testosterone and total testosterone levels are important.[11])

Testosterone tablets (Testoral) placed under the tongue, transdermal skin patches (Androderm), and topical gels (AndroGel) are less efficient than injections. Scrotal transdermal skin patches (Testoderm) require dry-shaving the scrotum daily and reapplying a fresh patch.

Oral testosterone has been the most common form used by American women. Low-dose testosterone injections may be the safest, most effective, and most economical option. Sublingual caplets and vaginal rings should be available soon.

Scientists are working on ways to get around problems with current oral testosterone medications. Future "courier" drugs will go directly to your brain, sneak through your brain's protective barrier, and deposit testosterone directly where it has the most impact.[12] This will avoid the problems mentioned earlier. Such systems are already under development.

Sex-Enhancing Oral Medications

Since we discussed Viagra at length in Chapter 9, I'll only mention it here to include it in our options. Men with erection difficulties can consider taking Viagra and the other phosphodiesterase type 5 inhibitor drugs to come. Severely gridlocked couples may benefit less from Viagra alone. (Men with severe relationship conflicts were excluded from the original Viagra clinical trials.) Lots of research says relationship problems are a major cause of treatment failure regardless of treatment method.

Penile Injections and Implants

Vacuum and constriction devices and removable cock rings are other options. Once you exhaust your reversible noninvasive options, consider reversible invasive methods, such as penile injection therapy. When reversible brief treatments are exhausted, consider surgical options like penile implants. If you go this route, be sure to include your partner in your plans from the start.

Sexual Pain (Dyspareunia)

For most people, pain during sex marks the end of sexual arousal. Pain also reduces desire and interferes with reaching orgasm. Dyspareunia is common among women and relatively rare among men (e.g., Peyronies disease). The first step in removing the source of pain involves diagnosing its causes. Symptoms of dyspareunia vary widely. They include burning and cutting pain at the labia at the start of intercourse; sharp, sore pain farther inside the vagina during intercourse, despite the woman being well aroused; and dull, aching pain close to an ovary during deep thrusting. Tampons, urination, oral or manual sexual stimulation, and sports can sometimes create pain similar to that experienced in intercourse. The pain can often be reproduced during a gynecological exam, when the painful site is touched with a cotton swab.

The most common form of nonmenopausal dyspareunia is characteristically a localized tearing or cutting pain at the vulva when touched or stroked (between the labia minora at the opening to the vagina). Some but not all cases show reddening or inflammation in the gland ducts in the vulvar tissue.

Postmenopausal women can have painful sex due to vulvar and vaginal atrophy caused by estrogen depletion. Thinning of the vaginal tissue and reduced lubrication also make inserting anything into the vulva or vagina painful. Other women report deep vaginal or pelvic pain. This can occur from ovarian cysts, vaginal ligaments stretched by childbirth, pelvic adhesions, endometriosis, and pelvic inflammatory disease.

Many women who have no observable gynecological problems report different kinds of pain in varying locations. Some experience more than one kind of pain. Regardless of cause, repeated painful sex predisposes a woman to another pain-related problem: vaginismus.

A wide variety of treatment options (medical, surgical, and psychological) are available to deal with sexual pain. Medical and surgical interventions include laser surgery, vestibulectomy, oral medications, topical creams, vaginal dilators, sitz baths, and diet. Over-the-counter lubricants can reduce discomfort during intercourse, but they work best when not used to gloss over emotional friction with your partner. Your local sexual boutique and numerous Internet Web sites offer scented and flavored versions.

At this point, many forms of dyspareunia cannot be eliminated. Moreover, once you anticipate pain, you have a second problem: Pain sensitivity can remain long after pain-producing conditions are removed. This readily builds a negative-feedback loop between you and your partner that can develop a life of its own. You have to address this in its own right by talking with your partner and taking steps to stop it. At the very least, this involves collaborating so that you don't have to worry about suddenly being hurt.

You need an active coping strategy that's long on finding solutions and short on catastrophizing. You have three goals:

- Eliminate or reduce your pain.

- Break your anticipation of painful or negative experiences.

- Build a positive frame for sex between you and your partner (which may or may not have existed previously).

If you have sexual pain, get a gynecological exam to assess for vulvar vestibulitis, vulvar and vaginal atrophy, and strength and flexibility of your vaginal and pelvic muscles. Laboratory tests can rule out viral and bacterial infections. Ultrasonography, colposcopy, and laparoscopy are sometimes required. Also rule out possible serious underlying disorders, such as lymphoma. In severe cases, your physiological, emotional, and interpersonal assessments are best conducted by a multidisciplinary team of experts.

When physical causes cannot be found, dyspareunia is often treated as a mental problem. Some women are told the pain "is all in your head," and shipped off for psychotherapy. Don't let yourself be treated like a mental patient. And don't ignore the psychological causes and impacts of your problem.

Consider the following when assessing your sexual pain. Your answers will help your physician pinpoint the cause of your problem:

- *Location*: vulva, vagina, deep or somewhere in between

- *Quality*: burning, tearing, shooting, sharp, dull

- *Intensity*: severity of pain, degree of distress caused

- *Circumstance*: things and activities that elicit the pain

- *Time and course*: duration and pattern of the pain

- *Degree of interference*: impact of pain on your sexual behavior and self-esteem

- *Pain meaning*: meanings you attribute to and derive from pain problem

Implementing Medical Solutions

Consider the timing and sequence in which you implement solutions in your relationship. I generally recommend that you try to solve things first without medications or sex toys if your arousal problem developed very recently (and you're in good health), if you and your partner are embittered and gridlocked, or if you are a young adult just starting sexual relationships. What you do first to solve your problems sends signals to your partner.

For example, "business as usual" stopped in Tammy's relationship *before* she started hormone replacement therapy. Tammy talked to George about being bored with their sex life. She missed having sex worth wanting, as much as she missed her own sexual desire. Most of all, she missed what she and George used to share.

Tammy used the occasion of hormone therapy to make it clear she wanted George and not just sex. Had Tammy taken hormones and then complained about sex, George probably would have thought Tammy was hormonally charged and pushing him around. The way she went about it made it clear she simply wanted him to be more present during sex.

Little things like this make a difference in your outcome. Remember, you need to focus on optimizing things, rather than just getting them "good enough." Be as considerate, kind, and helpful as you can be. Let your partner know your goal is getting together, not simply getting it up.

Optimize the Physical Stimulation You Receive

We've discussed lots of ideas and options, but there are always questions about how things really get applied and worked through. Basically, resolving arousal problems involves increasing the duration and intensity of the sensory stimulation you receive. You just keep going until your total level of stimulation exceeds your arousal threshold and your genitals kick into gear. But greater stimulation involves more than being rubbed harder or longer. It often involves being touched softer, more tenderly, more dearly, or more erotically—some way that brings you and your partner together in the moment. That's where the step between theory and practice can be a big one.

Sexual Techniques

Don't reduce the whole domain of physical stimulation to finding more or better ways to touch each other's body. Lots of couples need this too, but it's no substitute for positive emotional connection. Kissing, for example, takes time to perfect. But the refining process involves struggling through the meanings your kisses convey, as much as it does learning how your partner likes to play tongue tag. Puckering with pinpoint precision is not the issue.

Lots of books on sexual technique exist, and you may find some useful. There's the *Illustrated Manual of Sex Therapy, The New Joy of Sex and More Joy of Sex*, and *Sexual Secrets*—and hundreds more. Women may enjoy *Our Bodies, Ourselves*. No doubt you'll come across sensate-focus exercises, and you can try them if you like. However, I never use them with my clients. I recommend you try having sex where you don't get lost in your sensations.

Sensate-focus sex works for some couples but not for others. It is a breakthrough for some to just set things up so that one partner can lie back and "receive" with the other's consent and participation. However, if you and your partner typically lack a collaborative alliance during sex, you are less likely to find sensate focus helpful. Like the couples we'll discuss shortly, you'll probably reach your arousal threshold more easily, reliably, and enjoyably if you have an intimate physical connection with your partner.

Opening to Your Connection

When either partner has repeated difficulty getting aroused, many things encourage both of you to pull back from each other's touch. It's understandable that you start wearing emotional armor to bed. However, this encourages physical touch that's more firm and aggressive (or more tentative) than you or your partner might want. Being touched in ways you don't really like encourages you to tune out and break positive emotional contact all the more. Too many of us are too ready to break contact to begin with, whether we have arousal problems or not.

Once this vital link is lost, it's easy to feel awkward with each other. Repeated unpleasant experiences make you anticipate the same next time, which makes your fears more likely to come true. The end result is that couples with arousal problems lose positive emotional connection easily and frequently during sex. Many are completely out of touch, even if they make it through intercourse.

Your role in receiving your partner's touches, licks, and kisses is crucial to the outcome. You have to open up to your partner's touch for it to have optimal impact. You have to allow your partner to *touch* you. This doesn't involve making yourself vulnerable. It involves holding on to yourself, which minimizes your vulnerability.

You have to open yourself emotionally if you want to connect physically with your partner. If neither of you is good at this, connecting can be like two blind seekers in the desert.

Leaning into Your Partner's Touch

Here's something that can help. Think of making contact during sex as "leaning into" your partner's touch. This describes the mental image of connecting with your partner, as well as literally how you do it. Move your body toward your partner's touch, rather than pulling away. It only takes a millimeter, because it has a lot to do with intent. Pulling away changes how your partner's touch feels to you. Hand-holding in the early stages of a relationship epitomizes leaning into each other's touch. When it works, people experience it as melting into each other.

A large part of leaning into your partner's touch involves relaxing. It's hard to relax during sex if you have struggled with sexual problems for a while. Some people have better erections or more lubrication when they are doing the touching, rather than when they are being touched. They are good givers, but they have difficulty receiving. In other words, they lean into the touch more when they provide it.

People usually think of this as difficulty being passive. More accurately, many of us don't allow ourselves to be touched in deeply heart-warming or erotic ways. Opening to each other's touch always involves getting better at holding on to yourself. Let me tell you about three couples who went through this process.

Betty and Harry

Betty and Harry were a young couple whose medical problems severely curtailed their sexual relationship. Betty had two miscarriages interspersed with heavy irregular periods. Eventually she had a hysterectomy at age thirty-seven. Betty was depressed about losing her chance to give birth, and she knew Harry was disappointed, too.

For a while Betty and Harry stopped having sex altogether. Betty hadn't been very comfortable with sex up to that point, and things got worse after the hysterectomy. With the sudden end of her menstrual cycles, she was more a stranger in her own body than ever before.

On top of all this, Betty started having pain when they tried to resume sex after the hysterectomy. Betty didn't lubricate as much or as fast as she did before, and it was harder for her to get aroused. Betty used to flirt with men at her office and she knew about sexual vibes. Now the electricity was gone, and so was the warmth in her loins. She felt sexually "dull," like a switch had flipped somewhere in her brain.

Ultimately, hormone replacement therapy helped Betty a lot. But she had to hold on to herself along the way. When her initial medications proved ineffective, Betty was more depressed than ever. She was ready to give up on her sex life and her marriage.

This pushed Harry into a very difficult position. He didn't want to be selfish or overly focused on sex, but he also saw the end of his sex life—and possibly his marriage—looming before him. Harry was the proverbial nice guy, and he generally went along with whatever Betty wanted. This time, however, he spoke up.

Harry told Betty he wanted their relationship to continue in spite of their loss. He still had hope for the future they could have together. Betty pulled herself together and made another appointment with her physician. The next round of medications helped her a great deal. As her hormone levels returned to normal, her physical health, mood, and outlook improved.

Several months later, Betty was ready to resurrect their sex life. They had to repair their relationship, especially the tone and content of their sexual interactions. Emotional withdrawal, no sex for a year, and pain during their initial attempts had taken their toll: Betty lay in bed like a stone. As she felt time passing without becoming more aroused, she grew tense and despondent. She usually ended up in tears on her side of the bed, with her back to Harry.

This perfectly understandable pattern was tearing them apart. Harry was at a loss about what to do. He feared Betty would see his approaches as just pushing for sex, and he also didn't want to get rejected. On several occasions when he reached out to Betty, she shrugged his hand off her arm and withdrew farther to her side.

Then, on one repetition of this awful pattern, Harry refused to be shrugged off. Betty was so surprised she stopped crying and turned over to look at Harry. He said, "I know you feel defective for not having kids, and on top of that you had the hysterectomy. I know both are terrible losses for you, and it looks like our marriage is going down the tubes. But if that's going to happen, why don't you and I just hold each other for a while like friends?"

Betty was so moved watching the best in Harry stand up, she started laughing! Harry moved over and put his arm around her, with her head against his chest. They lay together as Betty's breathing evened out, and they sank into the warmth between them.

Gradually it dawned on Harry that he was getting aroused. His immediate reaction was to worry that he was doing something wrong. Then he realized it was coming from the warmth floating up between them. Harry looked over at Betty, who had been watching him for some time. Betty moved up so her head was on her pillow, level with Harry's. Betty got aroused and wet without any genital contact.

That night was a turning point for Betty and Harry, seeing it was possible for them to connect and get aroused. Many steps still remained to developing the sexual relationship they sought. But they had seen that the hysterectomy and miscarriages did not preclude having some things they wanted.

Heads on Pillows, Looking into Each Other

You can do what Harry and Betty did to establish emotional connection with your partner: lie down in bed on your sides, facing each other, with your heads on separate pillows. Don't lie on your back or on top of your partner. Your noses should be just far enough apart that your partner doesn't look like a Cyclops. Have enough light in the room that you easily see each other's face. Candles work better than fluorescent lights; mood and tone make a difference. *Heads on pillows* is a tool to increase intimacy (like *hugging till relaxed*, described in *Passionate Marriage*). Tools have any number of uses. For instance, you can use heads on pillows to

- Calm yourselves down and drain off anxiety

- Confront yourself by allowing yourself to be seen openly

- Increase in-the-moment connection with your partner

Byron and Vern

Men as well as women find leaning into their partner's touch quite challenging. Byron, for example, got together with Vern late in life when both were nearly sixty. Vern's first husband had died, and Byron's prior marriage had ended in divorce.

Byron frequently lost his erection in the middle of intercourse, and sometimes he had difficulty getting one at all. Vern didn't want to marry him if this was going to continue. Although Byron had intermittent erection problems in his marriage, Vern never confronted anything like this before. Neither Byron nor Vern knew quite what to do or make of their situation.

Byron visited his urologist, who found Byron's testosterone levels were low. A series of testosterone injections didn't help. This made Byron and Vern really wonder where their relationship was headed.

What Byron neglected to tell his urologist was that he was a bundle of anxiety when he got into bed—so much so that he frequently sopped the sheets with sweat. When Vern touched Byron's penis it usually went flaccid. Byron pulled back emotionally from Vern, because he thought she shouldn't have to help him. In Byron's world, he was supposed to do the holding and stroking. Byron had left home at eighteen because his father beat him, and he never saw his parents again. A career in the military gave him a home and a sense of direction, but not much experience allowing someone to hold him.

Byron's reaction to Vern reaching for his penis was the antithesis of leaning into her touch. He could see Vern take his loss of erection personally, as if his penis was measuring the goodness of her touch. Byron didn't want Vern feeling bad, and he blamed himself for not being able to discipline his body with his mind.

For her part, Vern wasn't sure she was cut out to be with Byron. Byron's erection problem pushed her to do what she deemed to be the man's job. She thought Byron should make the initiations. Unfortunately, Byron didn't initiate if he didn't feel "lucky" about getting an erection. Vern was uncomfortable initiating, although Byron never turned her down.

Vern liked sex. Sex was good in her marriage before her husband became ill. But stepping outside familiar sex roles made Vern question her identity and adequacy as a woman. Between Vern's hesitancies and Byron's sweat-bathed efforts, positive emotional connection between them was hit-and-miss during sex.

Shortly I'll tell you about how Byron and Vern finally got themselves together. But first let me introduce another couple, for whom opening to each other's touch was absolutely critical.

Vivian and Armand

Opening to your partner's touch is no small thing if you have vaginismus. Women like Vivian instinctively pull back and break connection to protect themselves, even if that's not really their nature. Vaginismus involves an involuntary contraction of the muscles surrounding the entrance to a woman's vagina, making intercourse painful or impossible. Vaginismus often results from repeated painful sex. Very quickly your goal shifts from maintaining positive emotional connection to just wanting it to stop.

The road back from vaginismus is an extreme example of the issues and dynamics all couples face in opening to each other's touch. Vivian was a thirty-year-old woman who six years previously developed inflammation in the gland ducts of her labia (vulvar vaginitis). In the second year of a reasonably good marriage, sex suddenly became incredibly painful. Vivian's husband was understanding at first, but he grew more demanding and less considerate when Vivian's gynecologist couldn't find a cause for her pain. Vivian went through many painful sexual encounters in efforts to save her marriage. She developed vaginismus, and her husband started having affairs.

After her divorce, Vivian went to a university medical center where her problem was accurately diagnosed. Laser surgery corrected Vivian's pain and she was able to use tampons again without difficulty. However, her vaginismus remained when she resumed dating and started having sex.

Vivian's solution required a collaborative alliance and a positive connection with a partner. Her sexual experiences with her husband were not much to build on. She started dating Armand, and although she got aroused and lubricated, her vagina tightened up whenever Armand touched her genitals.

Vivian and Armand were developing a style of sex all too familiar to her. She pulled back from Armand's touch, gave up any hope of positive connection, and tried to tolerate the experience. What Vivian needed was repeated experiences of leaning into Armand's touch. She needed to open to their connection. Fighting back the feeling that she was some kind of freak, Vivian sat down with Armand and told him about her problem.

When Armand realized Vivian's situation, he felt flattered that she wanted to work it out with him. He also worried that he was getting talked into another sexless relationship like his prior marriage.[13] But Armand was willing to stick around and see what happened. He thought Vivian was a beautiful woman, and he could hardly believe she had the problem she did. Their kissing and touching was terrific. Armand agreed he wouldn't touch Vivian between her legs until she was ready. No attempts, no playing around, no sudden grabs. Together, they constructed a sexual context in which Vivian could finally relax.

Before too long, at a time, place, and rate of Vivian's choosing, she had Armand gradually touch outside her genitals.[14] She was already well aroused, and she deliberately opened her legs to give him access. It was clear she could stop at any time. Vivian had to calm her fear that Armand would suddenly jam his finger inside her, but he just played with her pubic hair. Armand was amazed that Vivian opened her thighs to him. His wife had never done that at any point in their marriage. Vivian eventually gave a deep sigh of relief and relaxed. That was when she first appreciated how tense and anxious she had been.

Optimize Your Thoughts, Feelings, and Emotions

In therapy I help partners "dial in" the sexual stimulation they exchange. Dialing in gives you exactly the kind of stimulation you want and a whole lot more, because it is an intimate process. It involves working with your partner to create profoundly positive thoughts, feelings, and emotions to enhance your physical sensations. It takes a tractable emotional alliance with your partner, and the process of developing that resilient connection contributes in many ways. Feeling good about yourselves and each other for going the distance does more to create an optimal ambience than lighting candles (which helps too).[15]

Vivian's Story

When Vivian stopped anticipating pain and experienced real sexual pleasure, she was able to approach intercourse in a whole new way. She controlled the pace and duration as Armand inserted his penis. He stopped where he was when Vivian needed to relax and open to him. Eventually her vagina stopped tightening and she began to enjoy intercourse. Directing the action during intercourse turned out to interest Vivian more than she had ever realized.

As Vivian became more accustomed to intercourse, she and Armand started to experiment. One day Vivian climbed on top and initiated intercourse. She took her time getting used to this. Much to her surprise, Vivian got exactly the kind of stimulation she liked, positioning Armand's penis perfectly for greatest effect. This was a long way from lying back and getting "penetrated." The real story is not how Vivian got the muscles in her vagina under her voluntary control, but how a woman gained control of *herself*.

Whenever one partner grows, the people-growing machinery goes to work on the other. Vivian's transformation had an impact on Armand. Since Vivian first told him about her vaginismus, Armand had to handle his own feelings so he could participate with her. Coming from a machismo culture, it was a stretch for Armand to take sexual instruction from a woman. Vivian deciding when he could touch her, or enter her, pushed his unresolved feelings from his marriage: Was she trying to frustrate him too? Was she saying he was a bad lover?

Armand might have been a little macho, but he was no dope. He sensed Vivian wasn't playing "I've got it and you can't have it!" She was inviting him into a kind of alliance he'd never had with a woman. To have this, he had to keep his self-doubts and cultural training under control.

When Vivian sat astride Armand's penis, they both had to take a few deep breaths. It took a week for Armand to tell Vivian he'd never had that before. Armand was a little intimidated by Vivian's move, but also deeply touched. That was Armand's first taste of generosity in female sexuality. He was completely intrigued. How could Vivian let herself move as freely as she pleased? Armand actually got to *see* what she liked!

Armand and Vivian embarked on "dialing in" their lovemaking. Whether it was kissing, oral sex, or scratching each other's back, they worked together to get it just right. Dialing in sex takes two of you, because you both have to pay attention to what's going on. Collaborating with your partner to optimize physical stimulation increases your depth of involvement in sex while you're having it. You probably have done something similar when you get an itch you can't scratch and try to guide your partner's hand. Some aspects of dialing in sex are similar: "A little to the left. Lower, lower. More to the left. That's it! Ahhhhhh!"

Masturbation Is a Tool

Not all solutions to arousal problems involve sex with your partner. Sometimes it involves working things out for, with, and by yourself. Masturbation is a good way to do that. The issue isn't whether you like to masturbate or not. *How* and *why* you masturbate (or don't) always reflects your relationship with yourself.

By design, I didn't discuss masturbation earlier as a form of physical stimulation because that's the way most people think of it. We're discussing masturbation here as part of optimizing thoughts and feelings because I want you to see masturbation as a *tool*. Masturbation is a lot more than a tension release. Masturbation is your relationship with yourself in action. You can make new responses in real time to relate to yourself in new ways. Let me show you how this played out for the people we've met in this chapter.

Betty had a vague uneasiness about touching herself. She masturbated occasionally before and during her marriage, but she never found it very interesting or pleasurable. She couldn't figure out what her hesitancy was about because she didn't think her genitals were dirty. As soon as she settled in to touch herself, her feelings came up to meet her: accepting her body, grieving over her miscarriages, and losing her opportunity to give birth. All this came to Betty as she brushed back her pubic hair and spread apart her labia.

For Betty, touching herself gently was an act of accepting her life as it was. She used masturbation as a tool rather than simply as a form of physical stimulation. It involved equal measures of self-confrontation and self-soothing.

Vivian used masturbation to show herself she could be touched without pain and have pleasure without discomfort. Vaginismus treatments differ in how women go about getting the muscles surrounding their vaginas to relax. Traditional approaches have women insert progressively larger dilators while they relax into it. I encouraged Vivian not to use dilators or dildos, and use her fingers instead. This way Vivian would have better control of what she was doing, confront any negative feelings about her vagina, and touch herself to arouse herself rather than focusing on penetration.

Gradually Vivian made peace with her genitals. She had to ease up and be kind to herself, which wasn't easy for her to do. Touching yourself in caring ways is a powerful self-confrontation. This eventually allowed Vivian to ask Armand to help her resolve her vaginismus together.

Byron made similar gains with masturbation, but his process was different. Byron had difficulty keeping an erection when he and Vern had sex. However, he knew he'd have no difficulty if he touched his own penis. All his life, Byron was ashamed of how well he could do himself. (It's not typical barracks conversation.) He never told anyone until he came to therapy. Byron said he feared losing Vern if he didn't get a good erection. I asked him if he had the courage to do what he knew worked.

That evening Byron touched himself when he and Vern started having sex. He had no difficulty getting an erection. Vern was struck by Byron's courage and her own reaction: She found the whole thing incredibly sexy. She had never seen a man touch himself. Vivian couldn't believe how intimate she found it. The next time they had sex, Vern asked Byron to touch himself again. This was more than curiosity about how he did it. She found the openness of it incredibly erotic. Watching Byron made her feel brazen and out of character.

Vern thought to herself, "I'm almost sixty years old, my husband is dead, I'm thinking I'll never have sex again, and here I'm doing *what?!* And I'm doing it with the guy I'm thinking I can't marry because he can't stay hard! What's a girl supposed to do?" Vern thought about it briefly, and then she had no doubt.

Vern tied Byron's hands together with the tie from his uniform. Then she oiled and rhythmically stroked his penis. She looked Byron in the eye all the way into his orgasm. Byron had no difficulty with his erection.

How Desire and Sexual Arousal Interrelate

Sexual desire problems cause and result from arousal problems, and many intricate interactions are possible: Arousal problems reduce sexual desire. Repeated problems with subjective arousal, lubrication, and erections can kill your enthusiasm for your next sexual encounter.

Likewise, sexual desire problems increase your chance of arousal difficulties. Low desire contributes to trouble with subjective arousal, lubrication, and erections because you are less likely to become aroused when you're not involved or interested in the experience. It's easy to develop a sexual dysfunction from having repeated sex with a partner who has low desire.

Arousal and desire problems can arise from the same cause: Drugs, illnesses, situational problems, and emotional gridlock all interfere with arousal and orgasm and impair desire. After a while it's hard to know what is causing what. And once your desire problem and your arousal problem become entwined, it makes your situation harder to turn around. The end result is not surprising.

Lots of couples become celibate. If you are one of them, Viagra and other drugs may not overcome your sexual inertia. You need an approach that works the same for desire and arousal problems alike. That is what you are learning here: one integrated approach for one complex problem.

Looking back, you'll see it was inevitable that our three couples would have desire issues. And yet it's amazing how each couple's version of this generic process so elegantly reflected who they were. In each case, there was a developmental task each person faced that resolved their two-choice dilemmas.

Harry's task was to validate his own legitimate interest in sex while recognizing that sex was not all he wanted. For Betty, letting herself *want* again was a deliberate decision, even though she realized that it was not risk-free.

Vivian had to validate herself as a "nonfreak" in her determination to regain control of her life. Armand had to wonder if he was a pathetic dog sniffing out sex, willing to settle for a pat on the head.

Byron had to follow his heart's desire when his penis wouldn't obey commands. He had to master his anxiety and go after the woman he wanted. Vern had to validate herself as her sexuality erupted, while not getting so swept up in it that she married the wrong man.

In each case, people were challenged to hold on to themselves to pursue their heart's desire. In this process, they became stronger, more human, and more loving.

Resolving Desire Discrepancy

Couples frequently argue about low desire, but their real issue is *difference* in their desires. Neither partner's desire need be particularly low or high. Disparity in sexual desire is couples' most common sexual complaint.

Dealing with desire discrepancy requires holding on to yourself, because the solution always involves compassion and mutuality. Holding on to yourself allows you to adapt to your partner, without feeling like you've lost yourself in the process. Pulling this off *increases* your sexual desire, rather than diminishes it. That's because you feel *good* about yourself for doing this. This is no different than what happens as you open to your partner's touch.

This isn't the same as anxiety regulation through accommodation. This accommodation occurs because you can regulate your own anxiety and you know who you are. This accommodation is true mutuality, which is why you feel good—and desirous.

Resolving arousal problems doesn't always guarantee desire for each other. We saw this, for example, with men who find Viagra creates erections but not desire. Sex is easier when everything works like a charm, but that doesn't mean you want to do it with your partner. Long-term sexual desire in a committed relationship is more determined by self-respect and respect for your partner than it is by hormones and hardware. Fortunately, the process of resolving your sexual problem can increase your sexual desire, and mutual respect, in ways you've never dreamed.

Creating Desire and Hope

Does this sound hopeful? That's exactly what I'm hoping for. You probably could use a little hope if you're anything like our three couples. Each one had a dark night of the soul (or two) in the process of getting what they wanted. Therein lies a lesson about the role of hope in resolving your sexual problem.

Remember, a quarter of the men in the Viagra studies who took placebos got erections because they believed they would. Many had erection problems going back five years or more. Believe in yourself rather than in a drug, and then live up to your beliefs.

If you just barely resolve your sexual problem, you have to worry about slipping back into old patterns that will knock out your sexual function or desire. Your best shot at maintaining your gains over the long term involves how you create change to begin with: change your sexual relationship in ways that make you more capable of "desire out of fullness." Desire for your partner that emerges from feeling good about yourself lasts a lot longer than blue balls or horniness.

Like Betty and Harry, Byron and Vern, and Vivian and Armand, you probably need to stop avoiding your anxieties because you never know where they might lead. Harry started out making the best of a bad situation and ended up thanking his lucky stars. "How could we ever have known things would work out like this?" Harry thought one night, lying next to Betty after a particularly lovely encounter. Vern and Byron had that thought at one point, and so did Armand and Vivian. So have countless couples around the world.

Go about resolving your problems by drawing upon the best in you. Earn your own self-respect. You will create hope that is neither blind nor fanciful. It may lift more than your spirits.

So You Want to Have an Orgasm

Only the nose knows
Where the nose goes
When the door close.

—Muhammad Ali

Your first orgasm is an irrevocable, life-changing event, a boundary marker in sexual maturation from which there is no turning back. Orgasms are irreversible in other ways too. Every orgasm has its own point of no return. Given all these "set in stone" qualities, wouldn't you think orgasms would be easy once you joined the club? However, intermittent problems with orgasms are some of the most common sexual complaints.

Fortunately, having your first orgasm, or having orgasms more readily, more slowly, or more enjoyably all involve the same solution: getting your total level of stimulation *way* above your orgasm threshold. This makes perfect sense if you can't have an orgasm. But how can more stimulation help a man delay his orgasm? I'll explain this in Chapter 13, when we consider rapid orgasm in detail. For now, whether your orgasm problem is new or has existed for years, whether constant or infrequent, whether too fast or too slow, resolution involves these three things.

1. Removing possible physiological complications

2. Increasing your stimulation and creating more relaxed and more varied patterns of non-goal-oriented sex

3. Changing your sexual style to create more meaningful and satisfying realities

In this chapter we'll discuss how to deal with medical problems that could be getting in your way. Then we'll discuss ways to have an orgasm, whether with a partner or by yourself, whether you have medical problems or not. From the outset, keep a few things in mind.

Drugs. Remember what we said in Chapter 11 about hormones, medications, and drugs causing sexual problems. Drugs that interfere with sexual arousal (many antidepressants, antianxiety drugs, and antihypertensive agents) can impair orgasm too.

Gender. Men and women have difficulties reaching orgasm for pretty much the same reasons. I'll focus more on women's difficulties, since they have this problem far more commonly. Every man has difficulty reaching orgasm at some time in his life, and some have this problem often.

Multifaceted approach. No one thing in itself may cause your problem. A cluster of factors can combine to keep your total stimulation below your threshold. This might involve a combination of medicines, situational problems, and poor techniques. Consider your problem from different perspectives and take a multifaceted approach.

Focus on your potential. You are more likely to reach orgasm, and more likely to enjoy it, if you set your goals much higher. Explore your sexual potential. Take a leap of faith, rather than pushing yourself to have an orgasm. This is especially important if you have medical problems.

Optimize Your Body's Ability to Respond

Get a physical exam to rule out medical reasons for any difficulty with orgasms, arousal, or desire. This is particularly true if your sexual problems are recent or you have ongoing health troubles. Rule out things that could interfere with your body's ability to function. What you read next may motivate you to do this.

Illness and Injury

Couples are usually blissfully ignorant of things that can jeopardize their sexual relationships. When you become ill or injured you quickly discover how naïve you really were. I've worked with couples in this situation, so I know this can be difficult.

Illnesses, medical procedures, and medications make it hard or impossible to reach your response thresholds. Common syndromes like alcoholism, diabetes, kidney failure, and multiple sclerosis can cause vascular, neurologic, and hormone-based sexual problems. Endocrine problems (associated with thyroid and hormone problems) can dramatically impact your sexual function, interest, and satisfaction. So can neurological problems that affect your touch, vision, taste, hearing, and sense of smell.

Cancer and associated treatments can impact your sex and intimacy, your whole relationship, and your overall quality of life. Aside from the direct effects of cancer, the radiation (fatigue, skin changes), chemotherapy (nausea, loss of desire, hair loss), and surgery (amputation or scars) can take their toll. So can painful and embarrassing procedures, time apart during hospitalizations, and the threat of death.

Some genital cancers require removing a woman's cervix, vagina, labia, or clitoris, or a man's testicles or penis. Nongenital cancers can also have devastating impact. Breast or throat cancer, for example, can bring up every negative feeling you've ever had about your body, your sexuality, and your life.

Treatment for prostate cancer commonly involves eradicating a man's testosterone production with injections of Lupron Depot or Megace. (Testosterone accelerates prostate cancer.) This creates irreversible testicular atrophy. A new alternative, Proscar (finasteride), does not have this side effect. Some advanced prostate cancers require surgery. A nerve-sparing surgical procedure is available that does not impair a man's erections. If you need surgery, you want this version.

Although cancers are often nonfatal, they can drastically affect your sex life. Omar, for example, lost all sexual desire and couldn't get an erection after testosterone-suppression chemotherapy for his prostate cancer. He gained weight, his breasts enlarged, and he became sluggish and lethargic. It was difficult for him to share this crushing disappointment with his wife, Cerise. Cerise said Omar was lucky to discover his cancer in its early stages. Omar only saw how he'd gotten screwed. As his body changed, he withdrew from Cerise and sex dropped to zero. As time wore on, Omar's marriage was in shambles.

It took over a year and a half for Omar to face his two-choice dilemma and get his relationship back on track. On the one hand, Omar could keep raging about the loss of his erections and desire, and probably lose Cerise in the process. Or he could pull himself together, accept his losses, and enjoy what they could have together. Cerise could accept not having intercourse, but she wouldn't tolerate Omar taking his anger out on both of them. And withdrawing from her physically and emotionally for months on end had to stop.

Omar got a hold of himself and rebuilt his relationship with his wife. Depression medication helped a lot. He and Cerise focused on holding, cuddling, and mutual kindness. Omar brought Cerise to orgasm manually or orally when she wanted this. It was not perfect by a long shot, and certainly not what Omar wanted. But he didn't want to lose Cerise in addition to his other losses. This meant he couldn't indulge himself in an understandably difficult situation. He stopped inflicting further heartache on himself and the woman who stood by him.

Irritable bowel syndrome, ulcerative colitis, and Crohn's disease can have direct and indirect impacts on your sexual function and satisfaction. Joan, for instance, had Crohn's disease. Some people with Crohn's disease develop pelvic nerve damage that can impair sexual response, but luckily this didn't happen to Joan. However, she had painful oozing sores on her buttocks that she and her partner, Joey, had to avoid. Maintaining emotional contact during sex was a challenge, and sometimes Joey had difficulty keeping an erection. Joan had difficulty reaching orgasm with all the cramping, pain, and steroids. Once she had surgery, however, her general health and outlook improved markedly. Dealing with her ostomy and her appliance bag during sex was easy compared to what she'd been through. Joan's orgasms gradually returned and so did Joey's erections.

Work-related accidents and sport and recreation injuries can also affect your body's ability to respond. Pelvic and spinal injuries, for example, can interfere with neurological functions. Spinal injuries can impair a woman's ability to lubricate and a man's ability to get erections. You can lose your dexterity, mobility, career, and lifestyle in an instant. If and when that happens, you don't want to lose intimacy and emotional contact with your partner too.

Suzanne became paraplegic when she was thrown headfirst over the handlebars of her mountain bike. She was partially paralyzed from her waist down and learning to walk on crutches. In the year after her accident, depression and spinal shock clouded her return of function. Gradually she found she could get aroused when her partner, Larry, touched her genitals, but not when she engaged in fantasy.

Suzanne's leg spasms and her catheter made intercourse less convenient. However, she still liked taking Larry inside her, and they had intercourse when she had time to bathe and prepare. She and Larry liked oral sex and manual stimulation, and they added a vibrator to their lovemaking. There was some question as to whether Suzanne would ever have an orgasm again. But as her ability to walk returned, there was reason to be hopeful.

Indirect Impact of Illness

Many medical problems don't directly impair your ability to have an orgasm. However, they have enormous indirect impact through your thoughts and feelings. Sometimes the impact can so drastically limit your arousal and pleasure, you'd swear somehow your genitals were damaged.

The indirect impact of illness may not be obvious at first, but it always makes perfect sense. Menstrual disorders such as pain, excessive or prolonged bleeding, cessation of periods, and unpredictable periods (especially beginning menopause) can reduce either partner's sexual arousal and interest. Couples who generally avoid sex during menstruation have greater difficulty dealing with such problems.

Your ability to hold on to yourself greatly determines how well you adapt to your illness. Sometimes chronic illness can tap you out. Sandra's severe arthritis also created mouth and gum problems. Kissing hurt, moving hurt—just getting into bed for sex irritated her. Sex brought out Sandra's anger that this was happening to her. Sandra's doctor recommended hot baths before sex, and sex in the morning (before the physical wear and tear of the day), but she resented having to change her daily routine. Besides, Sandra considered herself a night person, her husband liked sex in the morning, and this seemed even more unfair.

Sandra spent months fighting with herself and raging over her health problems. She was angry about her constant diet of anti-inflammatory drugs, which themselves further slowed her sexual response. Her private emotional war limited the benefits she derived from the drugs. It was no wonder that Sandra rarely reached orgasm.

Slowly, Sandra's problems began to turn around. Medications and proper diet improved her health, and she grew accustomed to the changes in her daily routine. Her gums improved, and sex stopped hurting as much. As Sandra came to terms with her body and her life, she found it easier to get aroused and have orgasms again.

Your ability to hold on to yourself, and the stability of your relationship, determine how medical problems affect you. For example, your chances for satisfying sex after a heart attack are good if that's what you had before heart disease showed up. The physical demands of sex are usually not the problem. But whereas a triple bypass or heart transplant may be an everyday event for your cardiologist, it can shake up your life and your marriage. As with other life-threatening conditions, anxiety attacks and depression sometimes follow.

Helmut's heart attack at age fifty four was Helga's first real brush with death. Helga looked to Helmut for her stability, and this episode really rattled her. She wasn't about to risk losing him for the sake of sex. Helmut's doctor assured Helga that Helmut could reach orgasm without exceeding a safe heart rate. Helmut was eager to try. He promised Helga they'd go easy on gymnastics and make up the difference by "getting nasty." Helga agreed, but she was too distraught to reach orgasm. This went on for the next six months.

Helmut and Helga had been together a long time, but they didn't often talk about their feelings. When he finally insisted they talk, Helga said she was afraid Helmut would suddenly die. Rather than reassuring her or dismissing her fear as he usually did, this time Helmut didn't say anything. He thought about how close he came to dying, and then he looked at Helga. Helga realized the false reassurances were over. Their eyes remained locked in silent acceptance of the truth.

Helga and Helmut smiled and reached out to each other. They burst into tears as they held each other, grieving over the reality all couples face. Helga had no difficulty reaching orgasm that night, but it took months before this resolved altogether.

Like many couples, Helmut and Helga grew closer from going through serious illness together. They became more aware of each other and vowed to make the most of their relationship. This doesn't happen for all couples, because the demands of acute or chronic illnesses are simply more than some can handle. Medical problems challenge your ability to confront yourself, self-soothe, not overreact, and live up to your ideals and values.

Sometimes not having an orgasm is the least of your worries. When one partner develops Alzheimer's disease, dementia, or manic-depressive illness, both partners are at high risk for low desire and problems with arousal and orgasm. It's hard to have orgasms watching your partner progressively disappear before your eyes. The same can happen if your partner is chronically depressed. Divorce rates for couples with severe or chronic illnesses are high.

Adapting to Illness and Injury
Adapting to illness and injury is hard for anyone. A health crisis turns normal people into remarkable people with a remarkable marriage, or it breaks them down and tears their relationship apart. Sometimes turning pain into growth is the only way to salvage something. Illness and injury test your spirituality and your beliefs.

When you're struggling with serious illness or injury, it doesn't feel like a good time to broaden your sexual relationship. It is hard enough to change your relationship when everything is stable. Suddenly, you need to develop anatomy-independent eroticism to preserve your connection with your partner. Resurrecting sex after illness and injury can be a long-term proposition, and you have to hang in for the long haul.

For example, Judd developed difficulty reaching orgasm as a secondary result of Peyronies disease. The buildup of dense fibrous tissue in Judd's penis caused it to bend sharply in the middle, making erections and intercourse painful. Peyronies disease typically develops in midlife from unknown causes. These distressing changes can create sexual dysfunctions. Some men develop difficulty with erections or premature orgasm. Judd found it difficult to reach orgasm.

When Judd had sex with his wife, Holly, he thought about "that damn bend" and the discomfort in his penis. Antifibrotic medication

(Potaba) helped contain his Peyronies disease. Eventually Judd had plaque-removal surgery, which reduced the bend in his penis and permitted sex without pain. It took another six months for Judd to stop anticipating pain during sex and pay attention to Holly.

Judd continued to have difficulty reaching orgasm, especially during intercourse. He'd start thrusting faster and harder until he gave up in frustration and exhaustion. Sometimes Holly got tired or sore. Judd wasn't easy to live with when this happened. Their commitment to stay together got them through some very difficult times.

Working with oral sex (instead of intercourse) gave Judd the opportunity to relax. For one thing, he didn't have to worry as much about his penis bending. It also changed his picture of who was doing whom. Holly wanted to do it just right for Judd, and she made it easy for him to lean into her touch. He could feel Holly cherishing him in a way he never got from intercourse. This provided a better context for Judd to struggle through frustrations and disappointments about his penis, which stood in the way of connecting with Holly.

Gradually Judd began to reach orgasm reliably during oral sex. That helped his frustration and his self-esteem. He started to let Holly comfort him in ways he had shut her out. Optimizing oral sex was a big gain in intimacy for their marriage, and a change that Holly wanted. In the days following their encounters, she noticed he seemed much calmer and softer.

However, reaching orgasm during intercourse remained a problem for Judd. Holly generally let Judd have intercourse his way during sex, not wanting to upset him further. As time wore on and her patience wore out, she finally took control. Holly did something she had not done since early in their marriage, because Judd seemed uncomfortable with it at the time. Holly put Judd on his back instead of letting him thrust away during intercourse from on top. Holly mounted Judd and told him to relax. Judd seemed very awkward. Holly looked at him with her no-nonsense look and said, "I'm not kidding."

From on top, Holly straightened up and stopped moving. She took a deep breath and relaxed. Then she put her hands on Judd's chest and leaned forward so the weight of her body transferred to her arms. At first Judd thought she was pressing him into the mattress to make him relax and show she was in control.

Holly squatted above him, carrying her body with her arms and legs. Judd relaxed enough to experiment with this position. He gently held her buttocks in his hands. Judd found he could move Holly up and down and side to side effortlessly, any way he pleased. Her hips seemed almost weightless. He moved her so he had no fear his penis would bend. Judd was totally captivated.

Judd started watching his penis going into Holly. Eventually this changed in his mind to watching Holly's vagina take in his penis. At that point Judd looked up at Holly, and Holly smiled back.

Judd realized Holly was giving herself to him. Holly's vagina was Judd's to use until he had what he needed. He knew Holly wanted this for him. She wanted him to be happy. Holly smiled to him as he moved her up and down. Judd's orgasm flowed effortlessly from his loins.

Having an orgasm during intercourse was deeply meaningful for Judd and Holly. His inability to orgasm this way had been Judd's ultimate proof he was defective. Their experience together made this particular intercourse especially poetic and beautiful. Judd showed himself he could have orgasms without difficulty, once and for all. It wasn't that his problem was totally solved. But Judd knew he had the wherewithal to take care of it. The experience brought Judd and Holly closer together, and increased their determination to resurrect their sex.

All the medical problems we've discussed present somewhat similar tasks. Each one shakes up your life and challenges your identity, adequacy, and self-worth. There's usually lots of anger, helplessness, and feelings of victimization to deal with. Not all couples are successful. It's the people, not the illness, that make the difference.

Optimize Your Physical Stimulation

If you want to have an orgasm, it helps to recognize the sensations that lead up to it. Both men and women get a feeling called "orgasmic inevitability" when an orgasm is imminent. Your sense of inevitability comes from your body starting the cascade of physical changes involved in an orgasm. People usually punctuate this feeling of inevitability with exclamations like, "Oh, God!" or "Oh, baby!" or "I'm coming!"

People relax and enjoy themselves when they know their orgasm is about to happen. This hastens the process and makes it more reliable. Having your first orgasm is harder, because you don't know what you're looking for. As you recognize your sense of orgasmic inevitability at its earliest and faintest appearance, you get better at having orgasms.

THINGS YOU CAN DO ABOUT
ILLNESSES AND INJURIES

1. *Educate yourself.* Learn the medical impacts of your disorder and treatments you receive. Find out the sexual details. Locate physicians who specialize in your problem. Try your local medical center. Go on the Internet.

2. *Find a physician you can work with.* You want a doctor with whom you can discuss intimate details—someone who welcomes your input on medication and treatment decisions.

3. *Start with the attitude that adaptation is always possible.* Figure you'll have to grow into your new solutions.

4. *Work with what you have.* Focus on the strengths and abilities that you and your partner possess.

5. *Talk to other people with the same problem.* Get the nitty-gritty about handling sex from people who have been there. Attend patient support groups at your local hospital. Internet support groups offer good information, but don't avoid the intimacy and self-confrontation of face-to-face contact with others.

6. *Keep yourself rested.* You need to be well nourished and in good health. Once your responsiveness is impaired, getting the flu or a cold won't help.

7. *Exercise to the best of your ability.* You will feel better about yourself and your body and you'll have more physical endurance. Don't ignore your physical appearance.

8. *Expect to be challenged.* You'll probably have to change your customary sex repertoire and depart from conventional gender role stereotypes.

9. *Use your creativity.* Let your creativity and intention, not your physical limitations, determine what you and your partner do. Optimize your total level of stimulation and connect with your partner any way you can. Illness and injury create situations you've never had to face. Resolution requires doing things you've never done before or thought you'd ever do.

Organizing your sensations, thoughts, and feelings makes it easier for you to reach your threshold.

Directed Masturbation
If you've never had an orgasm, go about it the easiest way: masturbation. Most people have their first orgasm alone for good reasons. It's easier to figure out what you like and give it to yourself when you don't have an audience. It's also easier to recognize your sense of orgasmic inevitability without the distractions of a partner. Masturbation is the most reliable way to produce orgasms and produces the most physiologically intense ones.

Directed masturbation programs are a proven way for women to have their first orgasms; 80 percent of women who use them reach orgasm by themselves, and many go on to have orgasms with a partner. Instructions are available at your local bookstore,[1] or you can do this as a self-study. Deliberately masturbating (without pushing yourself to orgasm) challenges your self-worth and stretches your ability to self-soothe. That's why women who use directed masturbation report better acceptance of their bodies, increased satisfaction from intercourse, and less anxiety about sex and life.[2]

Getting Down to It
Whether your masturbation is programmatic or ad-libbed, you can learn who you are while you discover what you like. Masturbation is more than a way of deciphering your body's owner manual. It's a means of establishing self-ownership and self-mastery. Let me tell you about a woman who used it exactly this way.

When Nancy first told me about her problems having orgasm, she described her pattern of difficulties. She felt inadequate because she couldn't reach orgasm during intercourse, which in her view was the "right way" to have them. It was hard for Nancy to have an orgasm under any circumstances, and she felt she took too long to have one when she did. Nancy berated herself and wondered what was wrong with her. She was anxious and impatient even during sex by herself. Her touch was perfunctory, and she rushed herself through it. Based on this I suggested she begin with masturbation, using what she was already doing in a new way.

How you touch yourself (or don't) reveals your relationship with yourself, whether you are Ms. Multiple Orgasms or you haven't had your first. If you have more difficulty during masturbation than during sex with your partner, it tells you something's missing between you and you. Having an orgasm during masturbation sometimes boils down to touching yourself with simple compassion.

Once you can have orgasms, broaden the way you can have them. Try having an orgasm with your eyes open (presuming you close your eyes to focus on orgasmic inevitability). Vibrator stimulation can compensate for reduced sensory awareness when you open your eyes. This heads you toward being able to reach orgasm while you are with your partner.[3]

How Do You Know When to Stop?

When you're masturbating, how do you know when to stop? If you have difficulty with orgasms, you probably stop when you have lost hope. Compassion for yourself runs dry, and so does the "chance" you've given yourself. Nancy, for example, described her stopping point this way: "I feel pathetic, bored, frustrated, and disappointed. I know nothing is going to happen. Sometimes I'm in tears. I just give up." Nancy stopped touching herself after 10 minutes if she didn't feel highly aroused. She gave up emotionally long before that.

For Nancy, continuing past her usual stopping point was like stepping into wonderland. Just doing it longer wasn't the answer, and neither was pushing for an orgasm. Nancy had to learn to touch herself kindly, and pass through her self-doubts and self-rejections, to enter this unexplored territory. She discovered delicious sensations she didn't know she could feel. As her pleasure and self-respect began to grow, Nancy's masturbation became increasingly erotic and daring. She began to look forward to having orgasms during masturbation. Then she wanted to have this same sensation with her partner, Carl.

Inviting Your Partner to the Party

Lots of women and men who have orgasms by themselves find having orgasms with a partner problematic. This can happen for the following reasons:

- *Sex with your partner may not provide sufficient physical stimulation.* You may be able to reach orgasm if you do yourself just right, but you can't reach your threshold if sex with your partner is a little off. Perhaps your partner doesn't touch you as well as you touch yourself. Maybe the things you do together aren't nearly as hot as what you do on your own.

- *Your thoughts and feelings during sex with your partner are less optimal than during sex by yourself.* It could be something about your partner, your sexual relationship, being intimate, or your relationship in general. The content doesn't even have to be about your partner at all. It can be anything that surfaces for you when you two are together. One way or another, your mind-set during masturbation may be much more erotic than during sex with your partner.

For example, Nancy and Carl had the usual assortment of marital problems. They had the pressures of children and jobs and little time for each other. They were gridlocked over money problems and disciplining their kids, and they tried to ignore this as best they could. Nancy often broke contact with Carl during sex and just went through the motions. Against this background, any number of other things made it impossible for Nancy to reach orgasm. Sometimes they had argued recently, or Nancy had an upsetting phone call with her parents. Sometimes Nancy heard their kids in the next room. Sometimes Carl wasn't attentive, or his touch was mechanical. Often Nancy worried she was taking too long and felt Carl was getting bored or tired. Little wonder Nancy had difficulty reaching orgasm.

If you want an orgasm with your partner, here is how to do it: Talk openly with him or her before you have sex. Suggest taking turns "giving" and "receiving," rather than touching each other simultaneously. Here's the most important part: Put the receiver in control. This makes it easier for you to dial in stimulation and lean into your partner's touch.

This arrangement also gives you time to confront your inner demons. You probably need to struggle through conflicts that interfere with accepting what your partner offers. You can do this while you are the receiver, with your partner's full knowledge and consent. Sharing your inner process with your partner after you reach orgasm usually opens up whole new levels of intimacy.

Doing this was a big step for Nancy. It meant she had to hold on to herself with Carl. Instead of just following the pace and behaviors that he chose, Nancy spoke up about what she wanted. Much to her surprise, Carl seemed delighted with changes she proposed. This markedly increased the intimacy and commitment between them. Once she knew Carl participated of his own free will, Nancy confronted her own thoughts and fears that she was taking too long to have an orgasm.

One Step at a Time

With all the emotional turmoil that can surround having orgasms with your partner, it can help to have a logical and pragmatic four-step approach to turning things around. You can pick up the sequence at any point that fits your situation. Here is how Nancy and Carl applied this sequence to themselves:

1. *Have an orgasm while your partner is present.* It works best if you provide genital stimulation for yourself while your partner holds you. (You may be the only one who has successfully brought you to orgasm thus far.) Nancy and Carl continued experimenting with "receiver in control" sex, where Nancy took over stimulating her genitals when she wanted to have an orgasm.

2. *Have an orgasm while your partner primarily provides the stimulation.* The preceding step made the transition from masturbation to sex with Carl easier for Nancy. Between collaborating with Carl to dial in his touch, and knowing she could bring herself to orgasm if she wanted, Nancy found it progressively easier to have orgasms when Carl stimulated her.

3. *Make oral and manual sex reliable ways of reaching orgasm.* Nancy's orgasms with Carl got easier and more frequent. Relaxing further, dialing in the stimulation, and deepening her experience helped Nancy have orgasms pretty much whenever they got together. Both she and Carl began to look forward to sex with entirely different anticipations.

4. *Have an orgasm during intercourse.* You don't have to avoid intercourse, but don't drive yourself nuts trying to reach orgasm this way. I'll describe how Nancy went about this later in this chapter.

Don't be quick to decide you can't reach orgasm any particular way. There's a learning curve with any sexual behavior. Give yourself time to grow into it. You may like oral stimulation, for example, but not reach orgasm because you don't use it well enough yet. Men and women who can't reach orgasm during oral sex can get over it by using this same systematic approach. Think of it this way: People take decades to integrate eroticism, emotional connection, affection, and love. Give yourself time to integrate different types of stimulation.[4]

Orgasm Triggers

If you are close to having an orgasm, you may find particular behaviors work like a trigger. For example:

- *Throat extension.* Tilt your head backward as you lie on your back. Expose your throat. Sometimes it helps if your head hangs off the bed. Try arching your torso backward so your ribs are stretched. The movement of your abdomen should be outward and open, rather than curling inward and guarded.

- *Breathing.* Some people find closing their throat and holding their breath does the trick. Others find breathing rapidly (panting) helps.

- *Muscle tension.* Bear down on your stomach, pelvic, and rectal muscles. Tighten your buttocks or raise them off the mattress. Point your toes. Clench your muscles. Tense your entire body in pleasurable ways.

- *Scrotal stimulation.* As a man approaches orgasm, his testicles rise toward the base of his penis. Help the process along by gently cupping and lifting the scrotum.

- *G spot stimulation.* It's hard for a woman to reach her own G spot because it's located inside her vagina opposite her belly button. Her G spot surrounds her urethra (like a man's prostate gland), so stimulation may initially produce sensations of needing to urinate. Nancy emptied her bladder beforehand, so she could relax when Carl lent her a helping hand. At her request, Carl inserted two well-lubricated fingers about 3 inches into Nancy's vagina and raised his fingertips toward the ceiling.

As he gently rubbed, a 1-centimeter "bump" in the wall of her vagina swelled to the size of a dime. Nancy found this felt different from vaginal or clitoral stimulation. It turned out Nancy liked Carl stimulating her G spot with his fingers, while his tongue worked her clitoris at the same time. Nancy found she could reach orgasm almost every time they had sex this way.[5]

- *Door locks*. Nancy swore putting a lock on their bedroom door was an orgasm trigger. It told the kids they were not to be disturbed and signified their commitment to improving their relationship. The night after Nancy and Carl installed a lock on their door, they had better sex and laughed more than they had in a long time.

Stop Trying to Have an Orgasm

Orgasm triggers won't help if you try to force a climax. Besides losing your relaxed ambience and collaborative alliance with your partner, pushing yourself to reach orgasm is counterproductive, period. Orgasm triggers can make you feel pressured to have an orgasm *that instant,* so if you try one, don't do it as a "technique." Blend it into your lovemaking. Keep your focus on being together in the moment, and let your arousal continue to build.

Many people find it hard to not think about an orgasm when they're having sex, much like being told not to think about pink elephants. The injunction itself makes it likely that you'll fail. The solution requires focusing your attention on something positive, rather than fending off untoward thoughts.

Unfortunately, the opposite happened for Nancy when she had intercourse. She focused on creating the kind of experience she thought she was *supposed* to have, instead of what was actually happening at the moment. Nancy kept imagining a picture-book encounter that changed her life, satisfied every dissatisfaction, and made her feel equal to everyone else. Intercourse is actually the hardest way for most women to reach orgasm. Only a third of all women can reach orgasm with intercourse. The other 70 percent need additional clitoral stimulation to climax. This was "cheating" in Nancy's view. She thought she was supposed to reach orgasm the way most women never do.

When you get down to it, intercourse is like a man sticking his penis in his wife's "scrotum," because that's the corresponding anatomy. A scrotum develops from the same embryonic tissue as a vagina. The fact that 30 percent of women (and one man in a million) can reach orgasm with this stimulation underscores the power of female eroticism. The remaining 70 percent of women (and all men) don't have to feel inadequate because of it.

Intercourse is probably the most physically and emotionally complex sexual behavior there is. And given that a penis and a vagina are not equivalent body parts, there was no scientific reason why Nancy should expect to have orgasms during intercourse. If she wanted to have an orgasm, all she needed was the same kind of stimulation that worked for Carl: He could lick or rub her clitoris—the anatomical equivalent of a man's penis.

The Holy Grail Arrives

Nonetheless, Nancy wanted to have an orgasm while Carl was inside her, and he was willing to go along. It was less of a big thing to Nancy than in the past, now that she was adept at having orgasms. However, she was legitimately curious about what this would feel like. Nancy's best shot at her long-sought goal was continuing what had gotten her that far. She used a no-lose strategy to help her relax.

During intercourse, Nancy focused her attention on being with Carl. This way she won whether she had an orgasm or not. She knew pushing for an orgasm was counterproductive, not to mention inconsiderate and unkind. Looking at Carl gave Nancy something better to focus on than her doubts and self-rejections. Better to gaze into Carl's eyes than lie in the dark wondering where her orgasm was.

Nancy maintained the same erotic ambience and connection with Carl that originally got her aroused. She usually lost this once Carl inserted his penis. Nancy and Carl started gazing into each other's eyes during intercourse for long minutes at a time. But with all of this, Nancy still didn't reach orgasm during intercourse.

Then they tried having intercourse doggy style while Nancy used a vibrator. It was easy for Nancy to put the vibrator against her clitoris exactly as she liked. Nancy asked Carl if he could feel the vibrations inside her, and Carl laughed. He pressed himself into her and they leaned into each other. Carl stopped thrusting, and took hold of Nancy's shoulders. He slowly pulled himself in deeper while Nancy kept the vibrator on her clitoris.

Nancy wasn't worrying about orgasms. She wasn't wondering if she was having enough fun. She was having the best sex of her life. Carl was inside her. That's when Nancy was overtaken by the orgasm she always wanted.

13

Synchronize Your Pelvis and Your Inner Mental World

Where there is an ongoing relationship of caring, where there is a sense of humor, where there is a sense of mutual mercy, where there is a sense that God has given sex to you . . . there is nothing livelier. But when it is merchandised as a commodity for instant gratification, there is nothing deadlier than sex.

—Bishop William Swing, *Episcopalian* (1986)

Sex and intimacy don't seem to go together for some couples. Others have erotic maps that are a little "dark." Maybe you don't want cherubs singing during your orgasms. Maybe you climax better when you're playing with the devil.

In this chapter we'll link your mental world and the speed and ease of your orgasms. We'll discuss using fantasies to facilitate orgasms, getting your feelings and your senses synchronized, and letting go and holding on.

We'll also discuss how to slow your orgasms down. Thoughts and feelings can sometimes make orgasms happen faster than you want. Whether your orgasms arrive too fast, too slow, or on time, it often has to do with what's going on inside your head.

Fantasies and Your Mental World

We've talked a lot about emotional connection during sex and being with your partner in the moment. Given this, where do fantasies fit in?

Using Sexual Fantasies to Trigger Orgasms

Fantasies are normal by any scientific standard. Lots of people use them to facilitate their orgasms. Masturbation produces orgasms more reliably when you have a fantasy that works for you. Some people develop trigger fantasies they retain throughout their lives. In fact, fantasies are such a large part of masturbation you might find it hard to climax without one.

Fantasies aren't antithetical to good sex with your partner. In *Passionate Marriage* I describe role playing, a kind of joint sexual fantasy that brings partners together in the moment. But what about sexual fantasies of other people while you're having sex with your partner? Research says partner-replacement fantasies are the most common fantasy going.

Fantasies per se don't help or harm your sexual response or satisfaction. It greatly depends on how and why you use them. It's common to use fantasies to tune out your partner or compensate for his or her emotional disappearance. But you can use sexual fantasies to increase intimacy and connection.

Many people's notion of sharing fantasies involves revealing what they think about during masturbation. Developing a fantasy together is entirely different. It is a form of mental play and collaboration, ad-libbing the story as you go. For instance you could

- Pretend you are different people, living in a different place or time

- Make up various scenarios of how and why you meet anew and take things from there

- Assume the identity of characters from a movie or book you'd like to play out

Broaden your notion of sharing fantasies. It's no different than sharing your aspirations and living into the relationship you have always wanted. Shared fantasies can

- Put you in connection with your partner

- Create positive shared meanings in your current interaction

- Give you another means to become deeply involved in the encounter

- Help you relax in humorous play and keep you in the moment

- Raise your total level of stimulation and help you reach orgasm

Mind Noise

Not all mind traffic during sex has to do with fantasies. "Noise" can come from any number of different mental realities. Do you go away, tune out, or disappear during sex? Mental distractions and emotional disconnection can delay your orgasm, whether it's fantasizing during sex but hiding it from your partner or being anxious about possible rejection if you don't have an orgasm. Your mind becomes disconnected from your sensations or behavior.

Whether you have fantasies you don't want or you just seem distracted or absent, you can improve things. If you want to stop tuning out, recognize that you've mentally left the building, and figure out where you go. If you know where you go in your head, you're more likely to realize you've tuned out. Since some people haven't the vaguest notion what goes on inside them while they have sex, the bottom line involves bringing yourself back into the moment.

Once you identify distracting thoughts and feelings, ask yourself these questions.

- Why are these particular thoughts and feelings coming up?

- When did they start? Are they just surfacing, or have they been there all along?

- Why are these issues surfacing at this point in your life?

Cindy's Story

A moment ago I said that fantasies can rivet your attention on your partner, bring you together in the moment, and cut through your mind noise. For some people, however, fantasies *are* their mind noise.

What if you're bothered by your fantasies, whether you're with a partner or not? What if you can't climax with your partner without resorting to your fantasy? There's so little written about these fairly common problems, it's hard to know what to do if this is you. Dealing with your partner is often a difficult issue, too.

Fantasies are a particularly explosive topic for anxiety-avoidant couples like Boyd and Cindy. Their whole relationship hinged around keeping Cindy "safe" (read: not anxious). Some insecure women get reptilian when they discover their husband's *Playboy*. In Cindy and Boyd's case, however, the roles were reversed. Cindy dealt with her insecurities and need for validation by visiting Internet porno sites and trading sexually charged e-mail. Things blew up when Boyd found out.

Boyd got upset when he realized Cindy's sexual fantasies and masturbation were populated by people other than himself. He started ranting about "emotional infidelity" and demanded a full accounting. Cindy screamed at Boyd about invasion of privacy and invoked the Fifth Amendment.

Using Fantasies (and the Internet) to Make or Break Contact

In the same way some couples use fantasies to bring them together, some enrich their relationships through sex-related materials available on the Internet. And in the same way some people use fantasies to break contact with their partners, there are those who go online instead of being intimate with their mates. Sometimes the issue is defiance; sometimes it's avoidance. (Beneath this apparent show of independence, it's really emotional fusion.)

In Cindy's case, something else drove her online sexual flirtations: She got a charge from dabbling in the taboo and defying her spouse. In other words, Cindy got a general arousal rush from anxiety- and adrenaline-laced clandestine sexual behavior. Such things drive some people to have extramarital affairs. It drove Cindy to the Web. (I'll say more about this in Chapter 14.)

Cindy wasn't a thrill-seeking adrenaline junkie. Some anxieties turned Cindy on, and others made her run for cover. She didn't think Boyd would approve of her sexual interests, and she couldn't validate herself in the face of his disapproval.[1] She wasn't about to stir up a hornet's nest by proposing new sexy ideas. That kind of thing frightened her.

Besides, this made her secret a little naughtier and more electric. She was more likely to keep her marriage "stable," go to her computer, log on, and turn on. Lots of men do likewise. Cindy liked the sexual charge of having a secret mental world.

There was a downside to Cindy's adrenaline-laced sex life: When she and Boyd had sex, she had to break contact and fantasize in order to have her orgasm. She went off in her mind, and when she didn't, it took her much longer. Usually Boyd got bored, or his hand or mouth got tired. This made sex with Boyd frustrating for Cindy and made masturbation and the Internet more attractive.

Disturbing Trigger Fantasies

A number of my clients have been bothered by fantasies that reliably bring them to orgasm. Some find the content of their fantasies problematic. Some simply dislike being dependent on a fantasy to reach orgasm. Others don't like the way their fantasies interfere with being with their partners.

Cindy couldn't reach orgasm with Boyd without resorting to her fantasies. She usually had no difficulty having orgasms by herself and could climax within several minutes once her trigger fantasy started in her mind. It was harder for her to do this during sex with Boyd.

It bothered Boyd that this was so. It didn't help that Cindy obviously found sex with other men attractive. He wasn't upset by Cindy's masturbation per se—it was what he imagined she thought about while she did it. Boyd imagined that Cindy was having a better time by herself than she had with him.

To his credit, Boyd tried to make their sex more interesting. As a form of foreplay, Boyd suggested they tell each other what they fantasized about when they masturbated. Boyd went first and confessed that he fantasized about past lovers, Cindy's girlfriends, and women he met at work.

Cindy hesitated a moment. Then she told Boyd she fantasized about being nude in a room and having sex with any man who walked in. Boyd was shocked. He stopped their conversation and rolled over to think. After ten minutes staring at the ceiling in silence, Boyd turned off the light on his nightstand.

This impacted Cindy in ways Boyd never imagined. He didn't realize Cindy hadn't told him all of her trigger fantasy. She was so embarrassed by it, she finessed her disclosure to test out his reaction.

Cindy's trigger fantasy involved dancing and masturbating in front of a table of wealthy older men. Cindy never told Boyd about them, but the older men showed up almost every time he and Cindy had sex. They had watched Cindy dance and masturbate since she was an adolescent. Throughout their seventeen years of marriage, Cindy broke contact with Boyd during sex and danced for these men. Sometimes she felt a delicious sense of getting away with something. Much of the time, however, Cindy felt beleaguered by her fantasies.

What did this mean? Did she want to be debased or humiliated? Did she want to have sex with her father? Cindy thought her trigger fantasy, together with her Internet escapades and her difficulty reaching orgasm, proved she was really twisted.

While "subconscious" explanations probably leap to mind, the heart-breaking part for Cindy was that her fantasies replicated the kinds of relationships with which she was most familiar. The men in Cindy's sexual fantasies were a source of torment and solace.

Can You Change Your Sexual Fantasies?

The clients I've known with troubling fantasies presumed this was not something they could change. Usually this was not why they came to see me. The topic surfaced in the course of therapy for other problems. Often they struggled with their fantasies all their adult lives, deciding it was best not to talk about them. Talking about their fantasies was itself a major event in their lives.

Like Cindy, some of my clients find their trigger fantasies change spontaneously, by following the approach outlined throughout this book. Usually the changes aren't like night and day. They usually involve shifts in scenery, characters, behaviors, or tones of interaction. These small shifts often completely change the meanings of the fantasies, evolving friendlier and more palatable forms. This corresponds with my clients digesting their life experiences and addressing the unresolved issues involved.

To explain this process, I'll tell you about what Cindy had to digest. Cindy grew up in a chronically anxious household, a world of undeclared psychological warfare. People played with reality at will. Lying was common. Retaliation was the norm. Cindy's parents constantly bickered and sniped at each other, and at Cindy and her brother.

Cindy's parents treated any question or challenge from their children as disobedience and disrespect. Cindy's mother "unraveled" when she got anxious, and she'd say whatever reduced her anxiety in the moment, even if it was completely untrue. Her dad lost his temper when he was

RESOLVING UPSETTING THOUGHTS DURING SEX

- Don't overreact.
- Calm yourself down.
- Pay attention to your immediate surroundings (bed, partner, room).
- Distinguish fantasy from reality. Realize your thoughts are just thoughts.
- Stop judging and start watching. Don't catastrophize—analyze.
- Instead of justifying or blaming yourself, accept it is happening (for now).
- Look into your imagery and see the story of your life.

nervous or threatened or when he simply didn't know what to do. Cindy's father kept her older brother under his thumb, and the kid was using drugs and falling apart under the pressure.

During adolescence Cindy's brother frequently tried to touch her, and one time he tried to have sex. He stopped when Cindy slapped his face. Cindy was constantly on the alert in her house, waiting for the next major disappointment. It was impossible to count on a straight answer from anyone about anything. She never said a word about the sexual abuse until she went to college.

Earlier I described Cindy's taste for anxiety-laced sex. Many people who have not been sexually abused have the same anxiety arousal–sexual arousal pattern as Cindy did. This pattern can develop from the daily interactions of an emotionally fused family, where people don't regulate their own anxieties and impulses.

In Cindy's case, normal marital sadism between her parents trickled down as constant tension in their household. That's why Cindy couldn't see it when she scanned her memories. It was an everyday event. Cindy thought (and feared) that her fantasies stemmed from her brother's sexual gropings because she was looking for "traumatic events." Actually, her fantasies were eroticized forms of the kind of tormenting relationships she lived with every day.

The secret men's club was sly, hidden, all-powerful, and controlling. They knew she needed them to have an orgasm, and they let her know it. The men sat at the table watching her, making lewd comments as she danced. The men were tempting and taunting, and she was at their mercy.

Digesting Your Life

Now that you have some idea of what Cindy was trying to "metabolize," let me tell you how this played out. Coming from a chaotic family, Cindy picked Boyd for safety and low anxiety. Boyd was fairly easygoing but not *hot*. The big secret was that Cindy was sexually bored with him.

Cindy told herself she didn't want to upset Boyd by revealing she didn't find him sexually attractive. And given that, she certainly couldn't tell him about her clandestine Internet affairs and time spent looking at porn. More accurately, Cindy was protecting herself from the instability she knew the truth could create. She grabbed the moral high ground in her mind, as if Boyd's fragility kept her from the exciting sex life she wanted.

This was exactly the kind of self-aggrandizing maneuvering and blaming Cindy watched her parents do repeatedly. Cindy almost threw up in my office when she realized she was doing the same thing. It was a short step from there to realizing her Internet escapades replayed more of the same dynamics. Thereafter, Cindy stopped sneaking onto the Internet or exchanging provocative e-mail. It was one way she could stop acting as if she was living in the house she grew up in.

Looking at how she usually had sex with Boyd, Cindy saw herself dishing out the same kind of torment her parents had. She knew the heartache of trying to deal with someone you love, who simply won't confront himself and won't allow you to confront him either. Cindy started treating Boyd with more respect, and she became more sexually generous.

Being kind to Boyd brought forth *clean* pain about Cindy's own experiences growing up.[2] Cindy changed her life and her fantasies, not by feeling guilty but by behaving in ways incongruent with her past. As Cindy faced her marriage and digested the issues of her life, her sexual fantasies changed in deeply meaningful ways.

Resolving Disturbing Fantasies

If you are troubled by disturbing fantasies, use a two-pronged approach to resolve them. One part involves dealing straight in your relationship, and the other part works directly with your fantasies themselves. Don't think of your relationship and your fantasies as two separate problems. Think of them as one and the same: *They both involve relationships.* Being honest and fair with your partner is crucial to resolving disturbing trigger fantasies.

Think of this as resolving the past in the present: making a new response to your current relationship situation is how you resolve family-of-origin issues in real time. These issues are playing out in your fantasies. The links are sometimes hard to see, but they are there nonetheless.

Talk to the People in Your Head

In working directly with your fantasies, going further into them in specific ways can provide a new way out. You need to hold on to yourself and *talk to the people in your fantasies.*

Like many clients, you may be amazed that you can deliberately talk to the people in your head. You will learn profound truths about yourself and your life once you let the people in your fantasies talk to you. You may be intrigued, and perhaps a little frightened, by the thought that you can talk to the people you have sex with in your mind. The people in your fantasies will almost always respond—watch how you respond to them and they to you.

However, don't think you can predict what he, she, they, or it will say. Don't presume you're supposed to name them, although in some cases you are. You'll find many of them have their own names, and they expect you to relate to them in specific ways.

This shocking discovery often triggers a transformation. My clients find the people in their fantasies frequently become resources rather than tormentors. Disturbing fantasies become a means for self-exploration rather than self-destruction. Even if you like your fantasies just fine, developing a relationship with the people in your head can optimize a lot more than just your sex.

Since this is not something many people have experience with, here are some guidelines to help you. I help clients debrief their experiences so they get the most for their efforts. Here are ten questions you can ask yourself. If you want to understand how your sexuality is wired into your life and your relationships, the answers to these questions will help you. If the sexual world inside your head is troublesome, they offer a path to peace.

1. What do the people in your fantasies have to say?

2. What is each person like?

3. How would you describe the nature of your relationship with them?

4. What do they know about you?

5. What do they think of you?

6. How do they relate to you?

7. What do they think of themselves?

8. As they talk, what do you notice about them?

9. How do you act with them?

10. How is all this personally relevant to you?

My clients are sometimes surprisingly shy and bashful about talking to the people they screw in their minds. It helps if you start by introducing yourself, and approach this as if what you're imagining is real. Invite his, or her, or their help and watch and listen for what he, she, or they have to say. Let what happens evolve and take its own shape.

Look at the actual content of your fantasies to see what things really mean. When Cindy stopped apologizing for her fantasies long enough for us to really consider them, we found they had another side. In some ways, the men in her head were considerate and surprisingly kind. Cindy didn't have group sex with them. Each man took his turn taking Cindy into her room where she had sex with him in private.

In her fantasies Cindy enjoyed having sex, and the men didn't think less of her for it. In fact, she shared a camaraderie with each man, as two people finally at peace with themselves and each other. There were no more boundaries to cross. The men knew Cindy's secret: She liked sex. They knew her most lascivious and wicked thoughts. She opened herself completely and gave herself to them. With her deepest secrets revealed, she had a profound connection with the men in her head, with no fear of rejection. Cindy's fantasies were about a stable, profoundly intimate *relationship*.

During masturbation, Cindy produced the kind of relationship and sexual ambience she wanted. It's a lot easier to get your mind and body synchronized when you're having sex by yourself. When your thoughts, feelings, and physical stimulation get out of sync, it's harder to have orgasms. It takes some practice to keep your mind and body synchronized, and keep them synchronized with what's happening with your partner.

Going "numb" is a good example of your mind and body getting out of sync. Some men find their penises intermittently "go numb" during sex, much the way Cindy's clitoris did. When your mind and body are out of sync, more friction doesn't produce orgasms. The biggest part of getting your sensations and mind back in sync involves settling yourself down, not sensate focus.[3] Instead of trying to "let go," you probably need to hold on to yourself better.

Voluntary Control and Self-Mastery

The lack of voluntary control of her orgasms really got to Cindy. It epitomized her sense of deprivation and not being good enough. She kept wondering, "Am I holding back? Am I withholding my orgasm from myself? Why am I having difficulty letting go?" The answer she feared frequently came to her mind: "Because there's something wrong with me!"

This wasn't the best in Cindy asking questions. This was her way of dismantling herself. Constructive self-confrontation makes you stand up and go forward, rather than immobilizing you. The doubt, anxiety, insecurity, and petty mental torture Cindy experienced was just like what she grew up with.

Realizing she took herself apart in the same way people in her family dismantled each other was a big thing for Cindy. It helped her stop pushing herself to have an orgasm. She did this as part of her new relationship with herself, and she started taking better care of herself too. Boyd noticed changes in her manner and appearance and got frightened that this meant she was having an affair. He started badgering Cindy and dredging up her prior e-mail escapades.

At first Cindy felt betrayed by Boyd's accusations. But as she settled herself down, she saw Boyd was at the end of his rope, frightened, hope-less, and drowning in his own anxiety. She felt the urge to say something cutting, but she didn't do it. Rather than give in to her own feelings of frustration, deprivation, and being unappreciated, Cindy responded with generosity from the best in her. She went to Boyd and offered him a kind word. Cindy watched herself stop the pattern she grew up with and make a new response. She was kind to Boyd when he was vulnera-ble instead of using the opportunity to strike.

Stop Plodding—It's Time to Dance!

This had a tremendous impact on Boyd. He'd had his own stunning insight when Cindy didn't skewer him. Boyd grew up in a home where the emotional warfare was more open and violent. When Cindy didn't nail him, he saw the difference between his wife and the people he grew up with. He also saw himself once again frantically trying to hold his world together while it seemed to be falling apart.

Boyd pulled himself together and acknowledged Cindy had done nothing wrong. He embarked on a series of self-confrontations as seri-ous and productive as Cindy's. He also became less afraid of conflict and more direct with her. Previously, he had been just right for Cindy's fears, but a little "dickless" for her sexual tastes. Now he was starting to be more "phallic" in ways that Cindy found sexy and appealing.

Cindy and Boyd started dialing in the stimulation Cindy needed. They dialed in Boyd's stimulation too, much to his pleasure and amazement. They established a more stable, collaborative alliance both in and out of bed. Cindy started having orgasms more easily with Boyd. And the men in her fantasies became friendlier.

When Cindy first noticed subtle changes, they took her by surprise because she wasn't anticipating it. Bothersome aspects of her sexual fan-tasies lessened as she acted with compassion and integrity. The men no longer taunted her about needing them, and they no longer wanted to control her.

The secret all-powerful men's club became a group of men whose pur-pose was to teach women to enjoy their sexuality. The fantasy remained, but Cindy's use of it was less compulsive. She danced for her men when she wanted to. Now she had a choice. Cindy was developing more vol-untary control of her life.

There was more synchrony between Cindy's thoughts and feelings during sex, and her clitoris stopped going dead. She and Boyd started getting their thoughts and behaviors synchronized in ways they had never dared: they started constructing fantasies together.

One time, Cindy asked Boyd if he'd like to see her dance and masturbate. He said he'd be delighted, and Cindy danced for Boyd. In the past he would have been threatened by how she moved and thought about her with other men. However, after all they had been through together, Boyd was clear Cindy danced for him—and herself.

Boyd knew Cindy was showing him a side of herself he'd never seen before, the part that had taken her to the Internet. Boyd was relieved and honored. Cindy brought herself to orgasm while she talked to Boyd and looked him in the eye.

Boyd was astonished! He had never seen anything like this in his life, and the power of Cindy's eroticism amazed him. He reached down and started stroking his penis. Cindy thought Boyd was going to do what she had done. But when his penis was erect, Boyd walked over and brought her to their bed. Boyd took Cindy, and she gave herself to him. And, finally, they knew peace.

Turning Rapid Orgasms into Slow, Delicious Torture

The notion of holding on to yourself takes on very different connotations when you think about premature orgasms. Self-mastery and self-control are no less important than with delayed orgasms. Lack of voluntary control is what men and their partners find most difficult about this problem. Telling a man with chronic rapid orgasm that he can develop indefinite voluntary control is like waving your hands over his head and telling him he can fly. On the other hand, it's a lot easier to help men develop voluntary control of orgasms than it is to transform people's fantasies.

This should come as good news to the estimated 30 to 75 percent of men who have premature orgasms. Back in 1950, Alfred Kinsey's studies indicated that 75 percent of men ejaculated within 2 minutes of starting intercourse. Resolving men's most common sexual problem also provides opportunities for men to resolve some of their greatest struggles with mastery and control.

The idea of self-mastery really appealed to Jack, because he kept having his orgasm before either he or his wife, Brenda, was ready. Imagine what it is like to have no control over what happens to you whenever you have sex. This killed his sense of adequacy, which hinged on being able to do whatever needed to be done. It didn't help that Jack's rapid orgasms affected Brenda. She had difficulty reaching orgasm during intercourse, and she needed all the time she could get.

To Jack, normal loss of erection after ejaculation, and the subsequent refractory period (during which he couldn't get another one), was like adding insult to injury. Brenda was more than willing to continue having sex, but he preferred to sit out the time and she didn't push it. Brenda figured this was embarrassing and frustrating for Jack. In truth, she had no idea how bad this was for him, or what sex was like just before he climaxed.

Like Cindy, Jack's physical sensations and thoughts and feelings were out of sync. Jack tried to ignore the feelings in his loins, satisfy Brenda, ignore her sexual energy, thrust the way she wanted, not get nervous, fight his negative anticipations, ignore his cues of orgasmic inevitability, and more. There was a cacophony of noise and anxiety going on inside him. He was only half aware of what he was feeling, and hardly in the moment with Brenda.

Jack's world shrank to a little mental island where time raced and stood still simultaneously. He was so isolated and anxious during sex, he actually believed he lasted 10 minutes. It took Brenda a while to tell Jack she actually timed him to find out. It was closer to a minute, and maybe two at best.

Peace and Better Sex

When couples first hear me talk about better sex than they've ever had, they often imagine wild erotic fantasies and incredibly passionate encounters. They are often surprised and sobered to realize I'm referring to a sense of peace with the person you love.

Jack and Brenda struggled with his rapid orgasms through forty years of marriage. He was at the top of his profession, and on the surface he had everything. But Jack had never once relaxed in his wife's arms.

After a while, not relaxing in bed might have been good judgment. When they first came to see me, Brenda seethed with anger. It took her twenty years to ask Jack to get help, and he refused to get help for twenty years after that. Brenda fumed that Jack had not seen her pain and frustration, and she railed that he didn't care. Jack said his rapid orgasms really hadn't bothered him that much, and he apologized for being so insensitive.

Actually, Jack was saying it backward. In truth Jack was (and had been) so acutely sensitive about his problem, and so aware of Brenda's disappointment and frustration, that he couldn't bring himself to speak to her about it. What Brenda thought was Jack's insensitivity was actually his knowledge and avoidance of their situation.[4]

With a straight face, Jack said he thought he had a better deal than Brenda. At least he got to have an orgasm and she didn't. Jack actually believed he was one-up on Brenda, which was partly why he felt so guilty. At that moment, he had absolutely no thought in mind of how terrible the last forty years had been for him.

I turned to Brenda and asked her to imagine what it must be like to come to bed twice a week for over four decades, anxious and afraid of what you know is about to happen. You are proud and successful in other aspects of your life, but humiliated and ashamed in front of the one you love—so ashamed, in fact, you can't talk to her about it, and you can't bring yourself to go for help.

I turned to Jack and said, "This is your experience, isn't it, sir?"

Jack didn't know quite how to respond at first. But he rose to the occasion and acknowledged the accuracy of this depiction. As he spoke, a softer and less brittle man emerged. It was almost startling to see his appearance change in the session. Rather than being angry, Brenda found herself deeply moved.

That night Jack settled himself down, calmed his mind, and made contact with Brenda during sex. He paid attention and opened to her touch—and lasted longer. Waves of relief, grief, loss, and hope washed over Jack and Brenda. That night they began to explore the peace they had never experienced in all their sexual encounters.

Do you have any idea what it is like to confront yourself in the afternoon, and have some control over your orgasm for the first time in your life later that night? It's no assurance you won't have your problem again tomorrow, but you start to have hope for the first time in forty years that there is rhyme and reason to sex.

Jack's face relaxed, his eyes smiled softly, and Brenda's did too. To the degree you never get rid of your reflected sense of self, that's the kind of reflection you want to see. Many couples who have had sex for decades have yet to experience this. That's true for more people than you'd believe.

Hypersensitivity Theory
Men who have premature orgasms speak of "not being able to take too much of the good stuff." Some say sex feels "too good." Others say their genitals are too sensitive. Without realizing it, all three descriptions express a belief of being cursed with a low threshold for orgasm. While people do differ in response thresholds, it's not that simple.

One research study found no significant difference in penile sensitivity between men with rapid orgasm and those who lasted longer.[5] Moreover, some men with *diminished* sensitivity had rapid orgasms too. In other words, what drives premature orgasm is strong enough to "pop" guys who have neurological or hormonal impairments.

The key to resolving premature orgasm involves understanding what constitutes your total level of stimulation. Speed of orgasm can vary with circumstance, partner, relationship, sexual behavior, and time since your last sexual encounter. Latency depends greatly on the form of stimulation. Rapid orgasm (like delayed orgasm) is often specific to intercourse. Men with rapid orgasms usually last longer when receiving manual or oral stimulation. Likewise, they ignore the fact that they have much better staying power during masturbation.

Many a man mistakenly believes he reaches orgasm quickest during intercourse because vaginas provide the best sexual stimulation. This is how he rationalizes lasting longer during masturbation or oral sex.

It's interesting to watch men's reactions when I point out that orgasms from masturbation and oral sex are usually physiologically more intense than from intercourse. In other words, they have *better* control receiving more intense forms of stimulation and *less* control for the least intense one. At first glance this makes no sense . . . until you add anxiety into the picture.

Commonsense Solutions Don't Help
I want to show you a counterintuitive solution for premature orgasm, one that offers both short-term and long-term benefits. Resolving rapid

orgasms involves reducing the speed with which you reach your orgasm threshold. It's common sense to think the best way to do this is to reduce your sexual stimulation. Men with rapid orgasm try to reduce their stimulation one way or another, to keep from getting "too aroused."

Once men latch on to the hypersensitivity theory, their misguided stimulation-reduction strategies make perfect sense. These include reducing physical stimulation (e.g., refusing to receive during foreplay), reducing sensitivity either topically (e.g., multiple condoms, anesthetic creams, cocaine) or centrally (e.g., alcohol), or reducing eroticism and intimacy (e.g., biting your lip, ignoring your partner, or using distracting thoughts). All share a common attempt to reduce arousal.

There are three basic problems with these approaches.

- *They often don't delay your orgasm.* Pleasurable sensations and emotions are such small contributors to your total stimulation (compared to anxiety) that this has negligible impact on how fast you reach your threshold.

- *Sex won't be as satisfying for you or your partner.* It's not fun to make love with a guy who's tuned you out and suddenly becomes immobile in the middle of everything.

- *This can create erection problems later in life.* You can get so good at tuning out that eventually you can't reach your (rising) threshold. You can easily mistake this for medical problems.

A Broad-Band Two-Part Solution

So what can you do that might help and won't hurt? Start by recognizing that the basic cause of rapid orgasm is *anxiety*—the same anxiety that causes delayed orgasms in some men and many women. You can tell anxiety constitutes the vast majority of your total stimulation simply by the way you probably have sex. For instance, Brenda wasn't allowed to touch Jack's penis during foreplay because Jack was "saving himself" for intercourse. Several thrusts later—or sometimes during insertion—they were done. Jack's total stimulation basically consisted of the physical and emotional wallops of his anxiety.

In some ways, Jack didn't have the vaguest idea what Brenda's vagina felt like around his penis. He spent four decades trying not to feel it. He knew it felt "warm." But he never let himself feel Brenda's wetness or her moist heat. Jack had not the foggiest notion of how inviting, comforting, and nurturing Brenda's vagina could be.

He had an idea a vagina could be hungry and aggressive, and that scared him about being able to keep up. Jack also had difficulty with intercourse because he felt it was his time to perform. He was so afraid of his own performance anxiety, he didn't let himself realize how anxious he was.

Short-Range Solutions

To slow premature orgasms there are some mechanical techniques you can do. One is a stimulation-lowering method known as "stop-start." Another one, called the "squeeze technique," directly inhibits the orgasm reflex.[6] Some men find tightening their buttocks or performing Kegel exercises helpful. I've previously mentioned that testicles normally move upward toward the base of a man's penis as he approaches orgasm. Some men report having their partner tug down gently on their scrotum keeps them going longer.

Generally, I don't suggest using any of these methods, because they are less adaptive to long-term sexual function and satisfaction. They break the rhythm and mood of intimate sex, focus your interaction on whether or not you are going to climax, and perpetuate your anxiety about it happening. Instead, consider two other short-term solutions.

Reduce Your Anxiety

Think of your total level of stimulation as composed of anxiety and sex. If you decrease your anxiety, you can take a whole lot more sexual stimulation and still keep your total stimulation below your threshold. Even if you reach orgasm quickly, you'll enjoy it a whole lot more. That's because more of your total stimulation is actually *sexual* stimulation. Use what you've learned thus far about self-soothing to help you.

Off-Label Use of SSRI Antidepressants

The third short-term solution involves using prescription medications to raise your orgasm threshold. This is a new and promising treatment worth considering.

As mentioned earlier, antidepressants (especially the SSRI variety) are notorious for inhibiting orgasm in men and women. Some therapists and physicians are exploiting this side effect to advantage with men who reach orgasm too readily. Paxil and Anafranil have been used to increase men's latency. There's some research to back up this approach.

In several small studies, Anafranil increased men's orgasm latency to about 7 minutes (a 500 percent increase). Three wives reached orgasm during intercourse over the course of one study. When the study concluded, so did the men's increased ejaculatory control.[7] Another study showed similar results in some men with rapid orgasm, while others showed no benefit.[8] Anafranil and Paxil increase some men's control of their orgasms, but they can worsen erection problems too. These drugs are not appropriate for men with both premature orgasms and erection difficulties.

Using drug side effects this way is called off-label usage. That means a drug that received FDA approval for one heath problem is used to treat a different one. Dosage for orgasm control doesn't differ from normal dosage for approved reasons. Some physicians don't think this is wise to begin with. Others, particularly those trained in sex therapy, report good results.

Anecdotal reports suggest some men find Viagra slows their orgasms. Viagra taken for erection problems may change some men's sexual confidence enough to reduce their anxieties and slow them down. However, Viagra is generally ineffective in treating premature orgasm because it does not increase orgasm latency per se.

If you opt for SSRI-antidepressant treatment for premature orgasm, I suggest several things.

1. *Do it under your physician's supervision.* Don't play pharmacist.

2. *Use this chance to deal with your anxiety.* Settle down and stop performing rather than putting on the performance of your life. Lie back, relax, and take your time.

3. *Use the opportunity to create positive physical and emotional connection with your partner.* Rebuild your sexual relationship. Your partner will enjoy having less anxiety during sex too.[9]

A Long-Range Solution

Whether you opt for drugs or not, you can develop more voluntary control of your orgasms by raising your orgasm threshold. You accomplish this by repeatedly challenging your body with the densest, most intense, and most delicious stimulation of your life, delivered from the best (and sexiest) in your partner. This is why the long-term solution of raising your orgasm threshold is counterintuitive, given how you may try to delay rapid orgasms.

The key is developing more tolerance for *good* sex. This requires a resilient collaborative alliance with your partner. You need to stop damping things down, and your partner and you need to heat things up. Your part in this collaboration involves receiving this from the best in you (and reciprocating in kind).

Many mind-body processes, once thought to be beyond your conscious control, can be modified with biofeedback training (like controlling your brain waves and arteries). Your sexual response thresholds can also be conditioned. This process requires several months of intense sexual stimulation. That's why it works well to pair it with short-term strategies, like settling down and reducing your anxiety. If you try this, here are important things to keep in mind.

1. *Use lubricant during masturbation or manual stimulation from your partner.* You need to get good at stimulating yourself, if you aren't already. You may or may not have equally good control when your partner provides the manual stimulation. Help your partner get so good that you have the impulse to pull back from it. Then, don't pull back. That's collaboration. (Then do the same thing with oral stimulation.)

2. *Pay attention to your sense of orgasmic inevitability.* You need to get better at recognizing your cues of orgasmic inevitability, as do people with delayed orgasms. Just as anxiety prevents them from recognizing these sensations, it does the same to you. Your inner world just operates differently. When they feel orgasm is inevitable, they relax. You get nervous. Other people would give anything to feel that sensation. In your case, it's the last thing you want. Settle down and pay attention to what's going on inside you. You have to relax as your sense of orgasm approaches,

instead of tensing up. Keep your general anxiety arousal from spiking as it normally does, and you'll have better control.

3. *Don't hold back*. When receiving stimulation from your partner or yourself, don't attempt to control your orgasm. Open and lean into it. I know this is counterintuitive and contrary to your normal approach. However, you need to develop tolerance for *extremely good* stimulation, and you can't do that if you pull back or close down. This often requires reshaping your sexual repertoire and the emotional ambience of your bedroom. This, in turn, kicks the growth cycle in your marriage into gear.

4. *Go through your crucible*. Not holding back means you may reach orgasm more quickly in the short run, but with several important shifts. It now occurs because you are developing an ability that will help both you and your partner. The goal is to break the link in your mind between reaching orgasm and being inadequate. You have to believe in yourself, and open to your partner's touch.

I presume by now you can intuit the kind of integrity challenge this involves for men with chronic premature orgasm. By going through this, a man could feel stretched and become a better person. Getting your partner to knock your socks off sexually, and then not pulling back, applies the general approach you've learned throughout *Resurrecting Sex*. It involves holding on to yourself to do something that makes perfect sense, and would be good for you to do, but which can also shake your sense of self down to your core.[10]

This solution takes two of you. As with arousal problems and difficulties reaching orgasm, your and your partner's mental and emotional processes play a huge role in resolving premature orgasm. Effective treatment involves reducing *both* partners' anxieties. Many men are emotionally fused to partners who have as much difficulty self-soothing as the men do. Jack and Brenda were a case in point.

For years, Brenda blew her anxiety into Jack, and her anxiety and defensiveness kept her from being aware this was happening. She claimed the high ground in discussions about their relationship, and she was much chagrined to realize that she was a participant, not just a long-suffering spouse. In therapy the best in her came forward quickly, in part because she recognized the importance of how Jack was growing. She realized her anxiety was partly the reason why Jack couldn't take as much manual stimulation from her as he could when he masturbated. It was the same anxiety that sometimes made Jack feel a need to get away from her.

Brenda's self-confrontation lowered her anxiety and made her easier to be around. The stimulation kept getting better and Jack started lasting longer. Brenda thought of this as making a home for him and taking him in. She did this first with her hand and then with her mouth. Jack felt more and lasted longer than he had before. Then they increased the intensity and duration. Repeated intense stimulation, paired with deep connection with Brenda, raised Jack's threshold for orgasms.[11]

Jack was eager to transfer the gains they'd made to longer and more robust intercourse.[12] They did it by having Brenda use her vagina the same way she'd learned to use her hand and mouth. Jack stopped looking at intercourse as filling Brenda's vagina. He let Brenda take him home, within the core of her body. This same process also made it easier for Brenda to reach orgasms during intercourse. Jack's longer latency, and her own reduced anxiety, really helped. She could feel Jack was less anxious when they had sex.

Jack watched Brenda go through the same metamorphosis she'd observed in him. Through her determination not to be the weak link in the process, she became softer. As her face relaxed, she looked younger and more vivacious and inviting. By holding on to themselves through both terrible and incredible sex, Jack and Brenda came to embody the saying, "Life gives us partners who are diamonds in the rough, and when we finally lose our own sharp edges by grinding ourselves against them, we become gems."

Getting Your Mind and Pelvis in Sync Is a Lovely Way to Learn

The intricacies of holding on to yourself offer important lessons about life. Slowing your orgasm, or hastening it if you want, can help you learn what relationships have to teach. The lesson always seems to be the same: Marriage usually requires the Zen task of opening yourself to the very thing you dread. And holding on to yourself is crucial if you want peace, whether lying in your partner's arms, or in the world inside your head.

14

What Will It Take to Change Things?

For until it is generally possible to acquire erotic personality and to master the art of loving, the development of the individual man or woman is marred, the requirement of human happiness and harmony remains impossible.

—Havelock Ellis, *Impressions and Comments* (1924)

By now you probably have a good idea about what you can do to solve your problems. If you see ways to move forward that your partner will support, the two of you could be in for a lovely time. But what if you still have hesitancies about putting your ideas into action? After all, I haven't exactly encouraged you to anticipate an immediate cheer from your partner. And whether your partner applauds or not, count on an integrity struggle or two as you implement your plan.

However, if you're still afraid that changing your relationship (and your identity) will make you or your partner too anxious for sex, you are stuck. If you want to get unstuck, consider this. Your partner may, indeed, pressure you to return to former positions of accommodation, but that doesn't mean you two couldn't end up aroused by your process. What you may fear will be Armageddon might in fact ignite passion.

My goals for our last chapter go beyond encouraging you to move forward. I want you to see how resurrecting sex is part of something much larger, more important, and more worthy of respect than we usually appreciate. Sex, anxiety, and your ability to hold on to yourself are intricately intertwined no matter where you look, from basic sexual responses to ways family life shapes your eroticism. The arrangement has a wisdom, beauty, simplicity, and power far beyond anything humankind has yet devised, and I want to show you how holding on to yourself is your participation in that process. In doing so, I hope to reduce your fear of anxiety and leave you hopeful about your future.

Anxiety and the Spirit of Adventure[1]

Stirring up your relationship, and making your partner and yourself uncomfortable, are not to be taken lightly. However, neither one is antithetical to hot sex. We've seen how avoiding the natural growth processes in your relationship kills passion and desire. Going forward, with all attendant anxieties, does the opposite. This doesn't stem from the perverseness of human nature; it has to do with the biology of anxiety and sexual arousal.

Anxiety Can Be a Turn-On

Anxiety can *facilitate* sexual arousal. Lots of people like sex with a little anxiety mixed in. They talk about feeling daring or naughty, like they are breaking the rules or getting away with something. From the perspective of anxiety, it makes no difference if it involves particular sexual fantasies, racy lingerie, sex in the backseat of a car, or an affair with your spouse's best friend.

The arousal from anxiety-laced sex is not just between your legs—you feel it in your gut, chest, and face. Have you ever seen people get embarrassed by sex jokes and fan themselves with their hands to "cool" themselves? This is the kind of reaction I'm pointing to: sexual arousal, triggered by general physical arousal, which results from anxiety. The absence of low-level anxiety arousal makes sex seem routine and makes long-term partners bored and boring. A little adrenaline seems to pick things up.

Examples of Anxiety Arousal

To varying degrees, people's patterns revolve around this anxiety to general arousal to sexual arousal link (whether they realize it or not). For example, think about couples who have intense sex after reuniting when one partner might have been killed or injured—or couples who have intense sex when their gridlock reaches critical mass and divorce seems imminent. You might think discovering your partner is having an affair would be a turn-off. However, some people are amazed to find they are rageful, rueful, and sexually aroused.

There are many other versions. Couples who like to have sex after a fight. Couples who get turned on by verbal banter, taunting, and name-calling. These folks obviously like to get revved up before sex, but other examples aren't so dark. "The thrill of meeting someone new" is a common example of low-level anxiety triggering general arousal that creates sexual arousal.

Another beautiful example is *begrudging respect,* a far more powerful aphrodisiac than unconditional positive regard. Begrudging respect develops when your partner takes a legitimate stand that creates problems for you. He or she soothes himself or herself and remains resolute, without belligerence or overreaction. Although you may be perturbed and discomforted, sometimes you can hold on to yourself enough to look beyond your immediate feelings, and see your partner as a separate person with his or her own rights. Instead of getting angry or competitive, you find your partner surprisingly attractive and sexually interesting.[2]

Anxiety and Sex in the Laboratory[3]

There are physiological reasons why couples have passionate marriages amid the challenges of personal development that come to us through sex (sexual crucibles). Laboratory research indicates that sometimes anxiety facilitates sexual arousal. It's hard for your body to distinguish general physiological arousal from sexual arousal. For instance, research has shown that women have increased vaginal response to viewing sexually explicit movies if they first watch frightening films,[4] or do vigorous exercise,[5] or take a drug that speeds up their nervous systems.[6]

The relationship of general physical and mental arousal to sexual arousal and orgasm is not as simple as was once thought. For example, you are more likely to feel attracted to people you meet simply because your nervous system activity is heightened. Safety and security are important in sexual relationships, and so, it seems, are insecurity, danger, and anxiety.

What's most interesting about this research is that the sexually stimulating effects of general arousal held true for women with no sexual dysfunctions or those with low desire, *but not for women who had difficulty reaching orgasm.* Women who had difficulty getting highly aroused responded differently to becoming anxious than did those who didn't have sexual dysfunctions.

Another study demonstrated this same thing by manipulating anxiety and performance expectations for men who had sexual dysfunctions and other men who didn't.[7] *Anxiety decreased arousal and diminished erections in dysfunctional men. The same anxiety facilitated arousal and performance in men who didn't have erection problems.*

In other words, the issue wasn't anxiety per se; it was how people responded to it. Those who were presumably better at regulating their anxiety (no sexual dysfunctions) did better when confronted with more anxiety. Those who had difficulty regulating their anxiety (had sexual dysfunctions) did worse when their anxiety increased. When you have a solid hold on yourself, anxiety helps you focus on what's important. When you are brittle or flimsy, you become disorganized and ineffective as your anxiety mounts.

This holds true in many aspects of life. When you are sure of yourself, low to moderate anxiety makes you pay attention, hone in on what's before you, and take action. When you're unsure of yourself, the same level of anxiety hits you like a tidal wave, knocks you over, and leaves you floundering.

So how should you apply this to your situation? You could use this research to argue for maintaining the status quo in your relationship. After all, if anxiety reduces sexual function in people with sexual dysfunctions, what's the point of doing things that make you or your partner nervous? However, I suggest a different interpretation that can help your sexual relationship and your whole life.

When everything seems to be going downhill, you invariably have to make a different response to your anxiety to get yourself and your situation to function differently. This always involves holding on to yourself. You need to respond to anxiety the same way the functional people did: calm yourself down, pay attention to what's happening in the moment, and adapt and respond to changing circumstances. We've referred to this as responding from the best in you instead of running scared.

A crucial step in your development occurs when you stop seeing anxiety as scary or frightening. In a sense, this happens every time you solve a problem that terrifies you, engendering maturity and growth in the process. Growth starts *while* you are still nervous. It occurs when you take a new stance toward your anxiety. It makes no difference whether it's about sex or your life in general, and that's the point. You and your partner are going through the fabric of life, and the rules don't change when you're in bed.

Where Does Sexual Abuse Fit In?

But what if you or your partner has been sexually or emotionally abused? Are you left damaged or fragile from your experiences in ways that make you a special case? Does what I've described throughout still apply to you? What does compassion look like in your situation?

I've worked with a great many people who have been sexually or emotionally abused because, unfortunately, these terrible experiences are widespread. I've come to appreciate the huge impact abuse has on people, and I've developed more compassion and respect for what it takes to work it through. Many of my clients spent years in prior treatment trying to resolve their untoward experiences without success, making the assumption that this reflected how deeply they had been damaged.

In reality, my clients were blocked by inaccurate stereotypes about the impacts of sexual and emotional abuse. Also, much of their prior treatments emphasized (and glorified) trauma rather than resilience, which not only subtly promoted a "damaged goods" (pathological) view of sexual abuse, but also twisted their relationships by enforcing unique rules for how anxiety should be handled, especially concerning sex.

Working with my clients, I began to understand how the subtle impacts of sexual and emotional abuse play out in marriages and families. From this sprang a form of therapy that helped them stop seeing themselves as abuse "victims" or "survivors" and get on with their lives. An accurate picture of their erotic style allowed many clients to finally make peace with their sexuality, their partner, and their past.

Likewise, they were better able to address anxious sexual situations when they stopped looking at everything through the lens of their abuse and saw these as a normal part of *all* relationships (whether or not abuse occurred). They stopped seeing themselves as uniquely damaged, and allowed their (sexual) relationships to operate more effectively. Let me share with you some of the realizations that helped my clients.

People who have been abused often deal with sex and anxiety in entirely different ways than commonly recognized. Sexually exploited children undergo an early erotic awakening. They frequently *like* sex, especially the sexual jolt they get when their anxiety kicks in. That jolt is the result of anxiety arousal triggering sexual arousal. Their earliest sexual experiences are characterized by anxiety leading to general arousal and then sexual arousal. They frequently develop arousal patterns in which anxiety and sexual fantasies involving eroticism, power, secrecy, and humiliation play key roles.

When these folks marry, their behavior seems to make no sense. One might assume sexual abuse destroys people's sexuality by making them dislike sex. Indeed, sex in their marriages is often terrible, and many are celibate. Frequently, however, they are having extramarital affairs.

In other words, many people who've been abused are *hot*, not cold or asexual; they just hide their erotic interests in their marriages. They also have low desire for the tepid sex they create by misrepresenting their sexuality, by presenting themselves as asexual when, in fact, they are not. The results are all sorts of weird interactions in many bedrooms. (Cindy and Boyd, whom you met last chapter, were prime examples. Cindy snuck onto porn sites and had Internet affairs, while offering Boyd cadaver-like sex and struggling with troublesome orgasm trigger fantasies.)

This makes sense once you realize that children living in chaotic, emotionally volatile, or chronically anxious households often fare the same. This dominant anxiety–general arousal–sexual arousal pattern can develop even when emotional abuse does not involve sexual contact or innuendo.

Do You Like Anxiety-Laced Sex?

People who grow up with repeated emotional or physical abuse are prone to developing erotic templates in which anxiety and sexual arousal are intertwined. Going through childhood and adolescence in an emotional shooting gallery twists your erotic map and your anxiety arousal response together like a pretzel. In extreme instances this gives rise to sadistic rapists, stalkers, and twisted killers like Jeffrey Dahmer.[8]

Children from emotionally and physically abusive homes develop distortions in their anxiety arousal–sexual arousal link, more from daily household interactions than from specific instances of fondling or intercourse. In this way, parents who can't hold on to themselves *in general* affect the next generation and the marriages they enter into.

How does this ever stop? The approach you've learned in *Resurrecting Sex* applies to couples in which one or both partners have been physically, emotionally, or sexually abused. It is not just for "good marriages" or "people in good emotional shape." It's for real people with real problems and real difficulties dealing with them.

If your partner has been sexually abused, be compassionate and considerate. Don't go overboard trying to make things safe and secure. You want your situation relaxed enough to make contact with your partner, but don't be naïve or saintly—neither one makes you trustworthy or sexually interesting.

Differentiation: The Miracle of Self-Transformation

All too often, we ignore serious problems like abuse and emotional trauma, or we get hysterical about it and make it larger than life. Whether or not you have been abused, it helps to realize that your relationship is largely *not* determined by negative past experiences. Past experiences greatly color the way you look at things, but you're confronting forces far more powerful. Your past won't loom so prominently when you understand and accept that sexual anxieties are a normal part of sexual development, and that emotional gridlock and pressure-filled two-choice dilemmas (especially about sex) are inherent to intimate relationships.

On the other hand, physical and emotional abuse points once again to what we've seen repeatedly. The more people depend on each other to regulate their anxiety and identity, the darker their relationships. Likewise, the more people hold on to themselves, the more uplifting the example. This is called *differentiation*.

Differentiation controls how we act when we are with others, and how we function when we are alone. Whether we are driven by the best or the worst in ourselves hinges on our ability to confront ourselves, regulate our anxieties, not overreact, and tolerate discomfort for growth. Everything I've said from the outset of *Resurrecting Sex* has been about differentiation. Until now, I've referred to it as holding on to yourself.

Differentiation is the heart and soul of marriage, family life, and becoming a human being. Appreciating the beauty and elegance of how differentiation plays out in people's lives has occasionally brought me to tears. It has also brought more tears and struggles in my own life than I care to remember. In our closing pages, I want to share with you my love and appreciation of differentiation, as a way of integrating everything we've discussed in *Resurrecting Sex* and placing it in larger context.

As an individual, your differentiation governs your relationship with yourself, as well as with others. From a household perspective, differentiation governs interactions between family members. For instance, your and your partner's ability to hold on to yourselves controls the balance of comfort and growth cycles in your marriage.[9]

In other words, your willingness to confront, support, soothe, and prod yourself determines whether or not your marriage moves forward and the two of you grow. When you and your partner drive your relationship from your inabilities to regulate your anxieties and insecurities, differentiation within your marriage and your family stalls. This suppresses the differentiation of succeeding generations, who have difficulty regulating their own anxieties and are prone to developing negative anxiety arousal–sexual arousal patterns. These, in turn, create much human misery and drive seemingly irrational and self-destructive sexual behavior.

Differentiation: Creation in Action

I found with my clients that understanding and harnessing differentiation helped them make sense of—and do something about—all this misery. From this work, I evolved the first differentiation-based sexual and marital therapy, which I called the Sexual Crucible® Approach.

Watching so many things fall into place by simply studying sex and relationships has dramatically impacted my spirituality. For me, studying differentiation has fostered an appreciation for the spirituality of everyday life and the elegance of the Grand Design. I believe that any meaningful attempt to resurrect sex will make you question what you hold dear, and often involves a dark night of the soul. Any serious effort to integrate all we've discussed in *Resurrecting Sex,* from basic sexual function and dysfunction to how sexual relationships work, inevitably leads to spiritual matters.

Albert Einstein wrote a lot about science and spirituality. He found that the more he pursued the intricacies of the atom, the more his spiritual side developed. The same thing happened to Carl Jung when he studied our spiritual sense. It happened to me watching people resolve their sexual problems. According to Einstein:

> Everyone who is seriously involved in the pursuit of science becomes convinced that a spirit is manifest in the last of the Universe—a spirit vastly superior to that of man. . . . In this way the pursuit of science leads to a religious feeling of a special sort, which is indeed quite different from the religiosity of someone more naïve.[10]

Einstein said a scientist is possessed by a rapturous amazement about the harmony of natural law, which reveals a superior intelligence to that of humankind.[11] Buddha saw this same thing twenty-five centuries ago, and so has every subsequent spiritually enlightened individual. You can develop this spiritual sense by studying your marriage and your sex life, especially when they're not operating to your liking.

Differentiation is Creation seeking its own fulfillment through your development. Your struggles to regulate your own anxiety, identity, and self-worth while participating in your relationship are your contribution to the process. Your growth *is* human evolution. Differentiation is how our species propels its own evolution by interactions of people everywhere. It is the drive wheel and end product of emotionally committed relationships.

Throughout *Resurrecting Sex* I've tried to convey my awe and respect for how differentiation breathes life into marriages and makes them living entities, miniature systems with rules all their own. This is why the rules of intimate relationships preexist, and your job is to learn and heed them. It's why I said early on: Stop working on your marriage. Realize that your marriage is working on you!

If you aspire to change your relationship (and your life), get this incredible system working for you. To do that, act in accord with how differentiation operates. You're not going to have much impact by simply expressing your feelings. You are dealing with a process far grander than anything you've imagined, that's refined itself for humans over the last 500,000 years with countless billions of couples.

If intimate relationships are part of the Grand Design, wouldn't you think marriage would work in ways that enhance sex rather than kill it? Going through, rather than avoiding, gridlock and anxiety raises your level of differentiation. This is why doing what's necessary *while* you are scared makes you capable of greater love, commitment, passion, and compassion. Intertwining your integrity and sexuality triggers your differentiation, because your integrity and sexuality are the end results and driving forces of human differentiation. It works that simply and elegantly because the "it" is the Great Oneness.

Sometimes Differentiation Falters

All people, marriages, families, societies, and species reach a point at which irrevocable fundamental change (differentiation) occurs. This is called *critical mass*.[12] Your ability to hold on to yourself determines the intensity level at which critical mass occurs for you. The better your ability to hold on to yourself (better differentiated), the less anxiety and pressure it takes to reach critical mass. You, in effect, determine the level of anxiety and pressure it takes to make you pay attention and take action.

Differentiation is also an intergenerational process. You pass on your successes and failures in holding on to yourself to succeeding generations through your interactions with those you love. Your willingness to confront, soothe, and mobilize yourself to do what's necessary is your gift to others. Your marriage and your differentiation are legacies, good and bad, which you bequeath to your grandchildren and great-grandchildren whom you'll never live to see.

In some families, however, the anxiety and pressure level required for critical mass exceed parents' commitments to themselves, their relationship, and their children.[13] They simply refuse to confront themselves, and in so doing, they interfere with their children's differentiation. Their offspring become emotionally blind as well as hypervigilant and suspicious of others.

Anxiety and Adventure: Hold On to the Real You

I've counseled men who have premature orgasm, delayed orgasm, or erection problems, who have no idea how completely anxiety-ridden they are. Some women haven't a clue how anxious they are in bed because they've never experienced anything else. They can't relax because all they know is "red alert." Many people who read about performance anxiety still have no idea how tortured they are during sex.

Some couples tell me they get along quite well, but they want to make sex better. It turns out they live in an undeclared war zone, and they are far more alienated and fused than they realize. They are not misrepresenting themselves to me. The point is, they don't see it.

I'm not referring to people who are insensitive or out of touch with their feelings. Quite the contrary, often they have *loads* of feelings that they can barely contain. Some are psychologically minded, warm, creative, and successful. Others are incredibly brilliant but emotionally dry. Even moderately differentiated people are more out of touch with themselves than they imagine.

Emotional blindness is actually quite common. People go blind when they can't stand seeing their mate or parent perpetually dodge his or her inner self. We usually let ourselves see only as far as those we love can tolerate being seen, and then we blind ourselves to our blindness. The end result is a large number of adults so alienated from themselves that they don't know it.

Is it possible that you could be blind too? You could be the designated "feelings expert" in your relationship, and still be completely unaware of how unaware you are. That's what makes self-confrontation really tough. You have to let yourself see what you cannot see, and you can't see that you can't see it. Differentiation always involves establishing and extending emotional sight.

Meeting Yourself Can Be a Shock

Your task is to see the errors in what you think you already know. Yes, what you can't see yet, and what you don't know, can jeopardize the possibility of turning your relationship around. But what can *really* keep you stuck is what you're already sure of—the givens you accept about yourself, your partner, your relationship, and your past. Most people have a picture of themselves that's distorted enough to keep their anxieties down, and accurate enough to keep their integrity from getting suspicious. You need to look beyond this and figure out how your life story *doesn't* make sense.[14]

As your relationship with yourself (and your partner) grows, you may be in for a shock. Integrity-driven leaps of faith do interesting things to people. They usually run into themselves, having had no idea how out of touch with themselves they were. This often involves realizing you are more frightened, tense, anxious, and insecure than you thought—and more embarrassed, humiliated, intimacy-intolerant, angry, narcissistic, vindictive, self-centered, petty (add your favorite) than you imagined. Although these difficult realizations can trigger uncomfortable feelings of being unlovable, they will enhance your capacity to love. Just hold on to yourself, calm yourself down, and let yourself finally *relax*.

When People Relax They Often Become Sad

You may get nervous ("twitchy") when you finally relax, because it feels like you are dropping your guard. Actually, you're in the process of becoming *less* vulnerable. Nonetheless, in the midst of a growing sense of peace, you may find yourself becoming sad. Examine this sadness carefully and you'll probably find you're not depressed. This is *clean* pain. You have to relax when you experience clean pain if you want the full benefit. (Most of us have the urge to tighten up to protect ourselves, which makes us hurt more.) Clean pain hurts, but it doesn't reduce your ability to function. In fact, it usually does the opposite.

The subsequent rapid "brightening" that people experience after clean pain is remarkable and profound. I customarily photograph couples at the start and finish of our nine-day Passionate Marriage® Couples Retreats. Participants often comment to each other, "You look different!" referring to how people's faces are starting to relax. Everyone looks younger, more vibrant, and more attractive. For many people, clean pain is the doorway to a world where hope exists.

The Future You Want Is Not in Your Past

When you started reading *Resurrecting Sex,* perhaps you anticipated an old-fashioned psychodynamic approach, focusing on your unconscious and early childhood, or your personality disorders and emotional defects. Now you know better. It's not about unconscious anger or your partner reminding you of your mother or father. Instead, it's about attending to what's happening now, focusing on what you need to do and moving forward from your strengths.

I'm optimistic about your future, because you can seize this opportunity to make a real difference in your life! Whether your past contains sexual abuse, religious prohibitions, or resentments over recent disagreements, *you* bring your past into the present. The past recedes only when you stop acting in accordance with it in the present.

You have sexual dysfunctions for real, tangible, immediate reasons. This means it is never too late to turn things around. The present is where the final working through of your past takes place. You differentiate in the present by making new responses that are more appropriate to the here and now, and incongruent with your past. As you resolve your past in the present, your family's legacy is rewritten and human differentiation moves forward. If you take this step with your spouse and make your move from the best in you, your past will not control you.

Marriage Demands Compassion in Ways You Never Expect

We've covered an array of options and strategies for resolving sexual problems, from new medical wonders to old-fashioned consideration for each other. Through it all, I've tried to show you how it all fits together in one elegant system. My hope is that seeing the bigger picture gives you motivation and realistic expectations for what lies ahead. It also helps to recognize how compassion is built into the differentiation processes within marriage: Marriage holds your partner's happiness hostage, and the ransom price is always your own personal growth. One partner's sexual problem always impacts the other. The same holds true for illnesses, inhibitions, insecurities, and immaturities.

Marriage never offers you the simple choice: "Do you want to resolve your sexual problems or not?" The choice always includes: "Do you want to let this fall on your partner or not?" Often our response to both questions is a loud "No!" and that's where compassion comes in.

Compassion requires making room in your relationship for your partner. This involves not stealing your partner's choices by perpetually asking for more time before you buckle down and work things out.

Repeatedly, you will have to choose between stifling your partner's growth and happiness, or growing up yourself. Good sex involves compassion, openness, sharing, and generosity that are not confined to your sexual technique.

Create Hope, Find Peace

In this chapter, and throughout this book, I've tried to show how anxiety is part of the Grand Design. Anxiety weaves through the fabric of life, like a scaffold we climb, becoming more human in the process. Every generation struggles to free itself from anxieties that keep it from living out its highest values. This age-old lifelong process, the source of myths and legends, now confronts you in your bedroom.

So what shape does your relationship need to be in for you to address your sexual problems? If you hold off until your relationship is "better" you may never get the chance. That's especially true if sexual problems are creating havoc in your life.

Don't set lots of preconditions unless you want to stay stuck. Don't demand safety and security if you plan to make headway. Deep and abiding safety and security come *after* you've confronted your limitations. The sense of peace I've described comes from standing knee-deep in fear and insecurity and doing what you think is right.

Hope will get you further than safety and security, because hope is part of human resilience. Hope is what you have *before* change comes about. Hope is believing in yourself *while* you have doubts. Hope comes from understanding how life works and seeing yourself as part of the system. Hope helps you persevere through marriage's trials and tribulations.

The Moral of the Story

In our final moments together, stop and reflect on how far we've come. Think back to when you first read about two frogs in the buttermilk. I promised that by the end of this book, you'd understand how this applied to us all. The frogs went through anxiety and emerged transformed. It's no different for you or me.

The adventure of being human involves, at different times, being mammalian or reptilian. It also involves recognizing we are just like the frogs, thrashing about and stumbling into personal transformation. The trick is to not become a reptilian amphibian while you're floating in the buttermilk.

My Wish, My Hope

I wish you joy and peace and quiet connection with your partner. Peace that is more than the absence of strife. A spiritual peace. Sanctuary from the insanities of everyday life. Stillness filled with hope and potential, soothing and energizing like sunshine. I wish this for my daughter Sarah when she grows up. That is why I wrote this book for her, and for you.

Study Nature as it emerges between you and your partner. Let the system that made us all now make you what you can be. Align yourself with Creation seeking its fulfillment through your development. Hold on to yourself as tightly as you would hold on to your partner. You will become a better lover, a better partner, and a better parent. If you do this, and if our neighbors do this too, our children will grow up in a happier and kinder place to fall in love.

Appendixes

APPENDIX A
Referral Information and Resources

Although the sexual problems and relationship processes described in this book occur in every marriage, you may want or need a therapist to help you effectively harness them. Especially when dealing with sexual problems, you want a therapist who can do a lot more than empathize or teach communication skills. The therapist should be licensed to practice psychotherapy, counseling, or medicine in your state and have specific training in sexual problems. Preferably, he or she should be a *certified* sex therapist, who has met basic standards of preparation. The less you and your partner can hold on to yourselves, the more likely you will need the assistance of a therapist—and the more differentiated the therapist needs to be.

A good therapist can monitor important topics to keep you on track, help you observe your process, and assist in modulating and containing anxiety in your marriage to increase your differentiation. You may have to try several before you find one who can really help. A therapist can't bring you to a higher level of differentiation than he or she has achieved, because when anxiety and pressure in your marriage exceeds his or her differentiation, he or she gets "infected" too, and treatment effectiveness declines. Nothing in therapists' training or licensing requirements ensures that they are more differentiated, or know more about sex and intimacy, or have better marriages, than you.

Ask your friends for therapists they recommend, but ultimately, you'll have to assess their differentiation for yourself. Find someone you respect, but don't pick someone you are totally comfortable with—that's usually someone you're sure won't confront you. Find someone with whom you feel *productively* uncomfortable. A good match is not the same as your therapist "understanding" and "accepting" you the way you want to be seen; it's one in which you self-confront, self-soothe, and mobilize yourself to do what you need to do. On the other hand, therapists can be wrong— working with one is not the same as turning yourself over to him or her.

The Marriage and Family Health Center (MFHC) conducts a four-day fly-in Intensive Therapy Program, giving couples from across the United States and around the world access to treatment by the founder of this book's approach and selected associates. MFHC also conducts programs for couples and the general public. Passionate Marriage® Couples Enrichment Weekends are three-day weekend workshops addressing common but difficult problems in committed relationships, held in major metropolitan cities. Passionate Marriage® Couples Retreats are nine-day programs held in peaceful settings conducive to helping gridlocked couples get "unstuck." Audiotape series with listening guides and other materials are also available from MFHC to help you.

MFHC also conducts training for health-care professionals in the Sexual Crucible and Passionate Marriage approaches and maintains a database of therapists who attend our programs. Upon request, MFHC will inform you of such therapists in your area and the programs they attended. If a therapist presents himself or herself as a student of our approaches, be aware: Workshop participants' advertising guidelines require listing specific details of their training (for example, "a two-day Crucible® Approach Introductory Workshop," or "a six-day Crucible® Approach Sexual Desire Workshop"). Vague statements such as "studied with Dr. Schnarch" or "trained in the Sexual Crucible Approach" are misleading and potential misrepresentation. MFHC does not certify therapists' abilities and cannot be responsible for the actions of a particular clinician.

Several professional organizations are also available to help you. The Australian Association of Sex Educators, Researchers and Therapists (ASSERT) can refer you to a certified sex therapist (who may or may not be familiar with the Crucible or Passionate Marriage approaches). Likewise, Relationships Australia (RA) can refer you to a marital and family therapist whose training and preparation meet established criteria. Ideally, I recommend finding a therapist who has both credentials, although they are relatively rare. For information on sexual health clinics throughout Australia, contact the Australasian College of Sexual Health Physicians (ACSHP), which is devoted to the development of sexual health policy, training, and advocacy in Australia.

Marriage and Family Health Center
2922 Evergreen Parkway, Suite 310
Evergreen, CO 80439
(303) 670-2630
www.passionatemarriage.com

ASSERT
PO Box 224
Moffat Beach Qld 4551
(07) 5437 0357
www.assertau.org
ASSERT has offices around Australia

RA National Office:
15 Napier Close
Deakin ACT 2600
1300 364 277
(02) 6285 4466
RA has offices in every state and territory. For details of your local office, contact the Relationships Australia website:
www.relationships.com.au

ACSHP
Sydney Sexual Centre
Sydney Hospital, Macquarie Street,
Sydney NSW 2000
(02) 9382 7457
email: secretariat@acshp.org.au
website: www.acshp.org.au

APPENDIX B

Medical Conditions and Diseases Creating Sexual Problems

Endocrine	Gastrointestinal	Gynecological	Immunological	Neurological	Urological	Vascular
Acromegaly	Constipation	Dysfunctional bleeding	AIDS/HIV	Alzheimer's disease	Chronic kidney disease	Arterio-sclerosis
Adrenal dysfunction	Diarrhea	Dyspareunia	Arthritis and other bone or joint disorders	Brain lesions	Cystitis (acute, chronic, and postcoital)	Fistula
Diabetes mellitus	Irritable bowel syndrome	Endometriosis	Cancer	Dementia	Epididymitis	Hypertension
Hyperprolacti-nemia	Ulcerative colitis	Genital warts	Chronic fatigue syndrome	Diabetic neuropathy	Peyronie's disease	Ischemia
Hypogonadism		Infertility, pregnancy	Respiratory diseases	Epilepsy	Priapism	Myocardial infarction
Thyroid dysfunction		Menopause		Multiple sclerosis	Prostatitis	Stroke
		Menstrual cycle disorders		Parkinson's disease	Renal failure	Transient ischemic attacks
		PMS		Spinal injury or tumors	Urethrocele, cycstocele	Venous insufficiency
		Vaginismus		Stroke		
		Vaginitis (bacterial, fungal, trichomonal, viral)				

From Drugs That Affect Sexual Function. New York: W. W. Norton, 1996, p.17.

APPENDIX C

Drugs Associated with Sexual Dysfunctions

Prescription and Over-the-Counter Drugs

Antiandrogens

Antiarrhythmics

Anticancer agents

Anticholinergics

Antihistamines

Antihypertensives

Diuretics

Hormones
  Corticosteroids
  Progestins

Illicit and Nonprescription Drugs

Alcohol

Amphetamines

Cocaine

Heroin

Marijuana

Nicotine

Opiates

Demerol

Methadone

Psychotropics

Antianxiety

Anticonvulsants

Antidepressants

Antipsychotics

Sedatives/hypnotics

Stimulants

Source: Adapted from T. L. Crenshaw and J. P. Goldberg, *Sexual Pharmacology: Drugs That Affect Sexual Function.* New York: W. W. Norton, 1996, p. 20.

APPENDIX D

Drug and Medication Sexual Side Effects

Desire Problems
Reduced sex drive
Problematically high sex drive

Lubrication Problems
Lubrication response is slowed or
reduced in volume

Erection Problems
Complete inability or increased
difficulty to get or keep an
erection
Decreased firmness or sensitivity of
erection
Diminished nocturnal or morning
erections
Painful erections
Priapism

Dyspareunia
Pain during or after intercourse
Painful ejaculation
Painful orgasm

Orgasm Problems
Ejaculation with only semi-erect or
flaccid penis
Complete inability or increased
difficulty reaching orgasm
Ejaculation without orgasm, or vice
versa
Retrograde ejaculation
Decreased intensity or duration of
orgasm
Decreased intensity or volume of
ejaculation
Orgasm without pleasure
("anesthetic" orgasm)

Breast Problems
Galactorrhea
Gynecomastia
Breast pain or tenderness

Source: Adapted from T. L. Crenshaw and J. P. Goldberg, *Sexual Pharmacology: Drugs That Affect Sexual Function.* New York: W. W. Norton, 1996, pp. 6–7.

APPENDIX E

Side Effects of Drugs That Indirectly Diminish Sex

Body Image
Edema
Halitosis (bad breath)
Weight loss or gain
Physical comfort
Constipation
Dryness (skin, mouth, all mucous
  membranes)
Indigestion
Nausea
Pain
Rash
Urinary problems (retention,
  incontinence, cystitis, nighttime
  need)

Impaired Stamina and Movement
Angina
Shortness of breath
Exercise intolerance

*Mental States and Pleasure
Perception*
Aggression
Lack of desire or lack of pleasure
  (anhedonia)
Anxiety
Depression
Detachment
Irritability
Nervousness
Psychosis

Neurological Side Effects
Analgesias and parasthesias
Difficulty thinking
Dizziness
Fatigue and weakness
Headaches
Coordination problems
Nerve impairment
Pain
Perceptual distortions and deficits
Sedation
Sleep disturbances
Memory loss
Tremors

Endrocrine Problems
Alterations in insulin metabolism
  and thyroid function

Vascular Problems
Arrhythmias
Headaches
Excessive vasoconstriction or
  vasodilation

Source: Adapted from T. L. Crenshaw and J. P. Goldberg, *Sexual Pharmacology: Drugs That Affect Sexual Function.* New York: W. W. Norton, 1996, p. 10.

APPENDIX F

Organic Conditions Causing Diminished Desire

Medical Conditions That Lower Desire

Usually Lowers Desire
Addison's disease
Alcoholism
Chronic active hepatitis
Chronic renal failure
Cirrhosis
Congestive heart failure
Cushing's syndrome
Drug addiction
Drug ingestion:
    Antiandrogens (in men)
    Estrogen (in men)
Feminizing tumors (in men)
Hemochromatosis
Hyperprolactinemia (in men)
Hypopituitarism
Hypothyroidism
Kallmann's syndrome
Klinefelter's syndrome
Myotonic dystrophy
Parkinson's disease
Pituitary tumors
Tuberculosis

Sometimes Lowers Desire
Acromegaly
Amyloidosis
Anemia
Brain tumors
Cerebrovascular disease
Chronic obstructive
    pulmonary disease
Collagen diseases
Drug ingestion:
    Alcohol
    Alpha-methyldopa
    Antihistamines
    Barbiturates
    Clofibrate
    Diphenylhydantoin
    Marijuana
    Monoamine oxidase inhibitors
    Phenothiazines
    Propanolol
    Reserpine
    Spironolactone
Hyperaldosteronism
Hyperthyroidism
Hypoglycemia
Hypokalemia
Malabsorption
Malignancy
Multiple sclerosis
Nutritional deficiencies
Parasitic infestation
Prostatitis
Sarcoidosis
Wegener's granulomatosis

Source: R. C. Kolodny, W. B. Masters, and V. E. Johnson, *Textbook of Sexual Medicine.* Boston: Little, Brown, 1979.

Notes

Chapter 1: A Second Chance at Sex

1. Throughout this book I'll use the term "marriage" to refer to all emotionally committed intimate relationships, including those which may not be legally binding.

2. I don't plan to discuss the Internet at length. For more on sex and the Internet, see the 1997 special issue of the *Journal of Sex Education and Therapy* (vol. 22, no. 1), which is devoted specifically to this topic. Consult my article in that issue: "Sex, Intimacy, and the Internet."

3. Later on I'll show you how to use this "normal" situation to increase your sense of yourself and your capacity for intimacy, eroticism, and love.

4. W. H. Masters and V. E., Johnson, *Human Sexual Inadequacy*. New York: Little, Brown, 1970. Dr. Masters understood this problem, which is why he encouraged giving feedback to your partner and "telling your partner what you want" (personal communication, March 9, 1997). Sensate focus is really an innate capacity you use constantly, even holding this book. Ballet, high diving, and figure skating are examples of sensate focus raised to the level of creative art.

5. H. S. Kaplan, *The New Sex Therapy*. New York: Brunner/Mazel, 1974.

6. In the start-stop technique, developed by Jim Semens, the man repeatedly comes to the point of orgasmic inevitability and then stops all stimulation and relaxes. Develop good tolerance to manual and oral stimulation before

you try this with intercourse. The squeeze technique, developed by Masters and Johnson, adds the additional measure of squeezing the penis just below the base of the head when orgasmic inevitability occurs. See J.H. Semens, "Premature Ejaculation: A New Approach." *Southern Medical Journal* 49, 353–358, 1956.

7. H.H. Dalai Lama, and C.H. Cutler, *The Art of Happiness: A Handbook for Living*. New York: Putnam, 1988.

Chapter 2: How Sex Works

1. If you want the long technical version of the Quantum Model, consult my book *Constructing the Sexual Crucible: An Integration of Sexual and Marital Therapy*. New York: W.W. Norton, 1991. For a more concise and applied version, see *Passionate Marriage: Keeping Love and Intimacy Alive in Emotionally Committed Relationships*. New York: Owl Books, 1998.

2. B. Whipple, G. Ogden, and B.R. Komisaruk, "Physiological Correlates of Imagery-Induced Orgasm in Women." *Archives of Sexual Behavior*, 21, 121–33, 1992.

Chapter 3: What Is Happening When You Can't Get Aroused?

1. W.H. Masters and V.E. Johnson, *Human Sexual Response*. Boston: Little, Brown, 1966.

2. R.J. Levin and G. Wagner, "Heart Rate Change and Subjective Intensity of Orgasm in Women." *IRCS Medical Science* 13, 885–886, 1985.

3. Sexual aversion is generally a long-term problem. It typically comes from life experiences involving trauma (e.g., genital surgery), emotional and physical abuse (e.g., rape), congenital deformities, or gender conflicts. Sexual aversion rarely has an underlying physiological basis but still merits screening for medical disorders, medications, depression, and anxiety. Antidepressant medications such as Buspar, Effexor, and Paxil may help sexual aversion, phobias, and generalized anxiety disorders.

4. Systematic desensitization is a form of behavior therapy involving training in deep-muscle relaxation, which is used to reduce the anxiety and muscle spasms of vaginismus (and other problems).

5. Actually, this is a good example of Phil dominating Mary (although it doesn't look like it at first glance). In Part 2, we'll discuss how people who cannot regulate their own anxiety and sense of self invariably attempt to control and dominate the people around them.

Chapter 4: Do You Have Difficulty with Orgasms?

1. I am not referring to women intimidated by their own extreme sexual responsiveness, or those whose responsiveness causes their partners to become lazy. Some sex therapists encounter women who report reaching orgasm too quickly, meaning they have a series of small orgasms but seem unable to build up to a big one that is all-encompassing and deeply satisfying. This is relatively rare.

2. There is no scientific basis to Sigmund Freud's distinction between "mature" vaginal and "immature" clitoral orgasm.

3. I won't say much about multiple orgasms in this book. Multiple orgasms involve repeated orgasms without a long (refractory) period between them. About a third of women have them, lots don't, and many can develop this ability if they want to. Men can also develop the ability to have multiple orgasms (but not multiple ejaculations). But don't equate multiple orgasms with sexual development. I've worked with people who easily had multiple orgasms, who also had lots of difficulty with sex and intimacy. Your sexual potential has more to do with the depth and meaningfulness of your orgasms rather than how many you have. See Chapter 13, footnote 11, for suggestions on developing multiple orgasms if you're interested.

4. Some women experience "female ejaculation." This is not a widespread phenomenon, but it is not an abnormality. Women do have a vestigial prostate gland similar to men's. It is known as their "G spot." See Chapter 12.

5. R. C. Rosen, J. E. Taylor, S. R. Leiblum, and G. A. Bachman, "Prevalence of Sexual Dysfunctions in Women: Results of a Survey of 329 Women in an Outpatient Gynecological Clinic." *Journal of Sex and Marital Therapy* 19, 179–188, 1993.

6. The term "delayed ejaculation" might accurately describe a man who repeatedly reached orgasm without ejaculating.

7. E. Frank, C. Anderson, and D. Rubenstein, "Frequency of Sexual Dysfunction in 'Normal' Couples." *New England Journal of Medicine* 299, 111–115, 1978.

8. Both men and women have a saphenous artery.

9. P. Kilku, M. Gronroos, T. Hirvonen, and L. Raurumo. "Supravaginal Uterine Amputation versus Hysterectomy: Effects on Libido and Orgasm." *Acta Obstetrica et Gynaecologic Scandinavica* 62, 147–152, 1983.

10. R. C. Rosen, R. M. Lane, and M. Menza, "Effects of SSRIs on Sexual Function: A Critical Review." *Journal of Clinical Psychopharmacology* 19, 67–85, 1999.

11. Two-choice dilemmas are basic features of emotionally committed relationships: Often you want two choices at the same time but you get only one

(unless you steal your partner's choice). We'll discuss two-choice dilemmas in Part 2 and Chapters 10 and 14. You can read more about two-choice dilemmas in *Passionate Marriage*.

12. This procedure is often referred to as prostate "reaming."

13. Lots of people have difficulty subjectively distinguishing anxiety and sexual arousal. For people whose sexual experiences repeatedly mix arousal with anxiety (e.g., getting caught, being "naughty," defying parental control), sex without a little anxiety doesn't feel like much of a turn-on at all. We'll discuss this in Chapter 14.

Chapter 5: Twenty-two Ways to Resurrect Sex

1. In Chapter 2, you saw this very thing happened to Gordon as subtle changes in his erections showed up.

2. I'm not saying all you have to do is have "intense-enough sex" and all your problems will vanish. It's entirely possible to have a disease, injury, or medication side effect that puts your arousal or orgasm threshold beyond *anything* you might do. I've worked with people with irreversible physical problems, and their solution does not differ from what temporarily able-bodied people need. You have to focus on exploring your sexual potential, even (and particularly) if you never have another erection or orgasm in your life.

Chapter 6: Changing Is Often Difficult—and Worth It

1. *Passionate Marriage* contains a full description of comfort-safety and growth cycles in relationships, including a diagram outlining the details of both cycles and how they interact. Both comfort-safety and growth cycles are necessary for a vibrant, healthy relationship.

2. This is another example of a two-choice dilemma.

3. You won't find any discussion of listening and communications skills in *Resurrecting Sex* or any publications based on the Passionate Marriage® or Crucible® Approaches. The active ingredient in listening and communication skills programs is reciprocal validation, which reinforces the problem to begin with. The benefits of such programs often don't hold up when anxiety and pressure increase. The reason they show any benefit at all stems not from more accurate transmission of information but from anxiety regulation, reciprocal validation, and pseudomutuality inherent in "active listening."

4. You can read more about emotional gridlock in *Constructing the Sexual Crucible* and *Passionate Marriage*.

5. Gridlock may not be apparent in conflict-avoidant couples, who accommodate each other until the point of divorce. The moment lock-step accommodation stops, gridlock shows up in spades.

6. The incomplete personal development I'm referring to here is not "arrested development" (i.e., the result of childhood trauma); rather, it results from the simple fact that growth is a lifelong process. Few of us are highly developed when we marry—marriage itself makes us grow up. To the degree that you are not a well-developed human, you will be emotionally fused with the people around you.

7. This seems backward from conventional ways of seeing things in terms of attachment and fears of abandonment. But don't assume that "connection" with your partner calms you down and "lack of connection" makes you anxious. At the outset of your relationship, emotional fusion makes you feel wonderful. However, once the honeymoon phase is over, emotional fusion feels like alienation. This doesn't happen because something's gone from your relationship. It's the same emotional fusion that has always existed, but it's at a different phase of the process.

   Don't assume sexual problems create or result from emotional distance. Traditional viewpoints suggest your sexual problem successfully creates distance in your relationship. I'm suggesting the exact opposite: You probably *can't* find a good balance of closeness and distance that lets you regulate your anxiety effectively. If you can't regulate your anxiety when you are close to your partner, you'll be prone to low sexual desire, delayed or premature orgasm, and problems lubricating or keeping an erection. Alexia and Martin and Judy and Peter are emotionally fused couples. Start with the assumption that you and your partner are too.

8. The history of science follows the rule that the presence of something, more often than the absence of something, creates effects initially unintelligible to us. This principle allowed scientists to understand atomic particles so their existence could be proven, and to detect stars and planets too far away for visual telescopes to see. Decades of psychology based on attachment theory now blind people into thinking it's the absence of emotional connection with significant others—rather than subtle underlying emotional fusion—that drains their functioning and makes them anxious.

9. Most of us *do* function better when other people support us and everything goes our way. But that means others have to give up their own agendas, preferences, and options in order for us to function as we like. Being able to function on your own gives the people around you the freedom to devote their time, resources, and talents to their own lives (i.e., to have their own lives).

10. If you've been pursuing conventional advice to compromise and negotiate, what I've described may sound like industrial-strength solutions. If you've

been gridlocked for any length of time, you know that's exactly what you need. If you're not gridlocked, you and your partner should have no difficulty applying the information in subsequent chapters. If you haven't actually tried to change anything yet, you may find you're more gridlocked than you think.

Chapter 7: Hold On to Yourself!

1. This common form of borrowed functioning occurs in emotional fusion.

2. Self-soothing works best when the meanings you give your situation accurately reflect what's going on. Humans have a long and inglorious history of trying to soothe themselves with distorted infantile notions about sex and relationships. Soothing yourself with idealized images of marriage won't keep you calm and quiet when it looks like your relationship is falling apart. In fact, they have the opposite effect.

3. See E. Z. Tronick, "Emotions and Emotional Communication in Infants." *American Psychologist*, Feb., 112–119, 1989. Also see A. Gianino and E. Z. Tronick, "The Mutual Regulation Model: The Infant's Self and Interactive Regulation Coping and Defense." In T. Field, P. McCabe, and N. Schneiderman (eds.), *Stress and Coping*. Mahwah, N.J.: Erlbaum, 1988.

4. This is another example of borrowed functioning within an emotionally fused relationship.

5. Basically, this same vantage point lies at the core of aikido, a "soft" martial art. You have torque, or leverage, only as long as your partner (opponent) holds on to you.

6. There's plenty of time later to make your counterpoints. Holding off announcing your observations about your partner requires not overreacting and tolerating your feelings at the moment. The response you'll get later may be totally different if you can wait.

Chapter 8: Sex Devices and Surgical Procedures

1. Not all of these were men. Some unhappily married women want better sex or more desire without having to deal with their partners.

2. Single women who ask their partners to use condoms face the same emotional politics that surround the use of sexual lubricants.

3. Remember, other forms of birth control may be necessary.

4. For centuries, genital surgery has been performed on pubescent girls in some Arab and African cultures. This still occurs today among some immigrant groups living in Europe and North and South America. These procedures do

not improve women's sexual response—in fact, just the opposite. Women rarely undergo them willingly, and they are often scarred physically and emotionally.

Chapter 9: Sex Drugs: Better Loving Through Chemistry?

1. When a man has difficulty with erections and subsequent medical results indicate his hormone levels are borderline, it is not uncommon for physicians to adopt an "Oh what the heck, give it to him" attitude toward testosterone injections. Unfortunately, a "more is better" approach to hormones is not a good idea.

2. G. Forrest, *Alcoholism and Human Sexuality*. Springfield, Ill.: Charles C. Thomas, 1983.

3. R. C. Kolodny, P. Lessin, G. Toro, W. H. Masters, and S. Cohen, "Depression of Plasma Testosterone With Acute Marijuana Administration." In M. C. Braude and S. Szara (eds.), *The Pharmacology of Marijuana*, vol. 1, 217–225. New York: Raven Press, 1976.

4. The same holds true for injection therapy.

5. These were methodologically sound, randomized, double-blind, and placebo-controlled studies.

6. Any drug has side effects because many parts of the body (not just the target site) respond to it. That's why a drug that raises your mood can also raise your blood pressure, suppress lactation, and interfere with muscle function. The more "receptor sites" that respond to a drug (other than the target), the more the drug produces side effects. Viagra is unique in having few receptor sites. The enzyme Viagra blocks occurs in blood cells, muscle cells of some blood vessels, and the penis. One receptor site happens to be in the retina, which is why some men experience a mild visual color shift (like the difference between daylight and fluorescent light).

7. According to an FDA release covering March through July 1998, over 3.5 million prescriptions had been dispensed and 123 possible Viagra-related deaths had been reported. Of these, 69 deaths in the United States were confirmed. By the FDA's mid-November 1998 update, 6 million outpatient prescriptions (50 million tablets) had been dispensed and 130 American deaths were confirmed (excluding 55 foreign reports and another 57 unverifiable reports). Of these 130 deaths, 2 died from homicide and drowning, 3 had strokes, 77 had cardiovascular causes, and 48 were of undetermined origin. Significant risk factors for cardiovascular or cerebrovascular disease were found in 90 men (70 percent); 16 or more had nitrate medication–related complications. The average age of the dead men was 64. See *Summary of Reports of Death in Viagra Users Received From Marketing* (late March through July 1998).

8. Actually, men are more like women. All male embryos have female genitalia until their XY chromosomes trigger testosterone production, which changes the genitals (and brain) of the developing fetus.

9. M. L. Sipski, R. Fosen, C. J. Alexander, and R. M. Hamer, "Sildenafil Effects on Sexual and Cardiovascular Responses in Women with Spinal Cord Injury." *Urology* 55, 812–815, 2000.

10. Viagra research on men is simple by comparison, because the desired outcome is obvious: a good erection. The end point and method of evaluation for women is less clear (clitoral or vaginal vasocongestion? vaginal lubrication? subjective experience?). Preliminary laboratory studies of Viagra on women used photoplethysomography to measure genital responses while subjects looked at sex films and masturbated. Photoplethysmography shines an infrared beam from a vaginal probe against the walls of the vagina and measures the light that's reflected back. Greater genital vasocongestion reflects back more light. Measurement errors are common due to movement.

11. E. Laan, R. H. W. van Lusen, W. Everaerd, J. R. Heiman, and L. Hackbert, "The Effect of Sildenafil on Women's Genital and Subjective Sexual Response." *Proceedings of the International Academy of Sex Research,* 2000, p. 39.

Chapter 11: Solutions for Arousal Disorders

1. Medications can have side effects you wouldn't think of at first, which contributes to their emotional impact. They can create bloatedness or severe weight gain or loss, triggering body-image and identity crises and affecting how you think and feel during sex. Nausea, vertigo, blurred vision, intestinal disruptions, and ringing in your ears (tinnitis) don't inspire sexual interest or performance. The same goes for drugs that sap your stamina or make you edgy or depressed. Anticholinergic drugs used to treat side effects of antipsychotic medications (e.g., Benztropine, Procyclidine, Orphenadrine) can themselves cause bad breath, dry mouth, and taste changes that reduce pleasure and comfort with kissing. Antibiotics (and other medications) can change the vagina's chemical balance, causing odors that reduce women's interest and comfort. Some medications cause clitoral enlargement and hypersensitivity. Breast enlargement, pain, and tenderness occur in both men and women.

2. Testosterone levels change so rapidly in response to life events that blood samples in testosterone studies are often drawn every half hour.

3. Other forms include vaginal creams (Ogen), a transdermal patch, and a ring that remains inside the vagina for up to three months.

4. Progesterone is used in treating male sex offenders (to reduce their sexual interest) and prostate cancer (to minimize tumor growth) because it reduces testosterone levels.

5. J. Cullberg, "Mood Changes and Menstrual Symptoms With Different Gestagen/Estrogen Combinations: A Double-Blind Comparison With a Placebo." *Acta Psychiatrica Scandanavica* 236 (Supl. 1), 1–86, 1972.

6. Five studies by Barbara Sherwin and Morrie Gelfand at McGill University (Canada) found women who received monthly testosterone injections were less depressed, anxious, and hostile, and more clearheaded, confident, and energetic than those who didn't. Benefits were closely linked to rises and declines in the women's testosterone levels. Testosterone was twice as effective as estradiol, another female hormone. See B. B. Sherwin and M. M. Gelfand, "Differential Symptom Response to Parental Estrogen and/or Androgen Administration in the Surgical Menopause." *American Journal of Obstetrics and Gynecology* 151, 153–160, 1985; B. B. Sherwin, "Estrogen and/or Androgen Replacement Therapy and Cognitive Functioning in Surgically Menopausal Women." *Psychoneuroendocrinology* 13, 345–357, 1988. Estradiol can be prescribed as oral medication (Ortho-Prefest and Activella), a transdermal patch (Climara and Estraderm), and a vaginal ring (Estring). A new treatment (outside the United States) for women with low sexual desire uses low-dose testosterone-estradiol implants.

7. The little-known hormone DHEA shows you how much we have to learn. DHEA is the most abundant, the most poorly understood, and perhaps the most complex hormone in your body. Whereas men and women differ in testosterone and estrogen, they have similar DHEA levels. DHEA exists at higher levels (several hundredfold) than either testosterone or estrogen and has receptors in your brain, surface skin, breast tissue, and genitals. Decreased DHEA seems to be associated with reduced desire and sexual responsiveness (and increased osteoporosis in women), but no clear relationships have been found. Oral contraceptives and alcohol lower DHEA levels, as does Alzheimer's disease, lupus erythematosus, rheumatoid arthritis, ovarian cancer, and burn injuries. Wellbutrin and Trilostane increase DHEA levels.

8. J. H. Bancroft and F. C. Wu, "Changes in Erectile Responsiveness During Androgen Replacement Therapy." *Archives of Sexual Behavior* 12, 59–66, 1983.

9. There is another way to understand "male menopause." Research indicates men's testosterone level is as much the *result* of success and failure in life as it is the basis for aggression, assertion, dominance, and competitiveness. Studies at athletic events and military training show testosterone increases in winners and decreases in losers. Winning by chance (like a lottery) doesn't increase testosterone. Men (and women) take stock of their lives at

midlife, deciding whether they are winners or losers. In other words, low testosterone may be an end result, rather than a cause, of men's productivity and dominance. See A. Mazur and T. A. Lamb, "Testosterone, Status, and Mood in Human Males." *Hormones and Behavior* 14, 236–246, 1988; L. Kreuz, R. M. Rose, and J. R. Jennings, "Suppression of Plasma Testosterone Levels and Psychological Stress." *Archives of General Psychiatry* 26, 479–482, 1972; B. Ellertsen, T. B. Johnsen, and H. Ursin, "Relationship Between the Hormonal Responses to Activation and Coping." In H. Ursin, E. Baade, and S. Levine (eds.), *Psychobiology of Stress: A Study of Coping Men.* New York: Academic Press, 1978.

10. Mesterolone doesn't cause gynecomastia or promote tumor and cancer growth, and it improves depression in testosterone-deprived men. When mesterolone was given to men who fit the profile for "male menopause," it improved their energy and performance and they became more assertive and extroverted. The men showed no improvement in mood or sleep disturbance, headaches, and restlessness. See E. Kaiser, N. Kies, G. Maass, H. Schmidt, R. C. Beach, K. Bormacher, W. M. Herrmann, and E. Richter, "The Measurement of the Psychotropic Effects of an Androgen in Aging Males With Psychovegitative Symptomatology: A Controlled Double-Blind Study of Mesterolone versus Placebo." *Progress in Neuro-Pharmacology* 2, 505–515, 1978.

11. Men should also have their prolactin and estrogen levels checked. Low testosterone coupled with high prolactin often indicates a pituitary tumor.

12. M. Greer, "Carrier Drugs." *Neurology* 38, 628–632, 1988; N. Bodor and H. Farag, "Improved Delivery Through Biological Membranes, XIV: Brain-Specific, Sustained Delivery of Testosterone Using a Redox Chemical Delivery System." *Journal of Pharmacological Science* 73, 385–389, 1984.

13. Both men and women may experience sex as being emotionally controlled or penetrated. In different ways, both Vivian and Armand had to get over feeling this way. "Feeling controlled" is more a function of difficulty holding on to yourself than the strength of your partner's grip. The more you can hold on to yourself, the more you can give him or her ready access to your mind, heart, and genitals without feeling overwhelmed.

14. This took place *after* Vivian had learned to touch herself and relax by herself.

15. Stop struggling with your (or your partner's) body. It's hard to relax if you're fending off tasting or being tasted in ways you don't accept. It's hard to give oral sex like you've arrived at a banquet if you can't stand, or don't have much taste for, what's being served. Likewise, it's hard to relax and enjoy receiving oral stimulation when your partner is obviously ill at ease with your body. You both need to do more than get over your feelings

about oral sex—you need to develop some positive affinities for your partner's (and your own) genitals. Some people get nowhere approaching this as a matter of self-acceptance, until it becomes a matter of integrity and self-respect.

Chapter 12: So You Want to Have an Orgasm

1. J. R. Heiman and J. LoPicollo, *Becoming Orgasmic: A Sexual and Personal Growth Program for Women*. New York: Simon & Schuster, 1992; L. G. Barbach, *For Yourself: The Fulfillment of Female Sexuality*. New York: Signet, 2000.

2. R. Ersner-Hershfield and S. Kopel, "Group Treatment of Preorgasmic Women: Evaluation of Partner Involvement and Spacing of Sessions." *Journal of Consulting and Clinical Psychology* 47, 750–759, 1979; S. R. Leiblum and R. Ersner-Hershfield, "Sexual Enhancement Groups for Dysfunctional Women: An Evaluation." *Journal of Sex and Marital Therapy* 3, 139–151, 1977.

3. Kegel exercises were standard in sex therapy four decades ago. Strengthening your puboccygeus muscles with Kegel exercises was thought to increase sexual responsiveness and increase your comfort with and awareness of your genitals. However, according to research on women in directed masturbation groups, strengthened puboccygeus muscles may not in fact facilitate orgasms. (Both men and women can do Kegel exercises: Repeatedly contract and release the muscles that stop your urination.)

4. For example, one client I mentioned earlier masturbated using a pattern of stimulation his partner couldn't possibly reproduce: He stood alongside the bed and dragged his penis across the sheet. He had never had an orgasm with his wife throughout their relationship, because he was "unfamiliar" with the sensations of his penis being contained. This man had to learn to reach orgasm with the sensations of manual sex, oral sex, and intercourse.

5. Scientists think a woman's G spot corresponds to a man's prostate gland. Equivalent stimulation for a man is available only through his anus. Some schools of tantric sex encourage gentle prostate massage during sex to enhance a man's pleasure. It feels better when done by your partner than by your proctologist. If you try this, go slow and use lots of lubricant, just as you should with anal stimulation for women.

Chapter 13: Synchronize Your Pelvis and Your Inner Mental World

1. Sometimes people refuse to let their partner participate even if he or she is willing.

2. You can read more about clean pain (and dirty pain) in *Passionate Marriage*.

3. You can get out of sync during masturbation, just as you can during sex with a partner. Get back in sync by stopping long enough to settle down and refocus yourself, and restart with a kinder (and usually lighter) touch.

4. Successful avoidance always involves being able to see what you're avoiding so you can avoid it.

5. D. L. Rowland, M. Stefan, J. Haensel, H. M. Blom, and A. Koosslob, "Penile Sensitivity in Men With Premature Ejaculation and Erectile Dysfunction." *Journal of Sex and Marital Therapy* 19, 189–97, 1993.

6. The squeeze and stop-start techniques are described in Chapter 1.

7. S. E. Althof, "Pharmacological Treatment of Rapid Ejaculation." *Psychiatric Clinics of North America* 18, 85–94, 1995.

8. D. S. Strassberg, C. A. de Gouveia Brazao, D. L. Rowland, P. Tan, and A. K. Slob, "Clomipramine in the Treatment of Rapid (Premature) Ejaculation." *Journal of Sex and Marital Therapy* 25, 89–101, 1999.

9. What about using antianxiety medications to treat anxiety in men and women who have difficulty reaching orgasm? Unfortunately, these drugs generally interfere with both arousal and orgasm. Depressed people who take Wellbutrin (which doesn't have these side effects) often report sexual benefits, so much so that Wellbutrin initially sparked interest as a possible aphrodisiac. (It isn't.)

10. The personal stretch I'm describing is actually a process called differentiation. *Resurrecting Sex* is part of the first differentiation-based approach to sex and intimacy.

11. A note on multiple orgasms: Women and men can have multiple orgasms, but men usually can't have multiple ejaculations. If you're interested in developing this ability, pay particular attention to the long-term solution just described for premature orgasm. You need very dense stimulation. You need to reach the brink of orgasm and stay there for as long as you can. Repeatedly challenging your body this way often produces multiple orgasms.

12. Intercourse generally doesn't offer sufficient physical stimulation to raise a man's orgasm threshold. It also engenders the most anxiety of all sexual behaviors. Both factors make intercourse a difficult place to try to develop better control of your orgasms.

Chapter 14: What Will It Take to Change Things?

1. Edwin Friedman, a brilliant differentiation theory thinker and a wonderful presenter, died in 1998. His lecture by this name expanded my horizons. I use his title here in respect of his contribution.

2. You can read more about begrudging respect in *Passionate Marriage*.

3. The anxiety research literature is vast and complex. The few studies cited here don't do it justice, but they show that studies exist to support what I've seen repeated in clinical practice.

4. E. M. Palace and B. B. Gorzalka, "The Enhancing Effects of Anxiety on Arousal in Sexually Dysfunctional and Functional Women." *Journal of Abnormal Psychology* 99, 403–411, 1990; E. M. Palace and B. B. Gorzalka, "Differential Patterns of Arousal in Sexually Functional and Dysfunctional Women: Physiological and Subjective Components of Sexual Response." *Archives of Sexual Behavior* 21, 135–159, 1992.

5. C. M. Meston and B. B. Gorzalka, "The Effects of Sympathetic Activation Following Acute Exercise on Physiological and Subjective Sexual Arousal in Women." *Behaviour Research and Therapy* 33, 651–664, 1995.

6. C. M. Meston and J. R. Heiman, "Ephedrine and Activated Physiological Sexual Arousal in Women." *Archives of General Psychiatry* 55, 652–656, 1998.

7. D. H. Barlow, "Causes of Sexual Dysfunction: The Role of Anxiety and Cognitive Interference." *Journal of Consulting and Clinical Psychology* 54(2), 140–148, 1986.

8. Anxiety arousal is a strong component in pedophilia and the sexual exploitation of children. It is an element in sadomasochistic relationships, clandestine extramarital affairs, telephone sex, Internet chat-room innuendo, and many other sexual behaviors.

9. Here I refer to the level of differentiation between partners (which is the same as their individual levels of differentiation), which differs between couples. Within a given couple, partners are generally at the same level of differentiation.

10. A. Calaprice (ed.), *The Quotable Einstein*. New Jersey: Princeton University Press, 1996, p. 152.

11. Ibid., p. 151.

12. The shift in racial tolerance in America in the 1960s is an example of critical mass.

13. Think of well-differentiated people as the antithesis of emotionally fused couples. Both seek contact with their partners, but for different reasons. The better differentiated (less fused) they are, the more they're into sharing and true mutuality, and the less they participate in borrowed functioning. Because well-differentiated people can regulate their own anxiety better than emotionally fused couples, their relationships are more flexible and resilient.

14. If you want a head start at looking for things in your life that don't make sense, look at the stuff you do that seems fine to you but drives your partner nuts. It might not just be that he or she is nuts. Living with a nut who thinks he or she is insightful will drive you buggy.

Index